To citizens only vaguely aware that the United States is a federated republic, the Electoral College is a relic of a by gone era that needs to be jettisoned so that whoever receives the most popular votes throughout the country is elected President. Jerry Spriggs's deep and thoughtful analysis brings both a historical perspective and a contemporary reality to show the founders wisdom in the creation of the College; how the state based "winner take all" voting system, entrenched in all of our states, has corrupted the role of the College by disenfranchising the votes of millions of citizens; masking how truly close our electorate is divided; discourages voters in a state where they are in the minority party to even participate in elections; and decreases the chances of compromise. Jerry rightly points out that any attempt to amend the Constitution to eliminate the College is not a realistic proposition. But he shows how states can, through state legislative action or citizen initiative, replace their "winner take all" system which would allow the College to operate as it was intended to do.

Anyone concerned about improving America's voting process should find Jerry's book a refreshing read. He brings his considerable talents as a self-described geeky mathematician and game creator to a field dominated by lawyers, political scientists, politicians, and academics. His is a fresh voice, a balanced scientific approach, and an easy read. Jerry is the epitome of the informed citizen that the founder's said America will always need if the union of states is be perfected.

Jim Mattis, JD; served as President of the Oregon Law Institute;
Assistant Attorney General, Oregon Dept. of Justice; Legal Consultant,
Bureau of Governmental Research & Services, University of Oregon

Controversy swirls around the Electoral college. Twice in the last generation it has awarded the Presidency to a candidate with a minority of the popular vote. Strong voices call for it to be reconstructed. Is it obsolete? Is it fair? Should the rules be updated? What are the facts? What are the options? This well researched book is a 'must read' for anyone seriously interested in electoral reform. Jerry Spriggs concisely summarizes the issues surrounding the Electoral College, suggests a positive way forward and marshals substantial factual analysis to support his argument.

F. Gerald Brown, PhD, former Director, L.P. Cookingham Institute of Public Affairs, School of Business and Public Administration, University of Missouri-Kansas City

Presidential election mechanics – It's important to understand how we got here from there. Why did our founders think we needed the Electoral College? What does it mean to have a "fair" election? Why doesn't your vote matter? How can we change that? What can we do to end our quadrennial chaos and Presidential election disfunction?

These are the issues explored and questions answered by Jerry Spriggs in this powerful book about one of the most misunderstood and divisive aspects of our American Democracy.

If you take the time to read his clear and succinct explanation of the evolution of our election process, you will be surprised to learn everything you think you know about the Electoral College is wrong: Why you think it's unnecessary is wrong – Why you think it can't be made to work is wrong – Why you think it can't be changed to be more inclusive, fair and more democratic is wrong.

If you read and understand how the author suggests we change the counting of electoral votes, you will see the value and simplicity of his recommended way we can make the electoral process more inclusive and more valuable for our country.

This book is about making all votes matter! Spriggs explains how, despite the fact that you actually cast a vote, your vote may be irrelevant to the outcome. That's what divides us. That's the reason for voter apathy. And that's his point – the system has to work for everyone! Spriggs shows how we can still use the brilliant structure crated by our founders, but adjust the tally process to ensure all votes matter. His concept mitigates against the tyranny of the majority and brings us closer to consensus on who we think will be our best leader.

William H. Denney, Ph.D., ASQ Fellow, Organizational
Excellence Assessor, International Consultant

ALL VOTES MATTER!

JERRY SPRIGGS

ALL VOTES MATTER!

iUniverse books may be ordered through booksellers or by contacting:

iUniverse
1663 Liberty Drive
Bloomington, IN 47403
www.iuniverse.com
844-349-9409

Because of the dynamic nature of the Internet, any web addresses or links contained in this book may have changed since publication and may no longer be valid. The views expressed in this work are solely those of the author and do not necessarily reflect the views of the publisher, and the publisher hereby disclaims any responsibility for them.

Any people depicted in stock imagery provided by Getty Images are models, and such images are being used for illustrative purposes only.
Certain stock imagery © Getty Images.

ISBN: 978-1-6632-1533-8 (sc)
ISBN: 978-1-6632-1534-5 (hc)
ISBN: 978-1-6632-1532-1 (e)

Library of Congress Control Number: 2020925372

Print information available on the last page.

iUniverse rev. date: 01/15/2021

It is hoped that this book will be shared with others to spark interest, conversation and reform to make **All Votes Matter** when voting in our presidential elections.

Only by listening to the voices of many will this cause be successful.

The book has matured over time. I began writing this in 2012 and published it initially under the name of *Equal Voice Voting: Making Our Voice Count in the Electoral College*. That book covered the elections from 1980-2012. I rewrote the book, *Making All Votes Count: Using Equal Voice Voting in Presidential Elections*, in 2016 with improvements in the explanations to help clarify the issues and to cover all 15 elections from 1960-2016. This book is a further evolution to include the 2020 election, thus covering 16 elections in its analysis. Rather than being a quasi-data dump, (as the first two versions were) making it a rather dry read, this edition tells a fuller story and includes some Electoral College history, it's basic principles, and a fuller comparison with alternative voting approaches. Finally, the book ends with a call to action, encouraging you, dear reader, to not let this rest. Share the information. Engage in conversation. Encourage your state legislators to make this much needed change.

See more at: www.equalvoicevoting.com.

CONTENTS

Introduction xiii

Chapter 1 How the Electoral College Began 1
Chapter 2 A Purposeful Beginning... 17
Chapter 3 Consistency Matters 27
Chapter 4 Equal Voice Voting 41
Chapter 5 Interference 59
Chapter 6 Safety, Tests, and Benefits..................................... 73
Chapter 7 The Popular Vote.. 97
Chapter 8 National Popular Vote Interstate Compact (NPVIC) 117
Chapter 9 And Now This.. 139
Chapter 10 Next Steps.. 157

Appendix A 177
Appendix B... 183
Acknowledgements 201
About the Author.. 205

Voting and participating in the democratic process are key. The vote is the most powerful nonviolent change agent you have in a democratic society. You must use it because it is not guaranteed. You can lose it.

JOHN LEWIS (1940 – 2020), U.S. REPRESENTATIVE FROM GEORGIA)

INTRODUCTION

Paradigms are like glasses. When you have incomplete paradigms about yourself or life in general, it's like wearing glasses with the wrong prescription. That lens affects how you see everything else.

SEAN COVEY

(B. 1964, AMERICAN AUTHOR, SPEAKER, AND INNOVATOR)

It's not working.

That's the sentiment of many Americans when they consider the Electoral College – the mechanism used to select the United States President. Their frustration with the presidential voting system rises quickly if their preferred candidate fails to get elected. Many voters voice their disgust with a voting system that seems antiquated, out-of-step, racist, and possibly even anti-democratic.

The Electoral College awarded more electoral votes to Trump in the 2016 presidential election though Clinton won almost 2.8 million more popular votes across the nation. It did not seem to be a good example of democracy at work as the voices of the people were largely silenced. If the candidates themselves were not to blame, surely the voting mechanism could be.

Many now say, "We must change it!"

Americans want their presidential election system to be more democratic, much like other democratic countries wherein the victor captures the most popular votes. There's an eagerness for removing the Electoral College, dispensing with its awkwardness and associated confusion, in favor of a straight up-and-down system of voting. Yea or nay. It would be pure democracy at work.

Some caution that we should keep what we have.

This book favors neither side. Our presidential election voting process must change and the Electoral College should be preserved. Voting results such as we experienced in 2016, ignoring for the moment who won and who lost, ill-serve this nation's demand for voting fairness and inclusivity. This book examines an alternative voting approach, Equal Voice Voting (EVV), that can be incorporated on a proportional state-by-state basis. Without requiring a U.S. Constitutional amendment. The EVV promise is that all votes matter and every state is heard.

We can make the Electoral College work for us.

★ Historical Wisdom

Let's begin at the beginning when Alexander Hamilton, one of the Framers of the U.S. Constitution offered the following in the 68th Federalist Paper:

> The mode of appointment of the Chief Magistrate [President] of the United States is almost the only part of the system, of any consequence, which has escaped without severe censure. … if it be not perfect, it is at least excellent.

Hamilton thought that the Electoral College was one of the most ingenious elements of the U.S. Constitution. Yet it faces, and has faced hundreds of times, scorn and rebuke. How can one square his opinion with the oftentimes unnerving voting process we endure every four years?

Was Hamilton wrong? Were the Constitutional Framers unable to provide a voting approach that would encompass a changing nation over centuries? Was there perception of, "…at least excellent" simply not being good enough? If, in the beginning, there was (at least) excellence; where and how did it go wrong? How can we return to what the Framers had in mind – or can we?

Criticism of the Electoral College is nothing new, nor is it new to consider alternatives. To understand our dilemma, we must start at the beginning – the very beginning – when our Founding Fathers started with a blank sheet of paper; and, together, decided how our president should be elected. What would be most fair? What would be least vulnerable to fraud and corruption? What would be worthy of a new and democratic nation rising up in this western hemisphere?

If you count yourself among those who really don't know how the Electoral College works, you're among the many. Most people don't understand it. On the surface, it's much like the face of an analog clock. It seems simple. A quick glance reveals the time. Pulling the face off and looking into the clock's inner workings, however, exposes something quite different. The many wheels and axels and cogs spin and turn in a perfect sequence and rhythm to demarcate that elusive element of our lives: Time! Few things in our lives are so seemingly simple and yet are so complex, an ingenious system to mark the time originating from so long ago.

It's the same with the Electoral College. On the surface it's quite simple. People vote and those votes are proportionally translated into electoral votes on a state-by-state basis (some aren't even aware of this basic truth). Peel away this encounter with the voting process and the situation becomes far more complex and nuanced. There's politics involved, sure; but, as Sherlock Holmes would say, "There's even more mystery afoot." The voting process and results border on what might be deemed magic. Certainly, it's counted as one of our greater unknowns, at least among the vast majority of the voting public.

This book examines this seemingly mysterious system and provides answers to emerging questions. The importance of this exploration is to show how we can improve our presidential voting process and Electoral College results. There is a way we can engage the Electoral College to make all votes matter, allow all states to retain their independent voting sovereignty (as our Constitutional Framers intended), and underscore the inherent checks and balances originally desired. Making the Electoral College work for us is not difficult to do from a legal standpoint. The question becomes: do we really want to? Do we have the will to change, the strength to fix and improve what the Framers gave us?

★ A Paradigm Shift

It's only fair to warn you that this book is a description of and defense of an approach for managing all votes cast on a state-by-state basis. The system is called Equal Voice Voting (EVV) and allows the Electoral College to be exercised such that the voting citizenry can have confidence once again in this most basic of our democratic processes. What EVV cannot do is favor any political party or candidate. It is at once, fair, transparent, easily understood, and an encouragement for disenfranchised voters to cast their ballots for their preferred presidential candidate.

Importantly, *EVV demands a paradigm shift in our thinking.*

EVV requires that we think of the Electoral College from a different perspective. It asks that we look at our elections from a point-of-view that reveals that our voting process does not need to be complicated.

While paradigm shifts are common, they don't occur frequently. Consider the idea that the earth is flat. That used to be the way humans thought of the world (sadly, some still do). Long before Isaac Newton (17th century) proved the earth is an ellipsoid and even centuries before (around 300 BC), we began to realize the earth is not flat. It seems obvious now, but back then it was a big deal.

Here's another paradigm to consider: Humans can fly. Sure, we need an airplane to do so, but we didn't have such things a little over a century ago. Humans fly? Balderdash! Humans have no feathers. Humans are too heavy. God didn't intend for humans to fly, or even try. But someone proved humans can fly (albeit with mechanical devices) and now we do – all the time!

Speaking of time, consider how we humans have compressed time as yet another paradigm shift. A couple of generations ago, communication across this vast country was conducted by mail, which we now refer to as *snail mail*. Letters took days, sometimes weeks, to cross the country (if they successfully made the journey at all). Today, we send and receive emails every second. News, too, was distributed painfully slow and now it runs 24/7. Today we are able to pass text, pictures and videos in near real time, making the idea of long distance more out of this world than across the country. We have compressed time! In so doing, we look at the world and our reality differently. We invent faster. We build faster. We demand faster. Technology has brought the world close to us and our reality of time has shifted.

It's not easy to shift our thinking, to make a paradigm shift. Sometimes, we need a little nudge or some kind of event to make things clear. There's a story which illustrates this kind of invitation to consider a paradigm shift. Once upon a time Columbus was asking for sponsorship to sail west in order to get to India. He was told it couldn't be done. Some still thought the earth was flat, after all. It's said that Columbus then presented a chicken egg to his potential sponsors and asked if anyone could make the egg stand on one end without touching it or supporting it in any way. All attempts failed. It couldn't be done! Columbus then took the egg and smashed it down on one end so it could stand. You see, the egg had been previously hard boiled. Smashing the egg on its end allowed the shell to partially crush and support the egg on its end.

Standing the egg on end was a bit of a trick but the point is that it is often assumed that something cannot be done until it is shown that it can be. Then the truth becomes obvious. This book is an invitation to consider a paradigm shift in thinking regarding our presidential elections. EVV is not a parlor trick performed to amaze and intrigue, as was the standing egg. But the results are as readily apparent and within our reach if we consider all of the history, context and nuance of our presidential elections. EVV will emerge as a clear and obvious choice that has something for everyone.

EVV is perhaps not as significant as these first examples (round earth, human flight, technology advances) in terms of changing humanity's perspective of reality. But it does require we set aside a comfortable perspective for one that might seem strange at first. Just as standing an egg on its end is impossible until it's shown it can be done, EVV will indeed change perspectives for presidential campaigns, voter engagement, and the nation's confidence in our presidential elections.

The EVV paradigm shift, as do all paradigm shifts, requires that we change our thinking as our voting reality changes, at least insofar as our voting is concerned. This book will help you set aside current assumptions, biases, and perceptions of political control. You will see the EVV presidential voting mechanism adheres to successful principles: simple (easy to understand), fair (for all voters), and enticing (because all votes matter).

With that in mind, let's consider another fundamental reality:

Process is as important as results.

Any voting mechanism can identify a winning candidate as a result. A flipped coin or marbles counted in a coffee can will elicit results. Surely, there must be more to voting than that! The process is important!

Let's use basketball (you can insert almost any team sport, if you prefer) for an example. A basketball game is much more than the score. There are rules about how a ball is moved up and down the court, such as passing and dribbling. It's exciting to see which team gets the ball (rebound) if an attempted shot is missed. Markings on the floor itself guide the players where to stand to shoot free throws and where to stand to get the rebound if they're missed. The three-point line encourages longer shots to be attempted to score three points instead of two. Rules for defense ensure the competition is engaged and suspense enhances the excitement. Coaching strategy and on-the-floor skills help take advantage of or compensate for weaknesses. The process of the game keeps the excitement alive and the fans coming back for more. All the while, the clock keeps ticking. The game is not just about the score but includes how the score was made and when the score was made.

Basketball may be a crude analogy for a voting comparison, but it's an important one. The sport aims to entertain while a voting mechanism is fundamental to our democratic form of governance. The analogy points out the importance of realizing there's more to consider than just the voting result (i.e., who won). Voting processes must be fair, inclusive, and transparent. As you'll see in this book, the voting process is critical and worthy of much discussion and consideration.

This book examines what appears to be broken in our presidential election process and reveals the troublesome causes. This book relies on a state-by-state voting analysis of the previous sixteen elections (1960 through 2020). Evaluating the data reveals how broken our presidential election system currently is and how the voting process fails to serve our democratic values. Much of the voting citizenry simply are not being heard! Further, the voting data from those elections are compared with what could have occurred if EVV had been used instead.

Looking closely at our historical reality and posing the right questions allows us the opportunity – the awareness – to shift our perspectives. Correctly shifting our perspective to this new-found truth will clarify the focus on our voting process and will engender respect for the Electoral

College. We will clearly see that the purpose of the Electoral College outcome is basically threefold: (1) Reflect the popular voting sentiment, (2) Retain the voting significance of each sovereign state, and (3) Allow the checks and balances our voting system to deliver prudent and reliable results, preventing the risk of tyranny and mob rule.

EVV is the remedy that can allow the Electoral College to deliver what our Constitutional Framers had in mind. It removes the Winner-Takes-All (WTA) approach now exercised by every state and Washington, D.C. Instead, the proportional voting approach established by the Electoral College is honored such that all votes matter on a state-by-state basis. Every sovereign state retains its voting voice and significance. Giving no political party advantage, EVV ensures our presidential elections are fair and inclusive, giving equal voting voice to all voting citizens.

★ History Will Judge Us

David McCullough, one of our current premier historians, was interviewed by David M. Rubenstein. The conversation was recorded in Rubenstein's book, *The American Story*. It is offered here as a reminder of our responsibility for generations to come.

> ... *at the National Statuary Hall in the U.S. Capitol, there's a piece of sculpture commemorating the goddess of history, Clio. She's riding in her chariot, and there's a clock on the side of the chariot, and she's writing in her book.*
>
> *The idea behind putting the statue there was that the members of Congress would look up to see what time it is. That clock still keeps perfect time. That's a Simon Willard clock, made in Massachusetts about 1850. They would look up to see what time it is, and they would be reminded that there was another time – history – and that what you're saying today, what you're doing today, here on the floor of this legislative assembly, is going to be judged in time to come, in the long run.* *

McCullough reminds us that legislators have a responsibility. We do, too. What we preserve in our methods of governance impacts more than a current moment. It impacts our history. The Electoral College mechanism, complex as any clock, records our votes (our collective source of power) and our future. The voting system is not perfect. As Hamilton state, "It is at least excellent." Given the demands and purpose of such elections, perfection is probably not attainable. Ensuring its excellence, however, is easily within our reach.

We can make the Electoral College work for us!

★ Chapter Descriptions

All Votes Matter covers the topics described below. You are free to read them in any order. However, while there is no plot to follow, the chapters build upon each other in subtle ways that help provide the nuance and understanding needed to appreciate what they offer. It is suggested to read them in the order presented.

Chapter One – How the Electoral College Began
Any discussion of the Electoral College must consider its history. Introducing some basic terminology along with a brief treatment of what was considered when our U.S. Constitution was crafted forms a baseline from which a more thorough discussion can ensue. It will be noted that much discussion was enjoined by the Constitutional Framers to design a voting mechanism that would be fair to everyone enjoying a form of governance by *We the People*.

Chapter Two – A Purposeful Beginning
It's easy to say that the Electoral College was established to identify a winning candidate and next President of the United States. But it is much more than that. It is a mechanism that captures and gives representation to the voters. It also recognizes the sovereignty of the individual states. And, to add to this crossroads of vying interests, the

Electoral College mechanism was designed to provide a system of checks and balances to guard against corruption and fraud. In fact, it was put in place to guard against a pure democracy that, as history informs us, can give rise to mob rule and tyranny. It's a check to ensure our representative democracy can persist through times of challenge and stress.

As we consider a voting mechanism, it is beneficial to consider the concerns of our Constitutional Framers. The chapter discusses some basic tests that can be applied to any voting mechanism under consideration. Simply stated, there are three fundamental voting tests: all votes must matter, all states must be heard, and a system of voting checks and balance must work. From this perspective, these tests will be applied and considered for a simple popular vote, the National Popular Vote Interstate Compact (NPVIC) approach, and Equal Voice Voting (EVV).

Chapter Three – Consistency Matters
This chapter is a return to Electoral College basics. It demonstrates how the voting mechanism is a proportional allocation of votes on a state-by-state basis. It also shows the freedom states have for managing their respective allocated electoral votes. The Winner-Takes-All (WTA) aspect is discussed and is shown how it is applied in congressional district voting, which is used in Maine and Nebraska. The chapter finishes by showing how the states have chosen to switch voting methods in midstream, akin to a marketing bait and switch scheme.

Chapter Four – Equal Voice Voting (EVV)
Equal Voice Voting is explained, including the mathematical formula, with examples of what could have been experienced in past elections. The advantages of requiring neither a constitutional amendment nor an interstate compact are discussed. An examination of voting

disparities, differences between Electoral College and popular vote results, is provided. A few elections are closely examined to show the differences that could have been realized if EVV had been used instead. The voting device that the Constitutional Framers included should elections be narrow is explained, showing that there would be no need for Supreme Court interference to select a president. Finally, it is shown that EVV meets the aforementioned voting tests.

Chapter Five – Interference

Interference in our voting for a president, limiting us from experiencing an inclusive process, comes from various sources. Initially, the actual collection of ballots posed some challenges. Adding to the problem of interference was the fact that slaves, people of color, and women could not vote. Even white men who did not own property were excluded. Through the times since when the constitution was written, voters have been refrained from voting through various nefarious voter suppression techniques. Finally, due to the Winner-Takes-All (WTA) approach we still use, almost half of those voting are disenfranchised such that their votes for a president gain no representation in the Electoral College.

Chapter Six – Safety, Tests, and Benefits

This chapter discusses close elections with third-party candidates, explaining what happens if the Electoral College majority threshold of 270 electoral votes is not reached. The discussion reveals some of the ingenuity placed in the Electoral College to address such concerns.

The safety provided by the Constitutional Framers of state electors is discussed. Usually, electors vote as does the state citizens but sometimes disloyal electors surface, disrupting expectations.

Checks and balances, a hallmark of the U.S. Constitution comes into play with the requirement for candidates to capture the consensus of the people while also capturing a commanding coalition of states. It is thought that the current Electoral College process adheres to this intent but Winner-Takes-All (WTA) breaks down the election firewall. An ultra-wide variance in voting, comparing the popular and Electoral College results, shows that the popular vote can be terribly suppressed while delivering an electoral vote victory.

Voting tests are discussed, showing how the standards discussed in Chapter Two come into play. Each presidential election should be fair, equal, inclusive and engaging. Following the Framers' intention, such elections should also capture the popular vote (sentiment of the governed), the sovereign state voting voice, and still provide checks and balances. The chapter compares test results from our current presidential election process with what could be experienced with EVV.

Finally, the chapter shows how EVV provides the benefit of being nonpartisan. There is no political advantage realized by the election mechanism approach as all votes matter and all viable candidates gain representation. Further, the chapter discusses how the current swing state phenomenon could disappear as EVV would make every state that uses it significant.

Chapter Seven – The Popular Vote
Sensing something is wrong, many throughout our nation's history have wanted to change the voting process for a more popular vote approach. This chapter discusses how adopting this approach requires a constitutional amendment, showing what that requires. The popular vote is viewed from the vantage point of our Constitutional Framers, who abhorred a direct democracy. The dangers for sustainability and corruption of such an approach are

discussed. The chapter points out how ours is a very diverse nation and deserves a more sensitive treatment than using one process for all 50 states and the District of Columbia. For example, different states have different voting rules regarding voter identification and the treatment of felons. Further, the nation can be compared to Europe but not to an individual European country due the geographic expanse of the United States and the assimilation of a plethora of cultures. The chapter also reveals why the popular vote approach fails the voting tests mentioned in the previous chapter.

Chapter Eight – The National Popular Vote Interstate Compact (NPVIC)
The chapter on the National Popular Vote Interstate Compact (NPVIC) approach explains the idea and its requirements. It also explains how the approach is ridiculous, radical, and dangerous. The chapter shows how volatile the election results can become and, thereby, lead to a false narrative that can be foisted upon the nation by the media and political party agendas. Other concerns that possibly may emerge are identified further showing how NPVIC fails the voting tests and our nation.

Chapter Nine – And Now This
The ninth chapter is a collection of observations and considerations that may emerge in other discussions surrounding our election process. Gerrymandering, for example, is discussed with some congressional district formation principles that may lend credence to better representation. Ranked Choice Voting (RCV) is discussed showing that it is not at odds with Equal Voice Voting (EVV) but can, with some minor mathematical modifications, coincide well with what EVV delivers. Finally, the chapter delves into some general aspects of what it takes to meet the job requirement of being a U.S.

President. It shows that popularity alone is not enough and that an appreciation of and deep familiarity with our governing institutions, coupled with sound leadership skills, are needed.

Chapter Ten – Next Steps
This chapter is simply a response to the question, "So what?" It is realized that nothing in governance happens without first there being public awareness and public conversations that lead to legislation. Once you have read this book and are aware of how the Electoral College truly functions, and why and how EVV better serves the nation, you will be encouraged to share it with others. Such sharing, including contacting your state legislators with this information, will further enable your state to ensure better voter representation for all voting citizenry. Such legislation will ensure all votes matter and that your state is heard in the next presidential election.

Appendix A – Turning an Idea into Law
Used as an example, Oregon's legislature website provides a diagram of how an idea becomes a law. The steps are identified and explained to provide an overview of the intricate process. Appendix A also shows how initiatives are derived, including their purpose and the process used.

Appendix B – Previous Election Data
The sixteen previous presidential election data are provided, on a state-by-state basis, spanning elections from 1960 through 2020. The data compare what occurred during those elections and what could have happened if EVV were used instead.

* Rubenstein, David M. (2019). *The American Story.* Simon & Schuster

CHAPTER 1
HOW THE ELECTORAL COLLEGE BEGAN

We have the oldest written constitution still in force in the world, and it starts out with three words, 'We, the people.'
RUTH BADER GINSBURG
(1933 – 2020, ASSOCIATE SUPREME COURT JUSTICE)

It was 1787; a time to start. A new nation was being birthed and there was much to consider. What were these considerations? What labels would emerge to best define this new nation's form of governance and how would its power be best used and controlled? How would this nation of separate colonies meld into one and how could it be best led?

As you now know, we elect our nation's president through a process called the Electoral College. To better grasp how it works and to see how we can make it work for everybody, it's best to appreciate the context and early concerns our Constitutional Framers had. Theirs was not a simple challenge. They needed to address the election of a president, the only federal office elected by the entire nation, in a way that could be sustained far into the new nation's future.

★ Electoral College History

It wasn't the real beginning of the nation, but it was close enough. Independence from England had been fought for and won. The thirteen colonies had assembled themselves, each erecting their own centers of government realizing a new kind of independence. Each colony had at least one neighbor and all had concerns of safety and money (debt) and their independent exercise of liberty. They needed each other though some argued such interdependence did not necessarily point to merging into one new country. They already had the Articles of Confederation to help manage their relationships but it was not meeting the demands of a new nation. Others argued that a national constitution was warranted.

The summer of 1787 brought together delegates from twelve of the colonies (Rhode Island refused) with the objective of forming a new nation established on the bedrock of a constitution. Sadly, only 55 of the designated 75 showed up at all and none of them at the same time. The constitutional convention started eleven days late with barely a quorum of 29 (was this a foreboding omen?). The nation was born in conflict.

Some colonies already had formed their own constitutions. Now these delegates, whom we refer to today as our Constitutional Framers or Founding Fathers, were ostensibly assembled to revise the Articles of Confederation. The Framers knew much more was required and, working somewhat in secret by not disclosing their true intent, they were assembled to essentially construct a new government. Would it dissolve what each colony had already started? Would the new nation and all of the colonies be ruled by a king, abhorrent as the revolution had recently testified? What form would it take – what strengths, what freedoms, what promise would it wield?

These men relied on the best advice they could assemble. Earlier, in 1744, Iroquois Chief Canassatego had advised that the colonies be assembled as one, much as the Iroquois league (a confederacy) was assembled from six nations. There would be strength in the many not realized by the weakness of separate – and alone – government jurisdictions. He used the example of breaking a single arrow easily compared to the firmness when trying to break thirteen arrows. Today we see the thirteen-arrow reference depicted on many government seals as they are grasped by the bald eagle, the emblem of the United States of America. The seal of the presidency is one such example. It was a strong reference to the ancient republic of Rome (another influence): E Pluribus Unum – out of many, one. The inspiration stuck.

These were learned men of the day, steeped in languages, cultures, theology, philosophy, political science, agriculture, mathematics, and science. Madison, for example, studied history in depth as he delved into past governments. He considered their respective strengths and weaknesses so he could provide wise counsel to his fellow delegates.

Spoiler Alert: The following historical quotes about democracy may surprise you.

One influencer was the Greek philosopher, Aristotle. Jill Lepore's book, *These Truths*, points out:

> [*The delegates*] *borrowed from Aristotle the idea that there are three forms of government: a monarchy, an aristocracy, and a polity; governments by the one, the few, and the many. Each becomes corrupt when the government seeks to advance its own interests rather than the common good. A corrupt monarchy is a tyranny, a corrupt aristocracy an oligarchy, and a corrupt polity a democracy. The way to avoid corruption is to properly mix the three forms so that corruption in any one would be restrained, or checked, by the others.* [1]

History's lessons also came with warnings, one by Aristotle:

> *Republics decline into democracies and democracies degenerate into despotisms.*

Plato, Aristotle's teacher, advised:

> *Dictatorship naturally arises out of democracy, and the most aggravated form of tyranny and slavery out of the most extreme liberty.*

Even the Constitutional Framers themselves weighed in with their perspectives. Alexander Hamilton cautioned:

> *Real liberty is neither found in despotism or the extremes of democracy, but in moderate governments.*

John Adams, another Founding Father, contributed his own cautious historical sensitivity:

> Remember, democracy never lasts long. It soon wastes, exhausts, and murders itself. There never was a democracy yet that did not commit suicide.

Attorney Tara Ross, author of "Enlightened Democracy: The Case for The Electoral College," writes:

> Dean Clarence Manion of the Notre Dame University College of Law once observed: "The honest and serious students of American history will recall that our Founding Fathers managed to write both the Declaration of Independence and the Constitution of the United States without using the term 'democracy' even once. No part of any one of the existing forty-eight [at the time of writing] State constitutions contains any reference to the word."
>
> Half a century later, his statement remains true, with the exception of two recent additions to the Constitutions of California and Oregon. [2]

It is clear: The Founding Fathers abhorred the idea of a pure or direct democracy. It's a form of governance that is vulnerable to fraud, mob rule, and tyranny. As crucial as any other concern is that a direct (simple and pure) democracy gives control to majorities while silencing minorities. A direct democracy could give license to the governing bully, leaving the meek relegated to the fringes of society rather than actively participating in a form of self-governance intended to be of and by and for the people.

Are you surprised? It is common to assume that these United States is a direct democracy without considering what that truly means. A direct democracy is one in which the power of governance is controlled by the people rather than a central figure, such as a king or dictator. It might be helpful to visualize a few examples.

Suppose you belong to a five-member family. Suppose one evening it is decided that instead of cooking, the family will order out for their meal. The choice is presented that an order will be placed for either pizza or Chinese food. It is decided to put the decision up for a vote by a show of hands. The decision is made by whichever choice captures three votes (a majority). It's simple and pure and direct.

Suppose, however, that a city wants to build a highway that either cuts through the center of the city or runs along its outer border. A vote is taken for all the people (of voting age) to make a choice. Again, that would be an example of a direct democracy. However, there are a few problems that emerge. Where, exactly will the highway be? Which properties would be forfeited? How would it be paid for? Who would build it? Votes to decide all of these decisions would be cumbersome and time consuming. A direct democracy would not be a good way for a city to govern or make such decisions, let alone be good for governing a nation.

It gets worse. If a direct democracy is used, the situation becomes vulnerable to all kinds of fraud. Voters could be bought (persuaded) to vote a certain way, or be prevented from voting at all (voter suppression), or the votes cast be corrupted or lost (vote suppression). Fraud can enter into the equation in many forms.

A direct democracy, then, can be expressed as "one person, one vote." This notion is often voiced in our politics but it must be clear to what this is referring. It is not a suggestion that the nation reverts to a more direct democratic voting system. Rather, the "one person, one vote" idea is usually referring to the direct elections for state and local governing offices (i.e., council members, representatives, senators). It usually works that way but you'll see that the Electoral College provides a modification to the presidential election process for a variety of reasons, covered in a later chapter.

What could save this yet unborn nation from such perils? It was apparent, and is apparent still, that success and our future hinges upon power. Who has it? How is it used? And how is it transferred from one era, from one leadership entity, to another? It has been said that power corrupts. The Constitutional Framers, so forewarned, thought measures could be and should be taken to guard against such corruption. All of the Founding Fathers were concerned about the susceptibility of a new nation succumbing to future corruption or falling short of serving its people well.

Perhaps it was fear of such corruption as much as wisdom that cautioned the Constitutional Framers to build in checks and balances to ensure power was a liberating force rather than a corrupting one. Power limited would be people better served. Whatever the motivation and from wherever the historical lessons were derived, it was decided to divide the governmental powers into its three branches we recognize today: Executive (president), Congressional, and Judicial. Such division of power would contribute to the balance of powers, providing a system of checks and balances to stay any overreach of corruption from any corner of power that may arise.

The overarching principle for each governing branch was the rule of law, as defined by our U.S. Constitution. Each branch and their respective adherents would swear allegiance to the Constitution, ensuring each would serve it instead of an individual (a king, for example) or dominant group. The U.S. Constitution, then, would form the basis of the nation's government and would need to be able to withstand the tests of time.

Congress was tasked with making the laws, the Judiciary was charged with interpreting them, and the Executive was tasked for implementing and enforcing them. As they were designed to do, each branch checked and limited the other to provide a balance of power as the governing wheels turned and moved the nation forward.

★ Presidential Election Considerations

What form would the nation's congress take? Amidst much debate it was admitted that these colonies yearned for, indeed had fought for, freedom from a monarchy. Thus, the power of governance would be held in the hands of the governed: the people. While noble in its aspiration, it would prove to be yet another hill to climb to decide how, exactly, that would come to be.

It was already largely agreed that a direct democracy was a golden invitation to toss freedoms away. Majorities would soon dominate and minorities would be left wanting, painfully so. Given no recourse in a direct democracy, the minority voice would never be heard and injustice would infest the nation, again along with the temptations of corruption.

It was readily apparent that a central government could not long exist if every citizen weighed in on every concern, as a direct democracy prescribes. Instead, citizens would have to be represented by those in congress so the nation would be governed efficiently and sensibly. Representation would need to be managed so every citizen's interests – life, liberty, and the pursuit of happiness – could be realized among conflicting concerns. Thus, each colony would elect revered individuals, in whom they placed their trust, to meet in congress to collectively decide the affairs of the new nation. The notion of one person, one vote, while noble in its intention, would eventually falter both in its being unwieldly to manage and its vulnerability to fraud and corruption.

Another perspective emerged. If each colony wished to weigh in according to the interests of those they left back home, how many of these delegates (now called representatives in most states but still referred to as delegates among the original thirteen colonies/states) could they each send? If a colony was large and had many citizens, would it be entitled to send more delegates than a colony with fewer? Again, the need for checks and balances raised its head.

Added to this dilemma was the fact that some colonies were large, such as New York and Pennsylvania. Others were small, such as Delaware and Rhode Island. Simple geography would dictate that some states could have greater populations and greater costs and burdens than others and, thereby, deserve more legislative representation.

Combining both the desire to distribute governing power to the people and to also recognize the sovereign requirements of the individual colonies, the bicameral (two chambered) congress emerged. The House of Representatives would be populated by chosen citizens (delegates) of each colony according to the number of citizens each colony had. It became known as "the people's house." At that time, these delegates/representatives would then elect two to serve in the Senate for each colony. These senators would represent the colonies with each colony gaining equal representation for each of the thirteen, regardless of its size or population.

In case you may be wondering, Congress passed the 17th Amendment in 1912 that changed a portion of the U.S. Constitution's Article 1, Section 3, wherein citizens in each state now elect its two senators. The amendment was ratified the following year in 1913. Today, each state's voting citizens elect their two U.S. Senators.

It's important to point out the purpose, which still holds, for the bicameral congress. Consider how the House of Representatives is populated. Each state is divided, according to the census taken every 10 years, into congressional districts. They are divided according to the state's population providing a relatively equal division from a population-wise perspective. Citizens within those districts elect one U.S. Representative for their congressional district for a term of two years before he/she is eligible for reelection.

Each state's two senators serve at large, meaning they are elected by every voting citizen within the state. Each senator serves a term of six years before being eligible for reelection. The Senate is often referred to as the "upper chamber" giving it a distinction over the House of Representatives, as being considered to be more deliberative and not as reactionary. Whether it is a valid distinction or not, the length of serving a term three times longer than representatives gives senators a longer tenure and typically more governing experience.

★ Electoral College Representation

While Article 1 of the U.S. Constitution grants all legislative powers to Congress, Article 2 vests the executive powers to the President. The pressing question at that time was to establish just how a president was to be selected.

It was readily agreed that the new nation certainly did not want a king! They had just fought a war so they, as a collection of colonies, could be independent from Britain's King George III. As noted earlier, the seat of governing power would rest in the vote of the people. Electing a president, however, the only government position elected by the entire nation, proved to be a challenge. There already were voiced fears over a direct democracy, so opening the presidential selection process to capture votes by the nation's citizenry seemed fraught with danger. Could citizens of a few colonies (states), a separate majority, pick the president over a minority of voters scattered across the other colonies? Would some states not be represented at all though the new nation was formed as a federalist republic? Would these citizens, busy scratching out a livelihood, know enough or pay attention enough to wisely pick their leader?

How hard could picking a president be? The job description was sketchy, if known at all; but, wouldn't a leader emerge above the rest and be an obvious choice? Knowing that this person needed to be selected by a mechanism that could withstand the test of time, to be relied upon over and over again, presented a very imposing challenge. It couldn't be simple such as picking a General or flipping a coin or choosing the most senior legislator. This choosing process could not be frivolous because, simply, it would invite fraud and abuse and crush the new nation's governing structure.

Representation, decided by voting, had a questionable beginning. At that time, people of color, especially the slave population, were denied the right to vote, as were women. White men only, and men of means at that, held the power of voting. (More will be said on this in a later chapter.) Who and what would these men represent? Would they, could they, choose well? Were they educated and trustworthy enough?

Deciding how to pick a president was in keeping with the rest of the continental congress: highly contentious. A compromise was struck that incorporated the best desires put forth with a nod towards caution. Finally, a voting system was crafted that included the citizens voting from each colony (a colony-wide popular vote), an acknowledgement of each colony submitting a voting representation equal to each other colony, and a system of checks and balances so a runaway pure democracy would not cripple the nation by inviting mob rule and eventual tyranny.

The solution agreed to was what we now call the Electoral College. As Hamilton noted and quoted in the Introduction, "…if it be not perfect, it is at least excellent." The selection process is not vested in any one body, be it the general public or the judiciary or either chamber of congress. Rather, a proportional voting calculation was agreed to wherein each colony (states) were allocated a proportion of voting representation equal to the number of legislators they sent to congress. Today, representational and proportional voting remains at the core of the Electoral College on a state-by-state basis.

Today, just as it was in the beginning, each state gets two electoral votes because each state is represented by their two federal U.S. Senators. In this, all states participate on a level playing field regardless of their geographic size. For example, the large state of Alaska, almost encompassing an area (570,641 square miles) equal to about a third of the size of the lower 48 contiguous states, has an equal representation as the nation's smallest state, Rhode Island (1,034 square miles).

The nation's citizen voting (the popular vote) is also represented in accordance to the number of U.S. Representatives in Congress. Each state receives electoral votes in reflection of its population density. While some states have low population densities, a minimum of one electoral vote is allocated for each to reflect their U.S. Representative. Alaska, Delaware, Montana, North Dakota, South Dakota, Vermont, and Wyoming, as of this writing, receives one such electoral vote each. 428 additional electoral votes are distributed according to each state's respective populations across the remaining 43 states. A total of 435 electoral votes, then, are proportionally allocated across the nation.

A census is taken every 10 years to determine the number of citizens for each state. The population total is divided by the 435 number to derive an approximate number of people to be allocated for each state's congressional districts. This means that the number of a state's congressional districts is reflective of its population density and often changes from one census to another. This ten-year adjustment allows the Electoral College to be sensitive to the changing population densities on a state-by-state basis across the nation.

For example, when I was young, North Dakota (the state where I was born and raised), had two congressional districts and two U.S. Representatives. Since that time many residents have left the state and few have relocated there. In comparison to others states, North Dakota's population has shrunk. Consequently, North Dakota lost one congressional district (the entire state is considered as one now) and has only one U. S. Representative. California, on the other hand, had only 23 congressional districts when I was born and has added 30 more for a total of 53 congressional districts. The electoral votes are allocated according to where the people live.

Washington, D.C. is not a state but its population is granted Electoral College representation. Thus, it receives the same number of electoral votes as do the lowest populated states by receiving a total of three electoral votes, though it is a governing jurisdiction and not a state.

Combining the 100 votes allocated for the U.S. Senators, the 435 for the U.S. Representatives, and three for Washington, D.C. brings the total Electoral College vote allocation to 538. The U.S. Constitution is quite clear that a presidential candidate must win by a majority. A majority being 50% plus one means that the majority threshold needed for an election victory is 270 electoral votes.

The early elections had the majority winner of the presidential race be selected as the new President. The candidate who came in second would then serve as the Vice President. Well, that didn't work out well. Can you imagine after a tough-fought race, and the vicious rancor we witness today, that two contenders would work together in the Oval Office as President and Vice President? Fortunately, Congress stepped in and offered up the 12th Constitutional Amendment in December of 1803 and it was ratified by the states/colonies in June of 1804. It combines the election of the President and Vice President as a single ballot choice by the same political party, which is what we have today.

As the idea of a Constitutional Amendment surfaces in this discussion, it's important to understand what it entails. The Constitutional Framers realized that their creation, the Constitution, had to have some built-in resilience. Certainly, they understood, time could call for constitutional changes but they required such changes be difficult to make. They succeeded! A Constitutional Amendment requires a 2/3rds agreement by both U.S. Congressional chambers (Senate and the House of Representatives) as well as being ratified (agreed to) by 3/4ths (38) of the states' legislators.

It's not easy to amend the U.S. Constitution, nor should it be. Today, many are calling for an amendment to change the Electoral College or to get rid of it altogether. Alexander Keyssar noted in his book, *Why do We Still Have the Electoral College?* [3] that such amendments had, at that time, been attempted over 800 times. None of those efforts ever made it out of Washington, D.C. Given the political polarity we see in Washington today, it's safe to say that it is easier to impeach a president than to modify or eliminate the Electoral College!

As the discussion ensues over the pages of this book, and because a constitutional amendment is so difficult (almost impossible) to accomplish, the focus will be on other alternatives for improvement. Pressing forward under the assumption that attempting to eliminate the Electoral College in the near future is folly. Consideration will be devoted to alternatives for how our presidential election results can be improved to reflect the sentiment of the governed.

Still, though the Electoral College is not perfect, attention will be given to how it has been improved over the past two centuries. And, it will also be shown how it has been hobbled such that an added restriction limits its efficacy. It will be shown how Equal Voice Voting (EVV) can remedy the current malady and allow the Electoral College to serve us as it was originally intended.

★ Translating Popular Votes

When each presidential election occurs, the nation's citizens cast their ballots. The winning candidate, as noted earlier, must win by a majority. However, it is not a majority of citizen ballots. The majority refers to the number of electoral votes that are produced out of the Electoral College. There is a big difference!

The votes cast within a state are translated into electoral votes according to the proportion of votes that a state gets. For example, my home state of Oregon (as of this writing) has seven electoral votes (two for its two U.S. Senators and five for its U.S. Representatives). Oregon voters cast 2,374,321 ballots in the 2020 election. A plurality of these ballots (not all of them) were then translated into seven electoral votes to represent the voting sentiment of the Oregon voters. Every state's popular votes are translated in this manner, according to the proportional allocation of electoral votes each state receives.

The U.S. Constitution does not dictate how a state does the vote translation! This is a significant concern and will be discussed at length in other chapters. Suffice it to say that each state is free to do as it wishes in this regard. For example, Maine and Nebraska use a different vote translating process than do the other 48 states. It is their desire to do so and they are free to conduct this bit of voting calculation as they so wish.

The Constitution does dictate, however, that another method of checks and balances be in place. Founding Father James Wilson of Pennsylvania offered the idea of electors. Each state, it was suggested, would select electors to be part of the process in equal number to the number of legislators the state sent to Congress (the electoral vote count). These electors, it was felt, would ensure that astute and learned men would be able to intercede if the general public would be foolish enough to vote against the state's better interests. Thus, today, when you vote for a president (and vice president), your ballot is actually identifying (voting for) the electors to then cast the electoral votes. Yes, it's complicated, even a bit clunky, but it's part of the Electoral College apparatus.

When all of the electoral votes are summed up across all 50 states and Washington, D.C., the winning candidate will have captured the majority of them (at least 270). It's important to realize that this bit of calculating machinery causes the vote result to be spread across the nation rather than allowed to gather within a few states. A winning candidate, therefore, must win a majority coalition of state electoral votes, reflecting a majority consensus of the voting public across the nation; not simply from a single region of the country.

★ Forming A Republic

It's important to consider what these men accomplished that summer of 1787. It's remarkable that they crafted a constitution for the country but also consider what they endured while they did so. They met mostly in secret for fear of being noticed and mobbed. They met in a room without electricity which meant that they depended on light coming through the windows or light cast from burning lamp wicks or candles. It also meant that during those hot, sweltering days with no air conditioning and no fans, it was difficult to keep their cool.

Tempers flared, we're told, and there was little to assuage their angry moods. Remember, some didn't even want to be there. Most had at least some disagreement with the final outcome. Think of hot, tired, reluctant men debating in a darkish hot room where the air was still and, perhaps, a few flies to remind them of their physical misery.

These men pursued a goal of national unity knowing that many of their constituents would not favor the result, they would not be known as heroes, as we think of them today, and these bold actions could put their lives at risk. Their persistence (sometime stubbornness) accomplished much that went unnoticed.

This assembly of Constitutional Framers – these mere men – some earnest and some reluctant, each with their own individual weaknesses offering so many counter justifications, partook of the miraculous to even bring forth this unifying document: the U.S. Constitution. The new nation has proven to be a tremendously grand experiment in that a collection of colonies (now states) were formed under one umbrella of governance, a federalist republic. It's a national government of a collection of states, each with their independent sovereignties, as well as a voting public, that ensures their common interests and protection.

Benjamin Franklin, the eldest constitutional framer, was asked after the constitutional convention about what kind of government had been chosen. He replied, "A republic, if you can keep it."

His was not an idle musing or caution about the fragility of the nation's newly formed government. These United States were formed in a hot cauldron that mixed, and continues to mix, aspirations and conflicts and tensions. Often the nation exists purely out of compromise and sometimes it cools to allow growth and prosperity to flex its virtues. Events erupt to forge its citizenry to act as one, such as in World Wars I and II. Other times, this nation of self-governing humans, stumbles as it commits unforgivable sins that even history cannot forget.

The nation continues. We now exercise a representative and constitutional democracy; but it is a democracy shielded by a clever set of checks and balances to help withstand the dangers of mob rule and tyranny. It is a representative democracy with its power derived from the citizens themselves and their collective votes. These United States continue by adhering to the rule of law, recognizing and attending to the voices of minorities, and maturing in its governing wisdom as its citizens do. We are a nation of collective thoughts and words and deeds that both condemn us and exonerate us as best we collectively know how to do. This constitutional democracy promises no easy future. But it does promise a future that encourages its citizens to pursue life, liberty and the pursuit of happiness. Collectively, it further hints, we can succeed.

The calendar marking the beginning of the nation was started in 1787 when the Founding Fathers crafted the U.S. Constitution. Time has passed and some changes have been made to how we now elect the nation's president. Today we realize some flaws not originally considered in the process. It's time to consider another change.

★ Chapter Summary:

+ The Constitutional Framers abhorred a direct democracy because, history informed them, it invites mob rule, corruption, and tyranny.
+ The United States is a federal republic form of government, exercising a representative and constitutional democracy.
+ The power to identify (elect) a president resides with the voters.
+ The Constitutional Framers divided the federal government into three branches: Executive, Congressional, and Judicial to provide a system of checks and balances.
+ The Electoral College reflects our bicameral congress by allocating the same number of electoral votes as federal legislators.
+ Each state is allocated electoral votes equal to the number of their federal legislators (Senators and Representatives).
+ Electors from each state cast the allocated electoral votes to reflect how the state voters cast their ballots.
+ A winning presidential candidate must win an election by capturing at least a majority (270) of the electoral votes.
+ The Electoral College can only be modified or removed from the Constitution by an amendment, which is almost impossible to do.

1. Lepore, Jill. (2018). *These Truths: A History of the United States.* W.W. Norton & Company, p. 112.
2. Ross, Tara (2004, 2012). *Enlightened Democracy: The Case for the Electoral College.* Colonial Press, L.P., p. 15.
3. Keysaar, Alexander. (2020), *Why Do We Still Have the Electoral College?* Harvard University Press, p. 5.

CHAPTER 2
A PURPOSEFUL BEGINNING

We the people are the rightful masters of both Congress and the courts, not to overthrow the Constitution but to overthrow the men who pervert the Constitution.

ABRAHAM LINCOLN

(1809 – 1865, 16TH U.S. PRESIDENT)

Our world of experiences is based on principles. So it is with our form of governance. Our Founding Fathers formed our government on principles that would preserve the nation and grant its citizens the right to life, liberty, and the pursuit of happiness. It's the same with how we elect our president. There are principles involved.

The Constitutional Framers wanted the presidential election process to capture the sentiment of the governed – at least that of those who vote. Desiring the governing power not to be vested in a monarchy, they looked to the voting citizenry to hold the reins of government. Voting had to reflect the choice made by the people as well as each independent and sovereign colony (now states). At the same time, they wanted the system to be instilled with checks and balances to guard against fraud, corruption, and an unjust dominance that can emerge from a simple majority.

These principles outline the reasons for the Electoral College. Further, if we chose to make it so, the Electoral College can deliver a process that is fair, equal, inclusive, and engaging. We do not experience these principles at work today. Equal Voice Voting (EVV) can provide these fundamental principles, further ensuring that all votes matter, every sovereign state is heard, and that checks and balances are still at work.

★ Presidential Election Principles

Everything happens for a reason.

There are reasons for the weather, for wars, for how well we work with others. Science gives us reasons based on evidence. History gives us reasons based on 20/20 hindsight. Psychology gives us reasons to explain why humans, all of us in fact, seem just a little bit crazy from time-to-time. There are reasons I wrote this book just as there are reasons you are now reading it.

In other words, nothing really happens in a void. It's no different for elections. We can certainly analyze campaigns and give reasons for why a candidate wins or loses. That's fun to do sometimes, frustrating too. There are two perspectives to keep in mind: reasons regarding process and reasons regarding consequences. You may have heard it said that, "The ends justify the means." That's a little misleading. The ends do justify the means, just as the ends criticize, even condemn, the means. The means and the ends are, in many regards, equally important.

It's not enough to simply pick a presidential election winner (the ends). The process (the means) is important, too. For example, as the campaigns unfold, questions and concerns surround the many candidates leading up to the Democratic and Republican conventions. Gamesmanship strategies are found in every corner and hall and political broadcast leading up to these conventions. Some of the tactics are out in the open and discussed at length while others are orchestrated out of sight in back rooms. Often there are claims of nefarious fraud and corruption to further taint the legitimacy of the outcome. A widely held mantra is that *winning is everything* but the process tells us *why* and *how*, revealing there often are other things to consider.

So, let's look at the presidential campaign process.

The first thing all of us realize is that presidential campaigns take time. It seems the presidential campaigns begin as soon as a president is sworn into office in January after the election and they last, fatiguingly so, for the entire next three years and 10 months. Much of the early activities, of course, are unseen as the new power structures are assessed and new political alliances are formed. But it doesn't take long before conjectures are made about who will be best suited for the Oval Office when the next election occurs.

It all seems like one big game! There are actually multiple political games used when candidates run for presidential elections. We call them political strategies or simply call the whole mess, *politics*. Whatever we call the preliminary process it's readily acknowledged that a lot of time and thought and energy and money go into delivering the candidate and the messaging associated with him/her to succeed. Success becomes a marketing goal wherein candidates are packaged to appeal to the thoughts and emotions and impulses of the buying (voting) citizenry.

Is your head spinning yet? As if that's not enough, let's include the media.

As the campaign marketing strategies unfold, we are inundated with messaging from all media channels. It's not only television ads, for example, that we absorb. Television also delivers the impressions and reactions of political experts, pundits, and people on the street. Radio, Internet blogs, and podcasts compete with each other to capture our attention, shape our opinions, and lay claim to our future voting. Polling seems to be constant as multiple revered agencies elbow their way into our lives asking who we prefer, why we do, and – oh yes – are we old or educated or politically registered or where do we live or how much money do we make? Everyone has an opinion and it seems there's an abundance of prying eyes and ears and microphones and cameras to absorb them all. The results are captured and cross-checked and compared to historical data and prognostications are made about what they mean for upcoming election results. It all causes political fatigue.

I'm tired just thinking about it! But it gets worse. As outlined below, we're reminded that letting down our guard allows corruption to have its effect.

There's no denying that a fair amount of nefariousness creeps into the campaign process. Social media, for example, has exploded in recent years and is being manipulated to entice the voters to take sides, commit early, and sometimes to be swayed by false information. And, to make matters worse, other countries and foreign agencies are trying their hand at manipulating our public. The news even takes up time to report on who is doing what as the competition for our attention unfolds, knowing that the public has a large appetite for the tasteless, the sensational, and the extreme.

What did the Constitutional Framers think about all of this run-up to elections? Quoting Hamilton again from Federalist Paper #68 as he related discussion regarding the Electoral College, he said:

> *It was also peculiarly desirable to afford as little opportunity as possible to tumult and disorder. … Nothing was more to be desired than that every practicable obstacle should be opposed to cabal, intrigue, and corruption.*

It's not a stretch of one's imagination to assume that they had little appreciation for how corruption could influence an election as it can today. For example, news traveled slowly in the late 1700's and nobody then would guess that sound and video would travel instantaneously around the world via the airwaves and be available on a 24/7 basis. Messaging could become weaponized to a degree they could not have understood then. The combination of political science and media messaging was in its infancy compared to the sophistication it is today. The times have changed and continue to challenge. Still, the Framers were astute and diligent to ensure the Electoral College would sustain the future challenges.

What were the Framers' goals? They were not attempting to shape political campaigns when they created the Electoral College. Rather, they were striving to establish a resilient voting approach – a mechanism – that would adhere to certain principles to best serve the new nation's citizenry and their colonial jurisdictions. Certainly, their focus was on the consequences of the presidential elections – the reasons that would best serve the nation.

There's no denying that our presidential elections are spellbinding. The first Tuesday of November every four years is an exciting time as the whole nation – the whole world – takes notice as U.S. citizens vote, ballots are tabulated, and results are reported. Suspense fills the air as news networks hurry to be the first to declare a state has determined how their electoral votes will be cast for a given candidate. It's an exciting, nail-biting event that culminates in much fanfare, speeches, balloons, confetti, and dancing. For the winners and their supporters, it's time for champagne.

What would you want to see, if you could start from scratch, from the voting process? What goals would you want to see be fulfilled? It can be a daunting challenge and you may come up with several considerations. I think four principles will outline key concerns we can agree on: The election process must be: (1) Fair, (2) Equal, (3) Inclusive, and (4) Engaging. These four principles should be basic requirements for any voting process. Let's consider each.

The hope is that voters will participate in a **fair** voting process such that the voting options are clear, easy to understand, and that their choices (votes) can be easily and accurately counted. Voters should have their votes **equally** represented so no advantage is given to any candidate or political party. All votes should matter and be counted. The opportunity to vote should be an **inclusive** event such that no voters are denied access to the voting process. No voter should find the voting experience to be overly onerous or so challenging that they choose not to engage in this fundamental patriotic duty. The voting process should be **engaging** meaning that they should find it motivating to vote, due to the confidence that their vote will make a difference.

If you were tasked with that challenge, you'd have the benefit of history's 20/20 hindsight. The reasons and goals you might pick (perhaps those highlighted above) give you an advantage over the Framers. They argued over who should vote, true, but the mechanics of creating and issuing ballots, counting them, encouraging people to vote, and keeping accurate records of the elections were not their main objective.

★ Electoral College Principles

Now let's consider the reasons – the principles – the Constitutional Framers pondered as they crafted the idea for the Electoral College regarding election outcomes.

When the Constitutional Framers gathered in that hot room in 1787, keeping their intentions mostly secret, they set their sights on the voting consequences, rather than the voting process. They realized that much was at stake. If they got it wrong, the entire experiment to form a representative government for the newly united colonies under the leadership of a newly elected president would crumble – quickly and miserably. The reasons for creating the Electoral College were many and demanding.

The Framers had agreed that the source of power would reside with the people. As discussed in chapter one, they did not want a direct democracy. They were challenged with how to best capture the sentiment of the governed as they elected an individual to preside over the entire thirteen colonies. How could they accomplish this and still respect the individual sovereignty of the thirteen separate colonies? How could this be accomplished, fearful as they were of majorities dominating the process, while instilling a system of checks and balances? The consequence of their deliberations formed three principles:

- Capture the sentiment of the governed (a popular vote result).
- Capture the sentiment of each sovereign colony (separate and equal voices).
- Provide voting checks and balances.

The **first principle** had to be met: Capture the sentiment of the governed.

The Electoral College solved the Framers' concerns by letting the voters of each colony vote. Their votes would then be translated into electoral votes that were equal in number to the number of colonial legislators (senators and delegates) who were representing them on the federal level. The popular votes would not be aggregated all together as one nation, thereby respecting the concept of a federalist republic. Rather, voting tallies were done colony-by-colony as an independent exercise, albeit conducted at the same time and in concert with all the other colonies.

The **second principle** had to be met: Capture the sentiment of each sovereign colony.

By separating the voting voices via the electoral votes allocated to each colony, one from the other, the colonies would retain their independent sovereignty. Each colony would be represented by its own independent voting choice because they were members of a republic – separate but equal.

This is why, today, we do not have a popular vote election across the entire nation as if we were a direct democracy. The Electoral College calls for each state to run its own election, capturing the popular vote result within its own borders, and then translate those results into its allocated electoral votes.

The **third principle** had to be met: Provide voting checks and balances.

The checks and balances concern, permeating the newly crafted constitution, also emerged in voting for the nation's Chief Executive – it's President. A winning presidential candidate could not rely on a select region of voters from a small handful of colonies to capture the most votes, as in a direct democracy. Rather, the winner would have to campaign and garner the favor of a coalition of voters across the entire nation (all colonies), capturing a consensus of the voting citizenry.

The Framers were even cautious about the wisdom voters would have in selecting the best candidate. Would they be aware of the domestic and foreign issues? Would they be informed about what it took to govern this new nation? They placed a filter of sorts in the process, by having each colony select electors equal in number to the number of electoral votes the colony would receive. These electors, presumably called upon because of their intelligence, education, and community standing, would cast the colony's electoral votes. Hopefully, they would vote as the colony voters did, but if they recognized a poorly qualified candidate had been selected, these electors could save the day and cast their votes for a better alternative.

Electors are still used today and they seldom vote differently than do the state voters. In 2016, however, there were seven electors (sometimes called rogue or unfaithful electors) who did not vote in concert with their state's choice. This was the greatest elector defection in our nation's history and is considered an anomaly. Still, this form of checks and balances the Framers had put in place was exercised in that election.

Further, a standard was firmly set that the winning candidate would have to win a majority of electoral votes in order to win. There were only 69 electoral votes for the thirteen colonies at that time. A majority would be 50% + 1, or 35 votes. It would not suffice to simply win a plurality of voters (most of them) but a winning candidate would have to show a dominant voting result.

There was no need to worry over this detail in those early elections, however. George Washington won all 69 electoral votes, a unanimous election in the nation's first presidential election of 1789! Can you imagine such an outpouring and unanimous result today? Of course, that was before political parties emerged and the whole political process, as contentious as it has become, was just beginning.

★ Process Matters

We have exercised the Electoral College method for electing our nation's president for more than two centuries. The thirteen colonies have become thirteen states and the nation has expanded to include 37 more. The United States Constitution continues to hold true for all of them, binding them to an allegiance of unity as one republic. The Electoral College continues to be applied as it was those many years ago though it now includes the added 37 states. If the Constitutional Framers got it right, then the principles they established then should still apply today.

This book sets out to show that we have distorted the voting process. The principles are not as recognizable as they should be and voting results fall short of the desired goal. Failed voting results are not referring to which candidate or which political party was victorious in any previous election. Rather, the failed voting results point to our voting system – a mathematical construct – that now disenfranchises voters, denying the nation any true election accuracy.

One note of clarity: As you read the next chapters, you will be shown examples of past elections to illustrate concepts, highlighting voting successes and failures. It's important to realize that none of the examples are meant to present any political party bias. Rather, the intent will be to show that we fail to exercise the Electoral College properly and, as we do, not only do political parties and their candidates suffer, so does the voting public. As the chapters unfold, you will see that a simple remedy is available if the states adopt Equal Voice Voting (EVV).

You might be asking, "What's the reason for all this yakkity-yak?" The point I want to make is that as the Electoral College is discussed (including how it is and should be managed), consider both the process and consequence principles. As mentioned earlier, it's not enough to flip a coin to pick a winner. Process matters.

We will review how we engage with the Electoral College in light of these principles in subsequent chapters. The goals for both the voting process as well as the voting consequences will form a baseline standard to reveal success or failure.

The four voting process principles used for our presidential elections must be:

+ Fair
+ Equal
+ Inclusive
+ Engaging

The three voting result principles for our presidential elections must:

+ Capture the sentiment of the governed.
+ Capture each state's voting sentiment.
+ Provide voting checks and balances.

This is a high demand for a presidential voting process. It must be fair, equal, inclusive, and engaging during the event when voters cast their ballots. It must also capture the nation's popular votes, respect the individuality of the sovereign states, and provide a reliable set of checks and balances.

To be clear, we do not reach this standard today when we select the nation's president. Since we fail, election after election, we should be cognizant of the risk the nation takes during this important process. Not only do we run the risk of electing someone the nation's citizens really don't want, we also cannot claim any premier status among other democratic nations for our election process. We are not a nation to follow, in this regard, until we attend to these reasons that point to the *how* and *why* of both process and consequences.

The Electoral College has a rich history and subtle nuances. It is not complicated from a purely mathematical point-of-view. It is simple in that it only requires basic arithmetic functions: adding, subtracting, multiplying, dividing, plus the application of fundamental statistics. This book will reveal how easy it can be to restore the fundamental principles of sound voting practices and respect the intent of our Constitutional Framers and good voting practices.

One final consequence to all of this must be acknowledged. For a long time, the nation's voters have expressed that they feel disenfranchised (they are) and that they have lost confidence in the voting process. So much so that voter turnout across the nation is pitiful. Almost half of eligible voters do not register to vote. Around 40% of registered voters do not vote. Adhering to the principles noted above and shirking political distractions that shortcut the system will deliver a democratic voting system that will restore the confidence of all voters and the confidence of all candidates for the nation's future. Confidence in our voting system is critical for truly successful presidential elections.

★ Chapter Summary:

- ✦ Presidential campaigns are affected by politics, the media, and corruption.
- ✦ The Constitutional Framers desired an election mechanism that reflected the governing will of voters, colonial (state) choice, and the protection of checks and balances against corruption.
- ✦ Presidential elections should be fair: voting options clear, understandable, and easily and accurately counted.
- ✦ Presidential elections should be equal: voting should not give unfair advantage to any candidate, political party, or voting citizenry.
- ✦ Presidential elections should be inclusive: no eligible voters should be denied the right to vote.
- ✦ Presidential elections should be engaging: voters should be confident that their vote makes a difference.
- ✦ Process matters as small changes can lead to significant outcomes.

CHAPTER 3
CONSISTENCY MATTERS

> While imperfect, the electoral college has generally served the republic well. It forces candidates to campaign in a variety of closely contested races, where political debate is typically robust.
>
> WILLIAM M. DALEY
> (B. 1948, PRESIDENT OBAMA'S CHIEF OF STAFF)

We don't like change! People prefer that things remain the same. It gives us a sense of security, something to rely on. Sure, we like progress but never when it comes abruptly, upsetting systems or habits or our world views. We prefer consistency, be it as a young child, at our places of education, worship, work, or in our relationships.

When the U.S. Constitution was crafted and the Electoral College was established, the mechanism used for electing a president was a proportional system. It has remained that way ever since. The disruption of the election process begins at our state borders as we switch from a proportional system to one in which the winner claims all of the votes. It's called, Winner-Takes-All (WTA). (Sometimes, you'll see it called winners-take-all, implying there are multiple winners, which his true if you include all of the states. I prefer to pluralize the verb [Takes] to focus on each state contest.)

The voting public senses that something is amiss. Confidence is weakened when voting sentiments are not translated into representative outcomes and voters are left disenfranchised. The voting experience leaves the public yearning for a direct voting process wherein one person equates to one vote. Consistency is lost when the original proportional voting process is exchanged for a different approach by the states.

A consistent and fair voting process can be achieved if WTA is abolished and replaced with Equal Voice Voting (EVV). The proportional voting process established by our Constitutional Framers can be continued on a state-by-state basis, granting consistency throughout the process.

★ Proportional Voting

The Electoral College was set up as a proportional voting system wherein each state has electoral votes in proportion to their number of U.S. Representatives. The number of U.S. Representatives reflects the number of citizens a state has. Consequently, densely populated states have more U.S. Representatives than less populated states.

As of this writing, a congressional district contains about 747,000 citizens. This changes as the national population grows. Some states only have one congressional district (one U.S. Representative) giving them only one electoral vote. Every state also gets two additional electoral votes because of their two U.S. Senators. No state has fewer than a total of three electoral votes. These states include: Alaska, Delaware, Montana, North Dakota, South Dakota, Vermont, and Wyoming.

Meanwhile, the more densely populated states are allocated many more electoral votes to reflect their increased number of congressional districts and U.S. Representatives. Examples include: California has 53, Florida has 27, Illinois has 18, Pennsylvania has 18, and Texas has 36.

When the census is taken every ten years, the congressional district allocations shift according to the changes in state population densities. For example, when I was young and growing up in North Dakota, the state had two congressional districts. Now it has one. California around the time of my birth had 23 congressional districts while now it has 53. My how times change!

There is a fair amount of aggravation expressed over this proportional allocation convention. The objection stems from the idea that a person's vote is not worth as much in the more densely populated states than it is in the less populated states. Here's some math to illustrate what is meant:

California's electoral votes = 55
Wyoming's electoral votes = 3
California's citizens = 39,000,000 (2016 estimate)
Wyoming's citizens = 435,000 (2016 estimate)

Voting value tells us how much representation one's vote actually has. Dividing the number of citizens into the number of electoral votes provides a difference of voting value. It gives us a percentage that represents an individual's voting share of an electoral college vote in his or her state. The two states used here as examples provided these voting values in 2016:

California Vote Value = 0.0000014 electoral votes per voter
Wyoming Vote Value = 0.0000068 electoral votes per voter

Since that might seem a bit confusing, I will put it another way. Instead of asking what the vote value is, we can identify how many voters it takes for each electoral vote in a state. Here's how the two states compare from that perspective:

California voters needed for one electoral vote = 714,285.7
Wyoming voters needed for one electoral vote = 147,058.8

That means it takes fewer Wyoming voters than it does California voters for every electoral vote. In fact, in the example above, California needs 4.9 voters to be equal to one Wyoming voter.

The concern appears to be warranted from either vantage point. The two electoral votes granted for each state for their U.S. Senators is a leveling mechanism. It causes the more densely populated states to be slightly handicapped. Since it appears to take about 4.9 votes in California to equal one vote in Wyoming, it may seem unfair. But the leveling mechanism works as California easily dwarfs Wyoming when the population differences is 68.8 times greater.

There is another perspective to consider. As mentioned earlier, each state receives two electoral votes to reflect the number of U.S. Senators they have. These two votes put all states on an equal vote allocation footing, not counting the votes received because of their Representatives.

Let's experiment a bit. What happens if we remove the two electoral votes allocated for the two U.S. Senators from each state? The equation then becomes dividing by 53 instead of 55 for California and by one for Wyoming.

California Vote Value = 0.0000013
Wyoming Vote Value = 0.0000022

The voting value numbers are far more closely aligned, though they are still not the same. There is still more to consider. When statistics are involved, percentages are reflective of population pools, the numbers that make up a group. The population pools shown above (39 million versus 435 thousand) should NOT be the pools that are used when comparing the voting values. Instead, the correct population numbers come from the number of people voting. Let's compare the two states again:

California's voting citizens = 14,237,893 (2016)
Wyoming's voting citizens = 258,788 (2016)

Dividing the number of **voting** citizens into the number of electoral votes provides a difference of voting value:

California Vote Value = 0.0000038
Wyoming Vote Value = 0.0000115

Compare the results when using a pool of state citizens to the results using a pool of state voters:

California Vote Value of Citizens = 0.0000014
California Vote Value of Voters = 0.0000038 (an increase of 270%)
Wyoming Vote Value of Citizens = 0.0000068
Wyoming Vote Value of Voters = 0.0000115 (an increase of 169%)

The vote value difference shrinks between the two example states used above from 4.9 to 3.0. The difference is due to the voter turnout in these two states. In 2016, California's registered voter turnout was 73.35% while Wyoming's turnout was 90.86% (the highest in the nation). Please note that an eligible voter pool and a pool of registered voters is not the same thing. Our nation has an appalling record of eligible voters not registering to vote (44.3% in 2016)!

It seems, then, that if it's desirable to have a greater voting value, simply keep the voters away from the ballot box. After all, California increased its voters voting value more than two and a half times by having a low voter turnout. Wyoming didn't fare nearly so well in this regard by leading the nation in voter turnout.

Of course, that is facetious. We should still enable all eligible voters to participate in our presidential elections. It's not only the patriotic choice but the only way to truly determine the full sentiment of the governed. Every voter must be heard!

A lesson to take away from this example of voting math is that each state is not exactly equal to another. Our two state examples above proved they were far apart in their voting values along the voting value spectrum. If you live in a state with few electoral votes, your voting value is greater than those living in more populated states. If you live in a state with a low voter turnout, your voting value is greater than if you lived in a state with a high voter turnout. The simple truth is that your voting value is dependent upon the state in which you live.

Voting value differences is a troubling inconsistency of our voting process. However, in the grand view of presidential elections, the voting value differences is a minor voting distraction compared to other concerns that we endure in every election. We often do not consider, or even realize, that our nation is a composite of individual and sovereign states – a republic. Our Constitutional Framers included this mechanism to help level the voting power of state voters between states of high and low population densities.

★ Winner-Takes-All (WTA)

While consistency is desired in our presidential elections, the nation has endured another voting convention that creates a far more severe voter disadvantage. Given that the Electoral College was designed to be (and still is) a proportional voting system, it's not that way when we vote on a state-by-state basis. The rules change!

Each state, since the early 1800's, has chosen to translate its popular voting into a Winner-Takes-All (WTA) basis. A candidate that captures the most popular votes within a state also captures all of the electoral votes for that state. Votes not cast for the winning candidate from a state's voting are not translated into electoral votes, gaining no voting representation! They are essentially discarded!

> **NOTE:** Usually, the more common reference to WTA is written as "winners-take-all." It refers to winners (plural) indicating multiple winners across the multiple states. The preference used in this book is for the singular, "Winner-Takes-All" to highlight a winner being selected by voters of a single state. Further, the words are capitalized to facilitate using the WTA acronym.

The effect of the WTA change is that the whole presidential voting contest is upended! The rules change and the single contest (presidential election) is divided into 51 separate contests (50 states plus Washington, D.C.). You may be aware that when you vote for a president within your state, the goal for any candidate is to "win" your state. That means, your state's voting is a separate contest from the other 50 jurisdictions. The proportionality aspect gets discarded.

Imagine a football game at your high school or college. Imagine you're a player on the team. Suppose there is a big game this coming Saturday – it's Homecoming! You know your opponent is a tough team to beat and it's expected they will win.

Everyone on your team has practiced hard. Everyone has learned the plays and is determined to play their best. Everyone hopes, especially since it's Homecoming, the home team will prevail. You and the team and the homecoming crowd are pumped!

Imagine that every quarter is grueling. The opponent scores the first touchdown in the first quarter but your team regroups and fights back and scores in the second quarter. The defensive teams work hard to control the progress and neither team has scored in the third quarter. The third quarter ends and the game is tied seven to seven.

The fourth quarter is tense and the home crowd cheers as your team scores early, bringing the score to 14 to seven. Then in the very last minutes the visiting team breaks out and scores a touchdown. Instead of kicking the point-after-touchdown, they choose to run the ball into the end zone to score two points instead of one. The game ends with a score of 15 to 14 in favor of the visiting team. Your team lost the homecoming game!

Everyone's pretty sad on the home team. "Better luck next time," they say. You and your team members reply, "Yeah, we'll work even harder to win before we meet up with them again!" Fans applaud your effort and reassure you that you all made a valiant effort. The home crowd is still proud of you.

Then the paper comes out on Sunday. Everyone reads about the game. But what's this? The score is reported as being 29 to zero! This is the hometown paper and they're reporting that the home team scored nothing!

What do you think your fellow players are saying now? Will they be as willing to try so hard next time? Will any of your fellow players drop off the team? Will you inquire as to why the news reported the game's results as they did? What will the fans, the hometown crowd, say? What if they all agree with the paper, after all it is the trusted news. What if you hear derogatory comments and rebuke? What if you hear that some wonder how you could have let this important game slip by as you did?

Now compare this game to what happened in Florida in the 2016 and 2020 Presidential elections. Florida gets 29 electoral votes. All of these were awarded to Trump (Republican) because of WTA. If Equal Voice Voting had been used, Trump would have won 15 votes and Clinton/Biden (respective election years) would have won 14, the same as the example game above. The loss would have still occurred but the results would have reflected how voters actually voted.

How do you think the Democrats feel about their votes not counting? Will they be encouraged to vote next time, knowing that a Republican candidate in Florida won all of the electoral votes? Will Democrats be as eager to vote, to make their voices heard, if they know that Republicans can win such a victory and that their vote is really not needed? Will these kinds of results encourage future voter turnout?

If that scenario doesn't annoy you because you're Republican and you rather like having the Republicans win anyway, consider what happened in New York. In the 2016 and 2020 Presidential elections, 29 votes were awarded to Clinton and Biden in their respective elections. However, if Equal Voice Voting had been used, Clinton or Biden would have won 18 electoral votes to Trump's 11!

If Equal Voice Voting had been used in both states, Clinton would have won a total of 32 electoral votes to Trump's 26. But because of WTA in both states, Clinton won 29 electoral votes and Trump won 29. It is equal but unfair in both states.

Is it any wonder that so many voters do not vote in our presidential elections? If they know their vote will not really mean anything, many voters might say, "Why waste the time?"

There's a proverb that is applicable here: "Don't change horses in midstream." Abraham Lincoln used that admonition when he ran for his second term. As you can imagine, given the strife of a civil war, Lincoln had his detractors. To others, he advised that it would be unwise to pick a different president in the midst of the war. In other words, be consistent!

You may ask, "How bad is it?" For the previous 16 elections, 47.8% (average) of the ballots cast for a president have been set aside due to WTA! Over 63 million votes in the 2016 election and almost 69 million votes in 2020 did not count!

How does that voting value difference we spoke of earlier seem now? In my home state of Oregon, for example, we enjoyed a good voter turnout in 2016 of 80.33% and 81.19% in 2020, a significant voter turnout improvement over most other states. However, we also disenfranchised 51.15% in 2016 and 43.55% in 2020 of those voters because we used WTA! In other words, WTA worked against the gains we realized from improved voter registration.

If you cast your ballot in a state wherein your choice is for a minority candidate, you could have stayed home because your vote did not matter! Many voters do. Of course, this is not a good voting practice because, though a presidential ballot may not gain representation, there are other down-ballot candidates and issues that require all voters to be engaged.

One of the concerns all State Election officials have is voter turnout. Typically, across the nation, about a third (more or less) of registered voters do not bother voting. While there are many reasons why people fail to vote, feeling disenfranchised from the voting process (their vote not counting) ranks near the top of the list!

This brings us to a key issue for every presidential election. Given that we suffer low voter turnout of registered voters (ignoring for the moment the appalling fact that many eligible citizens are not even registered) and that we discard 47.8% of the ballots cast due to WTA, a shocking truth emerges:

Three registered voters are required to elicit one viable presidential ballot in any presidential election!

The reality is that one registered voter doesn't vote and one disenfranchised voter's ballot is discarded (due to WTA). Therefore, only one of the three ballots matters. This is a shameful situation. While steps can be taken to increase voter registration and to encourage greater voter turnouts, using WTA and tossing out 46% of the votes cast is despicable. This is especially the case when, as this book reveals, we do not have to continue this appalling practice.

There is another lesson to learn from this. The states are left on their own to decide how their popular votes are translated into the Electoral College. There is no U.S. Constitutional guideline as to how it is to be done. Over 200 years ago the states, individually, chose to use WTA and it's been used ever since.

There has been some discussion about Maine and Nebraska which, some say, do not use WTA. These two states use congressional district voting, which appears to forgo WTA in favor of a way to obtain a more proportional result. Congressional district voting is a recent change. Maine adopted the idea in 1972 and Nebraska did the same in 1992.

Congressional district voting translates a state's popular votes into electoral votes in two ways. First, the two electoral votes allocated to a state because of its U.S. Senators (each state gets two), are awarded to the candidate who wins the most popular votes in the state. This is one WTA application. Second, each congressional district awards its singular vote to the candidate who wins the most popular votes within that congressional district. This is another WTA application.

In effect, each citizen's vote is considered twice: once for the two votes awarded because of the U.S. Senators, and again for the single vote awarded within the congressional district because of its U.S. Representative. This means that your vote may not get representation within your congressional district but can on a state-wide basis, or vice versa, depending upon any given election.

Maine and Nebraska's electoral votes (Maine gets four, Nebraska gets five) were split only twice in each of these states. Maine split its votes in 2016, giving three to Clinton and one to Trump. The state did the same in 2020, giving three votes to Biden and one to Trump. Nebraska split its votes in 2008, giving four votes to McCain and one vote to Obama. The same result occurred in 2020 when four votes were awarded to Trump and one to Biden. It's a start to give voting greater representation to more voting citizens.

Equal Voice Voting (EVV) would have produced a better voter representation in those same years. Had the elections in Maine and Nebraska followed the EVV approach, their respective electoral votes dispersal would be as described below. Notice how every year had a more granular (more representative) result than what was experienced with congressional district voting.

Maine would have mostly split its four electoral votes, giving two electoral votes for the Democratic candidate and two for the Republican in eleven of the thirteen elections from 1972 through 2020. Two elections would have provided different electoral vote results.

- 1992 election: Clinton = 2, Bush = 1, Perot = 1
- 1996 election: Clinton = 3, Dole = 1

Nebraska would have split its five electoral votes in seven of the previous eight elections awarding two electoral votes for the Democratic candidate and three for the Republican except for:

- 1992 election: Clinton = 1, Bush = 3, Perot = 1

It's commendable that these states took it upon themselves to attempt a voting approach correction. They did not need to amend the U.S. Constitution because guidelines for how a state translates popular votes into electoral votes are not a part of that document. Each state is free to modify the popular vote translation process as its citizens and/or legislators choose.

The lesson here is that every state has the freedom to individually modify its approach. While both of these states recognized that the usual state-wide WTA fails to capture the true voter sentiment, they still used it, albeit in a modified way. Each state can, and should, recognize that WTA disenfranchises large portions of its voting citizenry. Each state can, and should, remove WTA for their presidential elections to improve voter representation and engagement.

★ Popular and Electoral College Results

Though you have just read about some of the truths revealed if one looks deeply into the voting process, many voters sense something is wrong even without this kind of scrutiny. It doesn't take a genius to realize one's vote doesn't count in an election. If you happen to live in a state wherein you tend to vote with the minority, your vote will not gain Electoral College representation for your presidential choice. Your vote will not succeed in getting your candidate into the White House, though he/she may win the national election.

For example, if you voted for Trump in 2016 but you lived in Oregon (my home state), your vote made no difference even though he won the presidency. Your vote did not get him there! But you're not alone. Trump's vote for himself in 2016 (he voted in New York) did not contribute to his win. Gore's vote for himself in 2000 (he voted in Tennessee) did not matter either.

If you do sense something is wrong with the voting process, it's likely that you don't totally trust the voting system. You may be a good patriot and continue to be a voting citizen, but you may do so because you know your vote for down-ballot candidates and issues deserve your attention. Good for you!

Distrust builds and you may find yourself among the many who want things to be different. Perhaps you wish the Electoral College was eliminated. Perhaps you wish the country would use a simple popular vote instead wherein each person's vote would matter. You might prefer the notion of "one person, one vote" that is desired by many. (This will be discussed further in Chapter 7.)

It is indisputable that our nation is a federal republic, composed of 50 separate and sovereign states. Recognizing this fact, the Constitutional Framers gave each state its own voting voice. A popular voting mechanism cast in one election across the nation would not have afforded this kind of election sensitivity for the sovereign states.

As mentioned earlier, the Constitutional Framers abhorred a direct democracy because history had proved that it gives way to mob rule and eventual tyranny. Knowing this, the Framers adopted a representative democracy with a system of checks and balances so a presidential candidate would have to gain a voting consensus across a coalition of states. One region or small group of states would not be able to tip the voting scales in their favor and override the voting sentiment of the rest of the nation.

Still, what can be done? The first step is hopefully apparent in this chapter: rid the country (on a state-by-state basis) of WTA. You have seen how WTA disenfranchises voters on a colossal level, forfeiting representation to an average of 47.8% of the ballots cast in every presidential election. Removing this approach can be accomplished without a U.S. Constitutional amendment, since WTA is not part of the Electoral College. Any state legislature can (and should) remove this encumbrance from its voting constituency.

If WTA is removed, a challenge emerges that calls for a mechanism that can fairly and equally translate a state's popular votes into its allocated electoral votes. Given that the Electoral College is a proportional system, it is logical to remain consistent for every state to adopt a proportional approach such as Equal Voice Voting!

★ Chapter Summary:

+ The Electoral College is a proportional voting system.
+ Every state uses a Winner-Takes-All (WTA) voting system to translate popular votes into electoral votes.
+ Two electoral votes are awarded to each state because of its U.S. Senators, giving some states a greater voting value than other states.

+ Voting value differences are a minor distraction from the more egregious disenfranchisement of voters due to WTA.

+ On average, the nation disenfranchises 47.8% of the voters in every presidential election due to WTA.

+ Due to low voter turnout and WTA disenfranchisement, three registered voters are required, on average, to elicit one valid presidential ballot.

+ States are capable of deciding, individually, how best to translate their popular votes into electoral votes. No U.S. Constitutional amendment is required.

+ Maine and Nebraska use congressional district voting. This is a variation of WTA and is not as representative of voters as EVV would be.

+ Voters sense that something is wrong with our presidential voting system. Their votes will not matter if they vote with a state's minority.

+ The lack of voting representation due to WTA disenfranchisement erodes voting confidence and contributes to low voter turnout.

+ WTA can be removed and EVV adopted in its place to make all votes matter and to ensure every state's voting voice is heard, thereby reinforcing the voting mechanism consistency.

CHAPTER 4
EQUAL VOICE VOTING

When you have mastered numbers, you will in fact no longer be reading numbers, any more than you read words when reading books. You will be reading meanings.

W.E.B. DU BOIS

(1868 – 1963, AMERICAN SOCIOLOGIST, HISTORIAN, AND ACTIVIST)

What is the answer?

You are now aware of how the Electoral College came into being, the principles upon which it was formed, and what we should expect of it. You are also aware that it is a proportionally based presidential election process that gets upended with the state-by-state usage of Winner-Takes-All (WTA). It's unnerving to realize that the nation disenfranchises about 47.8% of the voters in every presidential election because of the low voter turnout and WTA. It's unnerving to know that three registered voters are needed to elicit one viable presidential ballot.

Whatever mechanism takes WTA's place must meet the high standards a sound presidential election process demands. Namely, all votes must matter, every sovereign state must make a difference, and the constitutional checks and balances instituted by our Constitutional Framers must resist corruption and give representational balance to the nation's voting sentiment. Sadly, our current voting results fail our expectations causing voters to be disengaged as well as being disenfranchised.

Equal Voice Voting (EVV) is a process that consistently continues the proportional Electoral College voting process. Every vote cast for a viable candidate gains Electoral College representation. Further, every viable candidate can compete for a proportion of a state's allocated electoral votes, reflecting the proportion of a state's popular votes cast for her or him. Voting trust in the Electoral College can be improved with EVV as it restores voter confidence in the voting process. In so doing, EVV encourages greater voter turnout.

Equal Voice Voting is the answer.

★ Electoral College – A Proportional Voting System

History is more than an accounting of the past, putting everything in context and a sequencing of events. History illuminates our realities giving us perspectives we cannot comprehend from a current assessment of what we call *now*. History allows us to look back at presidential elections in the context of how this republic was formed and with the principles of governance our Constitutional Framers had in mind. We must be reminded that the election of our president – this one and only nationally elected federal office – is done so through a proportional process, giving both the nation's voting citizenry and the individual and sovereign states their voting voice.

EVV adheres to the proportional voting mechanism exercised by the Electoral College and honors the voting standards established in 1787. The EVV formula is straightforward. It incorporates two simple steps of division. The first division step produces a factor, used by each state, called the Popular Vote Value (PVV). The PVV is then divided into the state's total of popular votes cast for each candidate. The result is her or his share of the state's allocation of the Electoral College's electoral votes.

The next few pages illustrate the EVV formula and present some simple math equations. The formula is a simple two-step process. The illustrations also include number rounding rules, and some results adjustments that sometimes may be required.

★ The EVV Formula

To illustrate how this formula works, let's imagine a fictitious state that is allocated 10 electoral votes for the presidential elections. Let's also assume that three million voters cast ballots in the election.

The first step is to determine the state's Popular Vote Value (PVV). The state's three million popular votes cast in the election is divided by its 10 total electoral votes. The PVV for the state is 300,000.

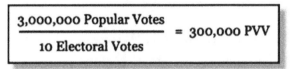

$$\frac{3,000,000 \text{ Popular Votes}}{10 \text{ Electoral Votes}} = 300,000 \text{ PVV}$$

Figure 4 – 1: Identifying the PVV

Now let's assume an election with two presidential candidates: Candidate "A" and "B". Candidate "A" does remarkably well and wins 1,920,000 votes compared to Candidate "B's" 1,080,000 votes. These votes are then translated (converted) into electoral votes by dividing each candidate's popular votes by the state's PVV.

Determining the electoral votes for Candidate "A":

$$\frac{1,920,000 \text{ Popular Votes}}{300,000 \text{ (PVV)}} = 6.4 \text{ Electoral Votes}$$

Figure 4 – 2: Candidate "A's" Electoral Votes

Determining the electoral votes for Candidate "B":

$$\frac{1,080,000 \text{ Popular Votes}}{300,000 \text{ (PVV)}} = 3.6 \text{ Electoral Votes}$$

Figure 4 – 3: Candidate "B's" Electoral Votes

★ Rounding Numbers

The Electoral College does not work with fractions, however. Some adjustments need to be made for our two candidates so that their electoral votes are whole numbers. The raw numbers for the electoral votes need to be rounded up or down to whole numbers.

The rule for rounding numbers is that half numbers (such as 1.5) are rounded up to the next highest round number. If we have 1.5, it gets rounded up to two. If we have a number less than that (such as 1.49), it gets rounded down to one.

In our example above, Candidate "A" received 6.4 electoral votes. That would get rounded down to a whole number of six. Candidate "B" receive 3.6 electoral votes so that number would get rounded up to four.

Let's do this again but include a third-party candidate in the race. We'll use Candidates "A", "B", and "C". Typically, third-party candidates win a much smaller percentage of votes and almost never gain any electoral votes. Using EVV, however, notice how Candidate "C" affects the outcome even with a small vote win.

Let's assume Candidate "A" wins 1,250,000 votes, Candidate "B" wins 1,080,000 votes, and Candidate "C" wins 670,000 votes.

Determining the electoral votes for Candidate "A":

$$\frac{1{,}250{,}000 \text{ Popular Votes}}{300{,}000 \text{ (PVV)}} = 4.17 \text{ Electoral Votes}$$

Figure 4 – 4: Candidate "A's" Electoral Votes

Determining the electoral votes for Candidate "B":

$$\frac{1{,}080{,}000 \text{ Popular Votes}}{300{,}000 \text{ (PVV)}} = 3.6 \text{ Electoral Votes}$$

Figure 4 – 5: Candidate "B's" Electoral Votes

Determining the electoral votes for Candidate "C":

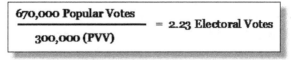

$$\frac{670{,}000 \text{ Popular Votes}}{300{,}000 \text{ (PVV)}} = 2.23 \text{ Electoral Votes}$$

Figure 4 – 6: Candidate "C's" Electoral Votes

This time, Candidate "A" won fewer votes than in the earlier example which resulted in 4.17 electoral votes. Candidate "B" won the same number of electoral votes and Candidate "C" captured 2.23 electoral votes, presumably, luring away some voters from Candidate "A".

When the rounding rules are applied, the candidates win these electoral votes:

+ Candidate "A" = 4 electoral votes
+ Candidate "B" = 4 electoral votes
+ Candidate "C" = 2 electoral votes

★ The EVV Threshold

The rounding rules only apply, however, if a candidate wins at least the PVV number of popular votes. For example, if Candidate "C" had won only 170,000 votes, the raw electoral vote count does not equal the PVV amount.

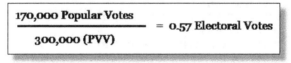

$$\frac{170{,}000 \text{ Popular Votes}}{300{,}000 \text{ (PVV)}} = 0.57 \text{ Electoral Votes}$$

Figure 4 – 7: Candidate "C's" Electoral Votes

The PVV forms a threshold that any candidate must reach to win any electoral votes. Reaching this vote threshold is what makes a candidate viable when applying the EVV approach. It means the votes won by a candidate are significant enough for Electoral College consideration.

In this case, Candidate "C" would not be able to round the raw electoral votes up to one because the candidate did not capture the necessary 300,000 vote threshold (the state's PVV). Once the threshold is reached (the minimum needed for any viable candidate) the rounding rules apply.

★ Third Party Candidates

But this may create a problem! Remember, this fictitious state is allocated ten electoral votes. What happens if a third candidate takes away enough votes to disrupt the allocation? Let's run the election again showing Candidate "C" winning the 170,000 votes and split the remaining 500,000 votes (formerly won by Candidate "C" in our example above) between Candidates "A" and "B", giving each of them an additional 250,000 votes.

Determining the electoral votes for Candidate "A":

$$\frac{1{,}500{,}000 \text{ Popular Votes}}{300{,}000 \text{ (PVV)}} = 5.0 \text{ Electoral Votes}$$

Figure 4 – 8: Candidate "A's" Electoral Votes

Determining the electoral votes for Candidate "B":

$$\frac{1{,}330{,}000 \text{ Popular Votes}}{300{,}000 \text{ (PVV)}} = 4.43 \text{ Electoral Votes}$$

Figure 4 – 9: Candidate "B's" Electoral Votes

Determining the electoral votes for Candidate "C":

$$\frac{170{,}000 \text{ Popular Votes}}{300{,}000 \text{ (PVV)}} = 0.57 \text{ Electoral Votes}$$

Figure 4 – 10: Candidate "C's" Electoral Votes

Here are the results when we apply the rounding adjustments:

+ Candidate "A" = 5 electoral votes
+ Candidate "B" = 4 electoral votes
+ Candidate "C" = 0 electoral votes

The total is nine, one less than the allocated ten electoral votes. The "lost" electoral vote is awarded to the candidate who wins the most popular votes. In this example, Candidate "A" would add another electoral vote to her/his total to make six. Candidate "B" would still have four electoral votes. The allocated ten electoral votes are reached.

+ Candidate "A" = 6 electoral votes
+ Candidate "B" = 4 electoral votes
+ Candidate "C" = 0 electoral votes

★ EVV Formula Adjustments

The reverse can also occur when the rounding adjustment causes the candidates' electoral votes to exceed the state's allotment. Let's use another example to show how this can happen.

Let's assume that Candidate "A" wins 1,350,000 popular votes, Candidate "B" wins 1,050,000 popular votes, and Candidate "C" wins 450,000 popular votes.

Determining the electoral votes for Candidate "A":

$$\frac{1{,}350{,}000 \text{ Popular Votes}}{300{,}000 \text{ (PVV)}} = 4.5 \text{ Electoral Votes}$$

Figure 4 – 11: Candidate "A's" Electoral Votes

Determining the electoral votes for Candidate "B":

$$\frac{1{,}050{,}000 \text{ Popular Votes}}{300{,}000 \text{ (PVV)}} = 3.5 \text{ Electoral Votes}$$

Figure 4 – 12: Candidate "B's" Electoral Votes

Determining the electoral votes for Candidate "C":

$$\frac{450{,}000 \text{ Popular Votes}}{300{,}000 \text{ (PVV)}} = 1.5 \text{ Electoral Votes}$$

Figure 4 – 13: Candidate "C's" Electoral Votes

Here are the results when we apply the rounding adjustments:

+ Candidate "A" = 5 electoral votes
+ Candidate "B" = 4 electoral votes
+ Candidate "C" = 2 electoral votes

The total is now 11 electoral votes, which is one more than the ten allocated for that state. One vote needs to be removed. Since Candidate "C" won the fewest popular votes, one electoral vote is removed from her or his total. The adjusted totals now are:

+ Candidate "A" = 5 electoral votes
+ Candidate "B" = 4 electoral votes
+ Candidate "C" = 1 electoral vote

The ten electoral votes are now the same as the allocated state's electoral votes.

It should be noted that these adjustments to add or subtract an electoral vote would not be common. They would occur only when there are more than two candidates running for the presidency and, even then, only in uncommon circumstances. In these situations, the total popular votes cause the rounding adjustments to nudge the electoral vote totals to be either less than or more than what has been allocated to the state.

★ EVV Voting Results

There are two more things to notice with these EVV voting results:

+ All votes matter!
+ All viable candidates gain electoral vote representation

It has already been discussed that large numbers of voters are disenfranchised in every presidential election. On average, 47.8% of the ballots cast do not gain representation. EVV gives representation to ballots cast for any candidate that is able to win enough popular votes to reach the PVV threshold, making them viable for Electoral College consideration.

In addition, even if you vote for Santa Claus, your vote makes a difference when a state uses the EVV formula. Every vote cast, whether for a viable candidate or not, affects the PVV. In our example above, our fictitious state was allocated 10 electoral votes. That means that for every ten votes cast, the PVV factor amount is increased.

Our example used 3,000,000 voters. The PVV for that number of voters was 300,000. If ten more voters were included to make 3,000,010, the PVV number would be 300,001. It may not seem like a lot but it makes a difference.

But wait – there's more! Imagine that there were only five more voters added to the total. Then we'd have 3,000,005 divided by the 10 electoral votes. The PVV in this case would be 300,000.5. The PVV number would be rounded up so, again, the PVV number would be 300,001. Which means, in this instance, every five voters affect the PVV number. All votes matter!

★ Voting Result Comparisons

What should we expect? Currently, many voters sense that something is wrong with presidential voting results given that the popular vote and electoral vote results do not compare well in relation to each other. We know that, because of WTA, the winning candidate captures all of the electoral votes from a given state. However, counting all votes from all 50 states and Washington, D.C., it's reasonable to expect (want) the two results to be similar, if not the same.

The following two graphs compare the voting results of the past 16 elections. The first graph shows the popular vote (dashed line) compared with the Electoral College results (solid line). These two lines represent the votes (electoral and popular) captured by the election winners. Obviously, there are wide variation between the two. They should be similar and because they are not, voters can sense that our voting mechanism does not portray how the country votes very well.

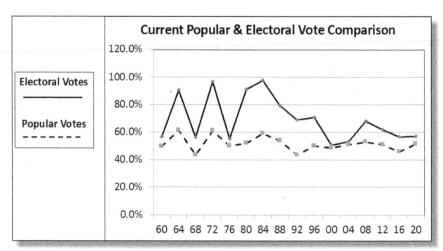

Graph 4 – 1: Popular and Electoral College Comparison

The graph below shows how the Electoral College results would have compared to the popular voting had it been used nation-wide in those elections. Notice how closely the two lines lie, sometimes merging, as the two voting results emerge.

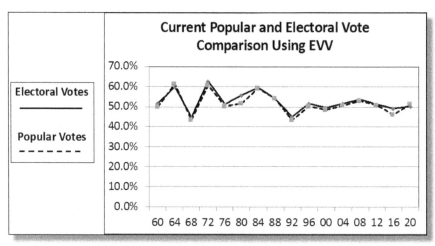

Graph 4 – 2: Popular and EVV Comparison

Clearly, if we want our Electoral College results to be similar to the popular voting, EVV provides a much better result. Remember, too, that these results can be achieved without the need for a U.S. Constitutional amendment.

★ Voting Results Disparities

There is yet another way to compare the voting results. It's a little more complicated but it points to yet another measure of how poorly our current Electoral College results fare in comparison to how the nation votes. Again, the poor Electoral College results are a product of employing WTA. EVV would remove that problem and provide a more accurate voting result nation-wide.

As we look at voting results, comparing popular and electoral votes, two terms will be used below to differentiate two concepts. The term *Difference* is used to show the difference between candidates, whether it is of the popular vote results or the electoral vote results. The term *Disparity* is used to show how the popular voting results compare to the Electoral College results.

The two graphs shown below illustrate what we might expect. If Candidate "A" wins 5% more popular votes nationwide than Candidate "B", it's reasonable to expect similar results from the electoral vote results. The 5% illustrated here is the *Difference* between the two voting results while the variation between the two voting type results shows a zero percent (0%) *Disparity* (The results are the same.).

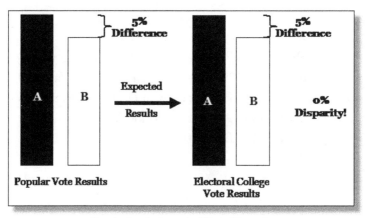

Graph 4 – 3: Expected Vote Disparity

If we look at historical voting results, we find that such expectations are dashed on the rocks of reality. The voting result *Disparities* between voting types are neither consistent nor predictable. The illustrations below show a couple of wide swings in voting results, from a voting disparity perspective.

The 1964 election shows there was a 21% popular vote *Difference* between Lyndon Johnson's 61% of the popular vote and Barry Goldwater's 40% of the popular vote. The electoral vote *Disparity* was 80% as Lyndon Johnson captured 90% of the popular vote and Barry Goldwater captured 10% of the popular vote. The *Disparity* between these two voting results was a 59% (80% - 21%)!

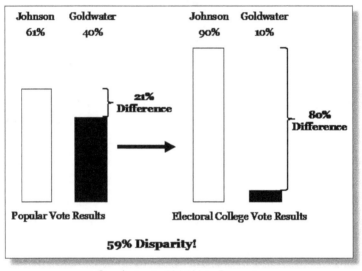

Graph 4 – 4: 1964 Vote Disparity

The 1984 election shows there was an 18% popular vote *Difference* between Ronald Reagan's 59% of the popular vote and Walter Mondale's 41% of the popular vote. The electoral vote *Disparity* was 96% as Ronald Reagan captured 98% of the popular vote and Walter Mondale captured 2% of the popular vote. The *Disparity* between these two voting results was a 78% (96% - 18%)!

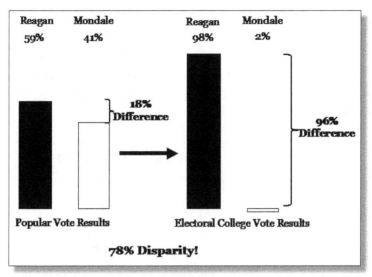

Graph 4 – 5: 1984 Vote Disparity

Consistency of results is not guaranteed but the wild disparity swings highlighted above should be a rare occurrence. However, looking back at the previous 16 elections, from 1960 through 2020, the graph below reveals that disparity swings from highs to lows is common.

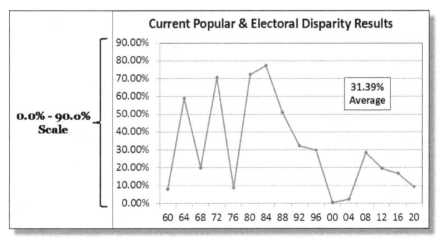

Graph 4 – 6: Disparities 1960 - 2020

Only once, in 2000, did the two voting results prove to be similar. The voting disparity average over the past 16 elections was 31.39%! These are not predictable results and contribute significantly to voter distrust in the presidential voting process.]

Compare these results with what would have happened if EVV had been used instead for these 16 elections. Note, however, that had EVV been used, the voter turnout may have been different and the results would not have been the same.

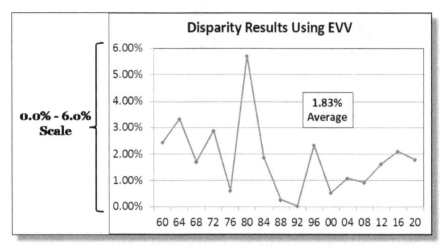

Graph 4 – 7: Using EVV Voting Disparity Results

While the graph line still swings up and down, two other things should be apparent. The left-side scale of the first graph ranges from 0.0% to 90%. The second graph shows a range of 0.0% to 6%.

The averages, too, are vastly different. The first graph shows an average *Disparity* of 31.39% while the EVV graph shows only an average of 1.83%. The voting *Disparities* we currently experience are more than 17 times as erratic as what would be experienced using EVV. In other words, the EVV voting *Disparities* would be much more in line with how the nation actually votes when using EVV.

A third graph, combining the two graphs above to further compare the two approaches, is shown below. Notice that the EVV *Disparities* are confined to the narrow band at the bottom of the graph.

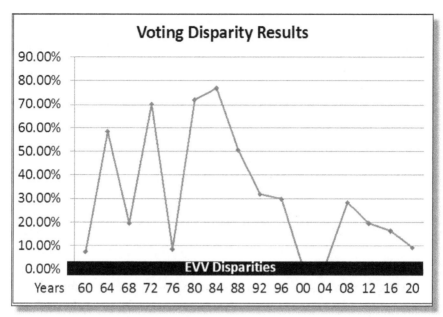

Graph 4 – 8: Combined Voting Disparity Results

The following table shows the results of the 16 elections from 1960 – 2020. Each election presents the voting results in percentages for the Democrat, Republican, and Other candidates. Other refers to those candidates who captured a significant number of ballots that could have also gained electoral votes had EVV been used. The 2016 Other column actually is a composite of the votes captures by Johnson and Stein.

The columns show the electoral votes (in percentages) that could have been captured if the nation had employed EVV. Those percentages, you'll notice, correlate favorably with the popular vote percentages, which are found in the next column. The third column for each political party shows the percentage of electoral votes that were actually captured. The percentages vary significantly from those of the popular vote column.

Election Years	Democrat			Republican			Other		
	EVV Electoral Votes	Popular Votes	Electoral Votes	EVV Electoral Votes	Popular Votes	Electoral Votes	EVV Electoral Votes	Popular Votes	Electoral Votes
1960	51.4%	49.7%	56.4%	48.6%	49.6%	40.8%			
1964	59.7%	61.1%	90.3%	40.3%	38.5%	9.7%			
1968	42.4%	42.7%	33.5%	44.8%	43.4%	56.0%	12.8%	13.3%	0.0%
1972	37.2%	37.5%	3.2%	62.8%	60.7%	96.7%			
1976	51.1%	50.1%	55.2%	48.9%	48.0%	46.6%			
1980	41.4%	41.8%	9.1%	55.8%	51.7%	90.9%	2.8%	6.5%	0.0%
1984	40.5%	40.9%	2.4%	59.5%	59.1%	97.6%			
1988	45.9%	46.1%	20.8%	54.1%	53.9%	79.2%			
1992	45.0%	43.3%	68.8%	39.4%	37.7%	31.2%	15.6%	19.0%	0.0%
1996	51.7%	50.1%	70.5%	43.5%	41.4%	29.5%	4.8%	8.5%	0.0%
2000	49.8%	48.8%	49.6%	49.6%	48.6%	50.4%	0.6%	2.6%	0.0%
2004	48.3%	48.3%	46.8%	51.7%	50.7%	53.2%			
2008	53.7%	52.9%	67.8%	46.3%	45.6%	32.2%			
2012	51.1%	51.0%	61.7%	48.9%	47.2%	38.3%			
2016	50.0%	47.9%	42.2%	49.3%	45.9%	56.5%	0.8%	4.4%	0.0%
2020	50.1%	51.3%	56.9%	49.3%	46.9%	43.1%			

Table 4 – 9: Combined Voting Disparity Results

It helps to look at history to see what happened so we can gain guidance moving forward. We see an erratic outcome when we look at the national voting results as popular votes are translated into electoral votes (employing WTA) on a state-by-state basis. Replacing WTA with EVV and using the same data over the previous 16 elections shows far more consistency. Further, it can easily be surmised that the voting public would realize that the Electoral College voting results closely reflect the popular voting across the nation.

★ Chapter Summary:

+ The Electoral College is a proportional voting system.
+ The EVV is a two-step process.
  ➤ Determine the Popular Vote Value (PVV).
  ➤ Determine a candidate's electoral votes.
+ Results are rounded to whole numbers.
+ Each candidate must win a threshold of popular votes to be viable.
+ Adjustments may be needed when third party candidates run.
+ All votes matter because it affects the PVV.
+ All viable candidates gain electoral vote representation with EVV.
+ EVV voting results closely align with the popular voting results.

- *Difference* refers to the difference of vote results between candidates, whether it is popular or electoral voting.
- *Disparity* refers to the difference between popular and electoral vote results.
- Our current voting experience caused voting disparities that averaged 31.39% over the past 16 elections.
- EVV voting experience would have caused voting disparities that averaged 1.83% over the past 16 elections.
- Less vote results disparity with EVV means voters can trust the presidential voting process more than what we currently experience.

CHAPTER 5
INTERFERENCE

We need to recognize that ... the disenfranchisement of voters, the suppression of votes, cuts across every community, and therefore, it cuts across partisanship.

STACEY ABRAMS

(B. 1973, LAWYER, POLITICIAN, AND VOTING RIGHTS ACTIVIST)

Do you matter? Does what you think or what you say matter? Does what you do or strive for matter? Do your values and your spiritual practice and your sense of right and wrong matter? Does the society and the neighborhood in which you live matter?

If you answered, "Yes!" to any one of these questions, and you are an eligible United States voter, then your vote for a president should matter. Your opinion matters. This nation was founded on the power of governance based on the people. Originally, the people who counted, the voters, were the few, not the many. Voting rights were horribly restricted in the early formation of the country, limited mostly to white men who owned property. Women could not vote. Slaves and people of color could not vote. The poor, too, were kept away from the ballot box.

We neither pledge allegiance to a king nor do we suffer under the tyranny of a dictator. "We the People," as the first words of the preamble to the U.S. Constitution declares, are the sole source of political power and we are either the benefactors or sufferers of how well or how poorly we wield it. It is often little understood that the power to move forward, to stand still, or to regress in the governance of our nation rests with the people.

This chapter focuses on the interference experienced during presidential elections either before or after ballots are cast. One interference, experienced in the earliest hours of this nation, was the mechanical challenge of collecting a viable voting result. Thankfully, these initial challenges and confusions have been met with today's technological advances. A second interference, revealing the dark side of this nation's history and human nature, is voter suppression. A third interference, emerging from a historical choice of convenience and habit, is vote suppression.

These three forms of interference have hobbled the ability to capture the votes, count them, and represent the voters in our presidential elections. Sometimes the failings stem from human imprecision and other times point to the workings of greed, unfounded fears, and a preference for power and control over others. Such interferences prevent election results from reflecting the true sentiment of the governed, a fundamental basis for our representative democracy.

★ Counting the Votes

It is helpful to imagine the context of how voting by the people was historically conducted. First, voting was not easy to do, given the limits of mobility and the distances separating the voters. Voting was not done secretly, as we so cherish today. It was a rather public affair. You might think it as being an awkward proceeding but, remember, only a few could vote – those white gents with property.

Second, voting did not start out using paper ballots as we have today. There were actually two ways to capture the votes. One was the caucus method wherein people stood with others who chose the same candidate. If you preferred a different guy (always a guy in those days), you stood with the other group. Then the heads were counted, as in taking a poll. Or, the guys voted by tossing something into a box; still a public and viewable action.

Quoting Jill Lepore in her book, "These Truths," she says:

> A "poll" meant the top of a person's head. ... Counting polls
> required assembling – all in favor of the Federalist stand here,
> all in favor of the Republican over there – and in places where
> voting was done by ballot, casting a ballot generally meant

tossing a ball into a box. The word "ballot" comes from the Italian "ballota," meaning a little ball – and early Americans who used ballots cast pea[s] or pebbles, or, not uncommonly, bullets. [1]

It certainly must have been arduous. Be they polls or ballots, they would have to be counted and recounted. Remember, there were no computers then, not even any calculators. Pens (quills), ink and parchment were all they had to record all of those tallies of peas, pebbles, and musket balls.

Imagine the process. First a collection of votes is made throughout the state (colony back then) and then, somehow, these votes by the people had to be converted into electoral votes. Messy. There would be fractions and decimals and questions would prevail about rounding numbers up or down or at all. These questions and answers were probably not consistent from state to state. More mess.

Thankfully, with the advent of computers and savvy statisticians, much of the challenge of voting capture is behind us. Presidential voting in the nation has vastly expanded from the original thirteen colonies to Washington, D.C. and 50 states. Ballots (no longer peas, stones, or musket balls) are either electronically captured or submitted via paper or both. Yes, we may still hear horror stories about hanging chads (nightmare of the 2000 election) or of systems being hacked; but, vote collection has mainly become an advanced science.

Still, vote capture and counting remains a concern and a worry that the nation's voting sentiment may suffer interference. Acknowledging the fits and starts of the early voting days, along with the modern-day challenges we face, one fact remains clear: Our votes are precious! We should not allow any interference for them to be cast or for the choices made to not be represented. All votes matter!

Voting still meets with interference in this country though much of the restrictions of gender, race, and ownership of property have been lifted. The mechanisms used to capture the sentiment of the governed has vastly improved but are now threatened by foreign entities and nefarious forces among us. Voting for a president is regarded as a prized patriotic duty, a right, and a privilege. We must take these threats seriously!

★ Dark Side of Human Nature

Foreign influence (interference) is a major concern. Russia, for example, hacked into the 2016 presidential election process via social media and data theft, causing inestimable harm. It is an interference that has cost the nation untold millions of dollars. More, it has eroded the trust voters have in the process, which is probably the most egregious form of destruction of all.

Foreign interference, and its aiding and abetting by sympathetic citizens, is an ever-present threat to our voting structure. Much has been written about and serious steps have been taken to counteract these threats. The significance for this writing is how it points to the nefarious side of elections, political conflict, and foreign relations. It points to the realities of our more undesirable aspects of human natures.

Man's inhumanity to man and the proclivities that emerge that give vent to untoward means and actions was a central concern for our Constitutional Framers. They knew full well that, left unchecked, the framework of governance they created could easily dissolve by common vices that serve a lust for power, fortune, and prestige.

Here are a few of their insights, as captured in the Federalist Papers, authored by James Madison, Alexander Hamilton, and John Jay:

> It may be a reflection on human nature that such devices [the constitution] should be necessary to control the abuses of government. But what is government itself but the greatest of all reflections on human nature? If men were angels, no government would be necessary. If angels were to govern men, neither external nor internal controls on government would be necessary. In framing a government which is to be administered by men over men, the great difficulty lies in this: you must first enable the government to control the governed; and in the next place oblige it to control itself.
> Federalist #51, Madison
>
> ... there is a degree of depravity in mankind which requires a certain degree of circumspection and distrust.
> Federalist #56, Madison

... men are ambitious, vindictive, and rapacious.
Federalist #6, Hamilton

These men who framed the U.S. Constitution also put their faith in the better angels of mankind, mainly realizing that they were forming a civilization that was built on hope for their futures. They formed a government based on the primacy of law, realizing that mankind is frail, subject to temptations of opportunity and gaining advantage.

Perhaps the Framers looked deeply at themselves and saw their own failings. Many owned slaves. Some were tormented by that injustice. Perhaps the smell of freedom won from England made them realize the importance of the values and standards taught them by parental discipline and religious guidance. Ignoring human frailty would cause their aggregated gift of the constitution to crumble away like riverbanks facing a flood.

★ Voter Suppression

It has already been said that only white men could vote when the U.S. Constitution was ratified. As far as a representative democracy was concerned, it was a feeble beginning that excluded so many from voting. It's especially insulting when the very first words of that constitution read: "We the people..."

The 14th constitutional amendment sought to partly remedy the problem by allowing people of color to vote. The year was 1868 when that amendment was ratified, 81 years after the U.S. Constitution was written. Things may have started out well, but as Gilda R. Daniels writes in her book, "Uncounted":

[In the early 1900's] The Jim Crow laws and violence effectively killed the right to vote for the newly enfranchised citizen. The right to vote was no longer a reality and democracy, a government for the people and by the people, ceased to exist. It took almost a century before the descendants of the former slaves would overcome the many obstacles set before them prohibiting access to the ballot in a meaningful way. An inability to register and vote existed across the South. [2]

Accounts are prevalent wherein voters are purged from voting rolls, denied access to the voting booth, and suffer hardship, indignity, and even death when attempting to vote. Gilda R. Daniels continues:

> From the 1860s to the 1960s to this millennium, voters of color endured poll taxes, literacy tests, grandfather clauses, violence, and murder as significant barriers to the ballot box. [3]

Meanwhile, women had to wait yet another 52 years until the 19th amendment was ratified in 1920 to allow women to vote. The year 2020 was the 100th anniversary of that right, a full 233 years after the constitution was written.

These amendments, along with the landmark 1965 Voting Rights Act (VRA), did not come easily or as a gradual "awakening" of the nation's legislative leadership. They came with sacrifice beyond measure up to and including torture and death. The cost paid has been heavy. The torment and exclusion have been a dark mark on our society.

Sadly, voting access limits are still being exercised. Voter registration rolls are still purged and barriers to voting are still erected. Sometimes these obstacles are creative: reducing the number of polling locations, reducing hours of availability, locating polling locations beyond the reaches of easy access, falsely advertising hours of operation, and so on. The antics seem to be without limit for those who can wield power to their benefit, excluding those in the minority or who are disadvantaged.

Silencing voters, by the tens and hundreds of thousands, even by millions, is a nefarious endeavor. It is not conducted by those who respect the ideals of a representative democracy. It is not conducted by those driven to truly serve a constituency. They are conducted by those who intentionally tip the voting scales in their favor to gain or retain power for their own advantage. These are criminal acts noted in the public court of common decency.

★ Racism and Sexism in The Electoral College

Some people claim that the Electoral College is racist. There is no denying that the voting mechanism, the entire U.S. Constitution in fact, was formulated in a terribly racist society. Several of the Founding Fathers owned slaves and were used to the benefits of their labor, attendance, and – worse – the power they wielded over the very day-to-day lives of these people they owned like chattel.

At its inception, the Electoral College incorporated the compromise that was previously established to determine the number of delegates each colony would have. Each colony's delegate representation was based on the number of people they had. The northern colonies did not want the southern colonies to have representative advantage (gaining more delegates in Congress) if the south also counted their slaves. The northern states feared that if the southern colonies had more delegates it would allow them to excessively tax the north.

A compromise was struck that considered slaves as three-fifths a person. It was a mathematical representation that effectively reduced humans to be mere numbers, partial ones at that. It resulted in the south not having as many delegates they would if slaves were counted as whole persons.

The formula used to determine the number of delegates affected the Electoral College. The number of electoral votes each colony had was based on how many delegates they sent to the U.S. Congress. The formula did not affect *how* the popular votes were converted into electoral votes. It only affected the number of delegates and, consequently, the number of electoral votes a colony was allocated.

The compromise should not be misconstrued to imply that it affected how slaves voted. They simply were not allowed to vote. There was no converting the slave vote by the three-fifths proportion because there were no votes cast by slaves.

These were despicable times that bore the fruit from decades of slavery. It was not a new venture, a turning of a new page of history, that found these learned men accepting a total disregard of human life while they wrote of such ideas that said, "All men are created equal." It was a lie then and the blood spilled over the years because of this societal sin speaks to the divide that still persists as racism.

We need to realize that racism is a world-view and an attitude that subjects a vulnerable set of people to a kind of hell on earth. Racism is not a "thing" in the sense that any object is a thing. It shapes who people are from the inside out rather than being some kind of outer shell, a uniform that identifies and separates some persons from others. It becomes a systemic state of one's very being.

For example, the nation's White House in which the President and family resides, was built by slaves. It is ironic that it is called a "white" house when people of color cut the wood, nailed the boards, and even applied the paint. Is the White House racist? Of course not, though it was certainly built during severely racist times by those subjugated to the pains of slavery. Today, we would no more tear the White House down because of a more awakened judgement of racism than we would erase the record of racism from our history. The White House is a thing erected during racist times. It is not racist as it stands, though it reminds us of those oppressively dark days.

We are left with the fact that the Electoral College is a voting mechanism – a mathematical approach. Yes, it emerged during the dark days of slavery and was originally based on despicable measures of people. Decades later, the three-fifths rule would be abolished as slavery was abolished. Still later, people of color would gain their rights to vote. The Electoral College still functions with its primary purpose to proportionally convert popular votes into electoral votes on a state-by-state basis.

Just as racism is a world-view and attitude, so is sexism. Though women have had a significant role in our history they often fall victim to the overwhelming and brutish power of men. Denying women their right to vote from the nation's inception is another form of oppression, engineered and reinforced by men. The lack of voting rights for women took 133 years to overturn. The taint of misogyny is still with us.

The problems persist. We can be encouraged that people of color and women can now vote, regardless of the fact such interferences should never have been entertained in the first place. Still, we have a long way to go both at the voting booth and in gaining equanimity in our legislative leadership. Many ancestors would be amazed at the progress made. Many other ancestors would wonder (some silently, some with a raucous roar), why has it all taken so long? Why have we not become more evolved, more mature?

Human nature has a dark side and cannot be wholly and naively trusted to not be tempted to invite fraud and corruption into our voting process. Our early history of slavery and sexism excluded many from the voting process, the very mechanism that fuels our representative democracy.

But the mechanism itself, now open to those excluded before, cannot be considered to be racist or sexist in spite of the past in which it was contrived.

There is much for white males to be embarrassed about as history points her accusatory finger at them, pointing out the shame because of how we as a people so easily mistreat each other. Racism and sexism are the yokes put upon us from the earliest days of this nation's founding because of selfish attitudes and limited views of reality. The Electoral College has broken free from much of the stink of its past. Everyone's vote should matter.

Should, but we are not quite there yet. We are not as inclusive as we need to be.

★ Vote Suppression

The U.S. Constitution is pretty adamant that the winner must win by a majority vote. A simple math trick then would be to take the box of pebbles or peas or musket balls or whatever that held the most thereof, and declare that box (that candidate) the winner. Efficient and easy! Winner-Takes-All (WTA) saves the day! No more mess!

Seriously, since the constitution did not delineate just how popular votes would be converted into electoral votes, early elections were a bit experimental. Some states attempted to divide the electoral votes allotted to them but their political leaders soon found they had a greater impact (read: could retain more political power) if they went with WTA. This is vote suppression (not to be confused with voter suppression). Vote suppression is a state choice. It is not an Electoral College feature.

To add a little insult to the injury, we must also realize that this habitually bad processing has been going on since the early 1800's. Two states used WTA in 1800. Six states used it in 1808. By 1836 every state used it except South Carolina. Whether it was a popular evolution or simply a quick way to convert popular votes into electoral votes, WTA was put in place and there was no going back.

Some contend that Maine and Nebraska do not use WTA today, but they do. As a reminder, they allocate two electoral votes for whichever candidate wins the state-wide plurality, an example of WTA. Each of their congressional districts award an electoral vote to the candidate winning the plurality of that district, causing WTA to still guide them. Certainly, the approach used by Maine and Nebraska is an improvement but WTA is still exercised in those states.

Many voters cast their ballots for their presidential choice only to have those ballots set aside without gaining any Electoral College representation. Ballots cast for any presidential candidate who does not win the state's plurality (most) of votes are essentially voided because their choice gains no electoral vote representation. This nullifying of large numbers of voters is due to WTA. It is vote suppression.

This book largely rests on the findings that emerged from a state-by-state analysis of the previous 16 presidential elections, from 1960 through 2020. The analysis included what effect WTA had on those elections. The results were stunning. An average of 47.8% of votes cast gained no representation. For example, the 2016 election was a rather average election in this regard, setting aside 46%! The 2016 election ignored (granting no representation) 63,176,680 votes. The 2020 election disenfranchised a lower percentage but still managed to not give representation to 68,955,450 ballots. Most striking is that nobody cried, "Foul!" or even complained. The electoral votes were converted from the popular votes as they have been for the past 200 years.

The following illustration shows a graphical representation of the representation the nation's ballots received in 2016. Each state is represented as a graph showing gray bars to represent the percentage of registered voters whose votes were represented in the Electoral College. The white areas represent the 47.8% (nationwide average) of ballots cast that did not gain representation. The white area also includes the registered voters who did not vote. Nationwide, the non-voting registered voters was about 30%.

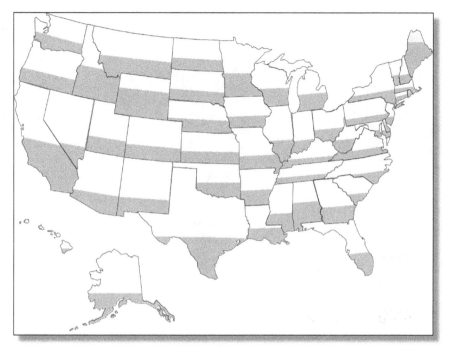

Figure 5 - 1: 2016 Election Representation

Compare the illustration above with the next one. Again, it is a graphical representation, on a state-by-state basis, showing the representation ballots could have received if EVV were used. The gray bars reflect the representation received by both political parties (Democrat and Republican). The white expanse only reflects those registered voters that did not vote in 2016.

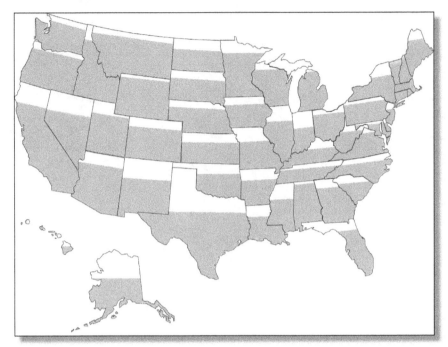

Figure 5 - 2: 2016 Election Representation Using EVV

As Hamilton wrote in Federalist #28:

Man is very much a creature of habit.

We are creatures of habit and we have followed along with the same tradition of using WTA for presidential elections for over two centuries. If something works, it's easier to just go with it without question. It's easy to imagine a deflection (and one I have heard from state legislators) defending the use of WTA as, "That's democracy for you." It is a knee-jerk response with no merit and no substance. It's just following tradition without acknowledging that the process disenfranchises voters.

There is no inquiry. There is no curiosity as to why, exactly, so many voters are disenfranchised from the presidential voting process. Some decry the whole thing and claim the Electoral College must be replaced but there is little understanding why the interference, the vote suppression, is there. Even deeper, there is little thought given to how to make the system whole again.

We have become used to WTA, even numb. We do not recognize the nullifying effects of WTA as it is used. We may sense something is wrong, given the odd Electoral College results compared to the popular voting, but the truth remains undiscovered and unchallenged. The silencing of votes is ignored. And we do the same year after year after year. Yes, we are very much creatures of habit. Vote suppression is an interference of the worst kind!

Ballots cast for a president are either represented in the Electoral College or they are not due to WTA. Many votes are suppressed in the process causing many voters to be disenfranchised, never having their rightful say. Vote suppression is a flaw in the voting system that is so pernicious, so systemic, that we have come to consider it normal, causing us to be blind to its injustice.

The idea of our votes being the seat of power is exciting and yet is so little understood and often under-appreciated. In one sense, given the wars and conflicts and lives lost to make it so, it is a gift none of us should take lightly. It is often said that voting is a patriotic duty, and it is; but let's not allow this action to turn into a mere habit or chore that must be done. Voting is a privilege and with it comes responsibility.

Voting is an occasion that requires a citizen of age to register and then act. Voting also assumes (demands?) that the voter makes educated choices about the issues and candidates vying for attention and support. Our collective futures depend on our voting; it depends on our active and intentional engagement. It must not suffer more interference!

★ Chapter Summary:

+ Early voting was a difficult process using caucus-type (counting heads) or ballot counting (items in a box). No paper ballots were used.
+ The Electoral College was created in times of extreme racism and sexism.
+ Only white men with property could vote. Slaves, people of color, and women could not vote as per the original U.S. Constitution.
+ The constitutional compromise that counted slaves as three-fifths a person only affected the number of colonial delegates.

- The Electoral College, a voting mechanism, is a neutral process innocent of the nation's historical shameful racism and misogyny.
- Instead of proportional voting, states chose WTA wherein votes cast for a candidate winning a state's voting plurality receives all of the state's electoral votes.
- Vote suppression is caused by WTA.
- Vote suppression causes many voters (about 47.8%) to be disenfranchised from the presidential voting process.

1. Lepore, Jill. (2018). *These Truths: A History of the United States.* W.W. Norton & Company, pp. 162-163.
2. Daniels, Gilda R. (2020). *Uncounted: The Crisis of Voter Suppression in America.*
New York University Press, p. 124.
3. *From the 1860s ... to the ballot box.*: Ibid., p. 173.

CHAPTER 6
SAFETY, TESTS, AND BENEFITS

The framers hated the tyranny of King George, but they were also afraid of the mob. That's why they put so many checks and balances into our system, to guard against the excesses of a government that might be inflamed by public passion or perverted by a dictator's whim.

DAVID IGNATIUS

(1950, AMERICAN JOURNALIST AND NOVELIST)

One of the ingenious and unseen of Electoral College mechanisms, a contingency election, kicks in when no presidential candidate captures a majority of electoral votes. The Constitutional Framers put this process in place if the winning threshold of 270 electoral votes would not be reached. Given that many elections are close and often have more than two viable candidates, reaching the majority electoral voting threshold may not happen. If the mechanism was not available, it would be a presidential election failure since the constitution requires a candidate win by an electoral majority.

Another safety net that was established as part of the Electoral College was the use of state electors. These intermediary delegates were to be among the trusted and educated who would choose (vote) wisely at times when the voters at large erred. Though they were expected to usually reflect a state's popular voting, they also were tasked to rescue the masses from themselves. It serves as a voting firewall should voters neglect their own best interests.

The second chapter outlined principles we should expect from any voting mechanism that elects the president of the United States. They form a test that measures whether our voting process is fair, equal, inclusive, and engaging. Since the voting includes all 50 states and Washington, D.C., the voting process must also capture the nation's popular votes while at the same time represent the voting voice of each governing jurisdiction. Finally, the voting mechanism must include a system of checks and balances to guard against corruption, fraud, or mob rule.

This book's introduction pointed out that the voting process is as important as the results, explaining it's not enough to just declare a winner. Yet, if a voting process succeeds in passing the tests just outlined, it is fair to ask of its benefits. It is beneficial if the voting mechanism succeeds in avoiding partisanship, for example. It is also beneficial that the voting process maximizes the voting voice of all voters while also increasing the representation every viable candidate is due.

At the same time, the voice of each state – every state – becomes significant when it employs EVV. Instead of a *swing state* designation being allocated to a meager few states because of their election power, every state becomes significant in presidential political campaigns as every electoral votes is up for grabs.

★ Contingency Elections

The Framers were not blind to the possibility that an election could fail to deliver a candidate who would win the majority of electoral votes, a fundamental Electoral College requirement. An additional mechanism had to be in place to guard against having this kind of election failure. Otherwise, the nation would be forced to conduct a second (maybe more) nationwide election(s) to meet the Electoral College standard.

A contingency election is usually only required when more than two candidates run for the presidency and none capture the majority of electoral votes. If only two candidates compete in an election, it is highly implausible for one of them not to capture a majority of electoral votes in the Electoral College.

A contingency election is conducted by the U.S. House of Representatives after the nationwide general election is completed. Each state is able to cast one vote, regardless of the state's size or population, for its preferred of the top three candidates. That means that the total of U.S. Representatives from a state must agree on how to cast their one vote. That is not a concern for states with only one representative. However, it gets a bit contentious when larger states must come to an agreeable compromise. For example, as of this writing, California has 53 U.S. Representatives, Texas 36, and New York and Florida each have 27. Whichever political party dominates in states with more than one U.S. Representative would have an advantage in a contingency election.

A contingency election has not been used since 1800 (Jefferson) and 1824 (John Quincy Adams). If a majority is not reached in a contingency election, the election is conducted again, and again, and again. The House of Representatives voted 36 times before the winner could be declared for Jefferson in 1800 (the contingency election was conducted in 1801). Those were, indeed, contentious times.

It can be argued that there is an advantage to using WTA because there is less risk that a contingency election will be needed. We came close in the 1968 election when there were three major candidates: Nixon, Humphrey, and Wallace. Wallace succeeded in capturing 46 electoral votes, which meant that if Nixon and Humphrey had run close elections, no candidate would have reached the 270 electoral votes threshold. Nixon dominated the election, however, capturing 301 electoral votes and thereby avoiding the need for a contingency election.

It could have been different. Imagine if Nixon had not won as many states and had not captured the needed 270 electoral votes. A contingency election would have been enacted. At that time, the U.S. House of Representatives had 243 Democrats and 192 Republicans. Further, the Democrats were in the majority for 29 states, Republicans for 18, and three states were evenly divided. Giving each state only one vote, Humphrey (a Democrat) could easily have won in that kind of election. Things would have been different.

As a reminder, there is a high cost for this bit of side-step maneuvering with the inclusion of WTA. It has already been shown that WTA disenfranchises large voting blocs. Because it does, viable candidates are also denied fair representation in the Electoral College. As said earlier, process is as important as results.

★ Checks and Balances

The Constitutional Framers worried a lot over the governing structure they were putting together, fearful of imbalances of power, the intrusion of corruption, and vulnerabilities to fraud. They knew they could not predict how this new government could be torn apart, but they knew enough to put elements in place to keep a tight lid on this boiling pot. They knew enough to slow the process down to ensure governmental power never rested in a single individual, government branch, or state. They also appreciated that a winning presidential candidate must find consensual favor among the majority of voters and across a span – a coalition – of states.

The Constitutional Framers constructed the Electoral College so it would prevent the direct voting by the people for a president. Instead, it calls for each state to have a list (slate) of political leaders to be the ones who actually cast their votes for a president. These electors, influenced by the state's popular votes, typically vote as the people do.

The process has been a confusing one as it is not clearly defined in the U.S. Constitution. Who picks the electors? What is their true obligation? Our nation's history of using electors in presidential voting has been a departure from what seemed at first to be simple.

Article II, Section 1, of the U.S. Constitution tells us:

> *Each state shall appoint, in such manner as the legislature thereof may direct, a number of electors equal to the whole number of Senators and Representatives to which the state may be entitled to Congress: but no Senator or Representative, or person holding an office of trust or profit under the United States, shall be appointed an elector.*

The Framers put this intermediary step into the process for protection. Their fear at the time was that the general public (voters) may not be well-informed about the political issues of the day or that they (voters again) may not choose well. Though we citizens cast our ballots for our chosen president, we are really indicating to the slate of electors which candidate we prefer.

Originally, not every state had the same system for selecting electors but there they were – these men. These learned, astute, and respected men, would take their little winning boxes of ballots (peas or pebbles or bullets) and then obligingly cast their own choice as electoral votes in the name of the state. Still messy, but the process hinted at caution, above reproach, an intermediary step to be trusted.

The aforementioned solution to the problem of extracting a victorious candidate from the mess may have been a bit different from one colony (state) to the next. But soon it became an acceptable, even preferred, way to derive the number of votes a candidate won from each state. Meanwhile, those other boxes of peas or pebbles or bullets are simply emptied out and reused again. Recycling began early.

Today, the process is now cleaned up a bit, though still complicated. The political parties within each state choose a slate of those they want as potential electors. They must do this before the general election. When the voters of the state cast their ballots for a president, they are really voting for these electors. The electors' names may or may not be on the state ballot, so this part may be a bit surprising and somewhat confusing. When you vote for a president you are, essentially, selecting an elector rather than the actual candidate.

Electors generally are observant of how the public votes and reflect the same result. Sometimes, though, a state elector casts his/her electoral vote contrary to how the public votes. The greatest example of disloyal electors was in the 2016 election when seven electors cast their ballots contrary to their state's voting. Typically, however, there are no *rogue* electors and the public voting is directly mirrored by the electors' voting.

Today, as noted in the Supreme Court case Chiafalo et al. versus Washington (state) decided in July, 2020: 15 states back up their pledge laws with some kind of sanction. Almost all of these States immediately remove a so- called "faithless elector" from his position, substituting an alternate whose vote the State reports instead. A few States impose a monetary fine on any elector who flouts his pledge.

The Supreme Court found that a, "State may enforce an elector's pledge to support his party's nominee—and the state voters' choice—for President." Further, the Court upheld, "… the power to appoint an elector (in any manner) includes power to condition his appointment, absent some other constitutional constraint. A State can require, for example, that an elector live in the State or qualify as a regular voter during the relevant time period. Or more substantively, a State can insist … that the elector pledge to cast his Electoral College ballot for his party's presidential nominee, thus tracking the State's popular vote. … It can demand that the elector actually live up to his pledge, on pain of penalty."

The electors meet on the first Monday after the second Wednesday in December after a general election. They assemble in their own states, cast their ballots (electoral votes), which are then certified. The Certificates of Vote are then sent to both chambers of the U.S. Congress where the votes are counted on January 6th and the presidential election is recorded.

★ When Checks and Balances Fail

The checks and balances the Constitutional Framers worried about is a key reason for having the Electoral College. By splitting out the voting on a state-by-state basis, a winning candidate must win the consensus of voters across a coalition of states. The 2016 election is a good example of how the checks and balances mechanism held fast.

Hillary Clinton won the most popular votes with a margin of about 2.8 million votes over Trump. However, she only carried 19 states and Washington, D.C. to Trump's 30 states. Clinton captured three electoral votes in Maine to Trump's one. Further, excluding California's voting, Trump actually won the nation's popular vote by a margin of almost 1.5 million votes. While Clinton did win the most popular votes across the nation, the majority coalition of states went to Trump. The checks and balances held.

Or did it? Will this kind of Electoral checks and balances always hold? Anytime a new invention is manufactured (such as a car or airplane), it is stress tested to ensure it totally works and is safe. The engineers set out to break it to either prove their concept or to learn how to better meet their expectations and standards.

If we apply the same kind of testing to the presidential voting process, we must consider the breaking points. Given that we always use WTA, we must ask, "Just how bad could the presidential voting process get in regards to an imbalance of popular votes versus electoral votes results?"

We can stress test the voting process in a purely hypothetical scenario (never to be a reality). We can use, for example, the election of 2016, wherein the winner of the popular vote lost the election. We can shift the votes, without changing the Electoral College outcome, and maximize the number of popular votes cast for Clinton. In the same test, we can minimize the popular votes cast for Trump.

Remember what we're doing here! We are trying to break the system, giving it a stress test to see what could have happened under hypothetical and unusual circumstances. It's kind of like seeing what happens to crash dummies when you drive a car into a wall. Then the analysts look at the broken pieces to discover what really happened. It's all for a good cause so let's continue with our stress test experiment.

We can pretend that in states he won, Trump won a simple majority by one or two votes. In states wherein he lost, let's pretend he got no votes at all. That will minimize his win by quite a bit. Meanwhile, in this hypothetical scenario, let's pretend Clinton barely misses getting a majority in the Trump won states by one or two votes. That means she got as many votes as possible without winning the award of electoral votes via WTA. In the states she did win, let's pretend she got all of the votes.

In the scenario just described above, Clinton could have won 70.7 million popular votes more than Trump and still have lost the 2016 election! It shows that her losing to Trump by 2.8 million popular votes was insignificant, given the margin for error that was possible.

The WTA makes the Electoral College fail this stress test of checks and balances. Extrapolating this evidence to all other presidential elections we have had since using WTA, then, the idea the Framers had for an Electoral College system of checks and balances has been corrupted. WTA is the problem. It is what is broken!

For those who might be alarmed at this finding, the test can be reversed. Let's put all the popular votes we can to Trump and subtract as many as we can from Clinton. Again, we do not want to change the Electoral College results.

Suppose Trump won every vote in states he carried and Clinton won no votes in them. Suppose, too, that Trump missed winning in states Clinton won by only one or two votes. How many popular votes could Clinton win and still lose the electoral vote race, and by how many electoral votes?

The results from this hypothetical scenario would show Trump winning an excess of 66 million popular votes more than did Clinton. The result using WTA would be the same as we experienced, with Trump winning 304 electoral votes to Clinton's 227.

The stress tests, using both scenarios, show that the Electoral College results do not reflect the large popular voting differences just identified. It means that the winning strategies used for our elections rests almost entirely on winning the largest coalition of states rather than capturing the sentiment of the governed as portrayed by the popular vote. There is a check on the power of the popular vote but it remains out of balance due to the unchecked power of the states.

The stress tests prove that what many felt about the Electoral College results, saying there was something wrong. The tests prove that there is not a good correlation between how the nation voted and the Electoral College results. The tests should also underscore the fact that Clinton winning 2.8 million more popular votes than Trump was just a casual walk in the park. It could have been much more extreme.

Let us examine the first scenario stress test. Clinton won the popular vote by a 70.7 million vote margin. Using EVV, 395 electoral votes would be awarded to Clinton and only 143 electoral votes to Trump; a much more realistic result given the popular voting disparity. Conversely, using the second scenario stress test with EVV, 397 electoral votes would be awarded to Trump and only 141 electoral votes to Clinton.

There should be limits to the influence of the checks and balances system in our election process. Certainly, one goal is for a majority coalition of states to be won by the winning candidate. A candidate should not be able to rely on a dominant popular voting bloc captured by a few highly populated states, which would be an imbalance. All states should matter. However, when the popular voting is as lopsided as these hypothetical scenarios are, a coalition of states should not prevail either. The intended checks and balances, now broken, needs to be restored.

The point in reviewing this kind of election stress test is to show that, with WTA, our presidential election checks and balances are weak, at best. The central idea put forth by our Constitutional Framers was to have an election system wherein a presidential candidate would not dominate with only a minority of states. The majority of the popular voting consensus was to be spread across all states. All voters would matter and every state would be significant. The checks and balances would make it so.

It is regrettable that the cautions and intent of the Framers regarding presidential elections have grown hollow. The checks and balances once instituted are now weakened because of WTA, which was adopted after the Electoral College was enacted. The guard rails still exist but they are wobbly and there are cliffs promising destruction if we do not recognize the problem and takes steps to restore them so they can function as once intended.

★ Election Test: What We Have

The most fundamental test we exact on our presidential elections is to see the results: who won? On that first Tuesday in November, when the ballots are tallied state-by-state, find many voters paying attention to the news coverage. Shortly after the polls close in any given state, projections are made as to which candidate carried (won) the state. Unless the race is extremely close (as in 2020), a state can be declared with just a small percentage of the votes coming in. The results are predictable because of the pre-election polling and scientific projections made based on careful statistical analysis.

We have already seen that there is much more to a presidential election than just determining the winner, however. Chapter two showed that we must have principles by which to measure the efficacy of the election itself. As a review, it was shown that a presidential election should be:

- **Fair** – The voting options need to be clear, easy to understand, and the voting choices can be easily and accurately counted.
- **Equal** – The votes need to be equally represented so no advantage is given to any candidate or political party.
- **Inclusive** – The opportunity to vote should not deny any voter access to the voting process.
- **Engaging** – Voters should be motivated to vote having confidence that their vote will make a difference

These four principles form a kind of assumed backdrop for our voting expectations and only surface if they are egregiously trampled upon. We have already seen how prevalent voter suppression often is, which causes all four of these standards to be broken; yet, we tend to be most incensed if the infractions are experienced locally. On the national stage, these standards erode into assumptions and seldom generate worry.

Chapter two also pointed out three more principles that we should expect the following from the Electoral College process:

- **Capture the sentiment of the governed** (a popular vote result).
- **Capture the sentiment of each state** (separate and equal voices).
- **Provide voting checks and balances.**

The office of the presidency is the only federal office elected by the citizens from all of the nation's governing jurisdictions (50 states and Washington, D.C.). Consequently, the voting process must capture the popular voting and the voting voice of each separate state. It must also do so with an eye towards voting safety. No single state or minority region of the country can be able to pick the nation's leader. Each election requires that the winning candidate gains the consensus of the people while, at the same time, captures a commanding coalition of the states. Given what has been presented thus far, it is fair to ask how our presidential elections measure up against these standards.

The following pages present a scoring of the presidential elections in relation to what we currently experience by the 48 states and Washington, D.C., and by Maine and Nebraska using congressional district voting. The scoring is also applied to the voting process if EVV were used. You may not totally agree with the scoring and may wish to nudge a grade up or down, depending on your own perspectives. However, as you compare the grades, you will recognize the great disparity between the approaches that remain even under a more generous assessment.

Current Voting Approach	
Standard	Grade
Fair	A
Equal	F
Inclusive	A
Engaging	F
Popular Voting	F
State Voting	F
Checks & Balances	F
Grade Point Average	**D**

Figure 6 – 1: Current Voting Approach Grading

+ **Fair** – The voting process is clear. A lot of attention has been given to ensure ballots are clear, easy to mark, and counted fairly. There has been a lot of discussion about voting clarity being an issue. Florida's concern over hanging chads in the 2000 election is an example. Voting machine security is another pressing issue. Overall, across the nation, these concerns are aggressively addressed and corrections made when needed. Generally, it can be said that the election process is fair. **Grade: A**

+ **Equal** – State electoral votes suffer the WTA process causing large percentages of voter representation to be forfeited. Further, WTA also causes viable candidate representation to be discarded. **Grade: F**

+ **Inclusive** – In general, voters are not denied voting access. However, voter suppression has its negative effect. Since this is not due to the voting mechanism, per se, it is not reflected in the grade. (See Note below.) **Grade: A**

+ **Engaging** – Voters who are inclined to vote in opposition to the plurality of state voters do not experience fair voter representation, due to WTA. Such disenfranchisement discourages voters from voting. **Grade: F**

Note: It should be noted that voter suppression emerges in various nefarious ways causing many to not be able to cast their ballots. No voting mechanism or approach alone can change this. Corruption and fraud have interfered with the nation's voting throughout its history. Such interference should be recognized for what it is, when it happens, and steps be taken to correct it. It is not part of this grading assessment though it certainly remains a challenge for a true democratic voting process.

This is not a good grade. If the test were put on a four-point scale, as many college courses are, the national Grade Point Average (GPA) for presidential voting would be 2.0, or a solid "C." The national voting process does not do well.

Let's continue with the other three measures.

+ **Capture the sentiment of the governed** (a popular vote result). The popular votes of the nation are captured but 47.8% of them are discarded, due to WTA, as they are converted into electoral votes. **Grade: F**
+ **Capture the sentiment of each state** (separate and equal voices). Each state weighs in with their respective voting voice but it does not reflect the true sentiment of the state voters. Again, the problem is due to WTA. **Grade: F**
+ **Provide voting checks and balances.** It might seem that the Electoral College system of checks and balances are in place. The intermediary step of electing electors still functions as originally designed. However, because of WTA, the checks and balances to protect the voting process fails the stress test. A large disparity between the nation's popular voting and the electoral votes captured by the states shows the system grievously out of balance. **Grade: F**

Three more "Fs" are added to the total bringing the presidential election process GPA to an embarrassing 1.14, a "D." It is easy to see, given this kind of measurement, why many may wish to discard the entire Electoral College system. Students with this kind of GPA often drop out of school, seldom getting an opportunity for remediation.

★ Election Test: Using Congressional District Voting

Maine and Nebraska are the only states that use congressional district voting. As explained earlier, two of their electoral votes are cast according to the candidate who wins the state-wide popular vote plurality. The two votes are awarded using WTA. The remaining votes are awarded on a congressional district basis (hence its name). Any candidate who wins the plurality of popular votes in a district gains an electoral vote. WTA is used to determine which candidate gets these votes. To be fair, awarding a single vote on a proportional basis would reduce it to fractions, which is not desirable and could create some confusion and complexity to the process.

Measuring congressional district voting against the standards established earlier shows it is an improvement over what the rest of the states currently experience.

Congressional District Voting	
Standard	Grade
Fair	A
Equal	C
Inclusive	A
Engaging	C
Popular Voting	C
State Voting	C
Checks & Balances	F
Grade Point Average	C

Figure 6 – 2: Congressional District Voting Grading

+ **Fair** – The voting process is clear. A lot of attention has been given to ensure ballots are clear, easy to mark, and counted fairly. **Grade: A**

+ **Equal** – State electoral votes suffer the WTA process causing large percentages of voter representation to be forfeited, but less so than what is currently experienced. Likewise, WTA still causes some viable candidate representation to be eroded if not discarded. **Grade: C**

+ **Inclusive** – In general, voters are not denied voting access. However, voter suppression has its negative effect. Since this is not due to the voting mechanism, per se, it is not reflected in the grade. (See note below.) **Grade: A**

+ **Engaging** – Voters who are inclined to vote in opposition to the plurality of state voters do not experience full voter representation, due to WTA. The process is improved over other states, but such disenfranchisement still discourages some voters from voting. **Grade: C**

Note: It should be noted that voter suppression emerges in various nefarious ways causing many to not be able to cast their ballots. No voting mechanism or approach alone can change this. Corruption and fraud have interfered with the nation's voting throughout its history. Such interference should be recognized for what it is, when it happens, and steps be taken to correct it. It is not part of this grading assessment though it certainly remains a challenge for a true democratic voting process.

This is a passing grade. If the test were put on a four-point scale, as many college courses are, the national Grade Point Average (GPA) for presidential voting would be a an even 3.0. Congressional district voting gets a "B."

Let's continue with the other three measures.

+ **Capture the sentiment of the governed** (a popular vote result). The popular votes of the state are captured but a percentage of them are discarded, due to WTA, as they are converted into electoral votes. It is an improvement over what is experienced by the other 48 states. **Grade: C**

- ♦ **Capture the sentiment of the state** (separate and equal voices). The state weighs in with its voting voice but it does not fully reflect the true sentiment of the state voters. Again, an improvement but the WTA problem still remains. **Grade: C**
- ♦ **Provide voting checks and balances.** It might seem that the Electoral College system of checks and balances are in place. The intermediary step of electing electors still functions as originally designed. However, because of WTA, the checks and balances do not fully protect the voting process. A disparity between the state's popular and electoral voting results is still out of balance, though improved over what other states experience. **Grade: F**

Two more "Cs" and one "F" are added to the total, lowering the presidential election process GPA to a solid 2.0 average, or a "C" grade. The approach is a marked improvement over the other 48 states, but is not really deserving of applause.

Congressional district voting has only been used by Maine since 1972 and by Nebraska since 1992. As a comparison, it's informative to see how Maine and Nebraska's congressional district voting would compare with EVV, had it been used instead in those states during the elections it was used. Maine has had four electoral votes and Nebraska has had five during those elections.

Using congressional district voting, Maine only split its electoral votes in 2016 and 2020. Clinton captured three of the votes in 2016 as did Biden in 2020. Trump gained one electoral vote in both of those elections. Nebraska only split their electoral votes in 2008 and 2020. Obama captured one electoral vote and McCain was awarded the other four in 2008. Biden captured one electoral vote and Trump retained the remaining four.

Using EVV, however, a different and more exact reflection of how people voted emerges. Maine almost always would have split their four votes giving two to the Democrat candidate and two to the Republican. The only exception is that in 1992, Bill Clinton would have captured two, Bush one, and Perot one. Similarly, Nebraska would have always split their electoral votes, giving the Democrat candidate two votes and the Republican three. The exception would have been in 1992 where Bill Clinton would have captured one vote, Bush three, and Perot one.

Three points can be made with this analysis. First, EVV electoral vote results are more reflective of the popular voting in both states as compared to congressional district voting. Second, it shows that any state can be successful in modifying its approach to how electoral votes are distributed among candidates. Third, the states are free to do so without a U.S. Constitutional amendment.

The two tables below compare the totals of electoral votes over the years comparing the number of electoral votes captured in Maine and Nebraska with the number of electoral votes for those states if EVV had been used instead. The table for Maine covers the elections of 1972 through 2020. The table for Nebraska covers the elections of 1992 through 2020. The single vote in the "Other" column in the EVV section shows the single electoral vote that Perot would have captured in 1992, if EVV had been used. Notice how the states' popular voting is much more reflective in the EVV columns.

Maine					
Congressional District Voting			EVV		
Dem.	Rep.	Other	Dem.	Rep.	Other
30	22	0	27	24	1

Figure 6 – 3: Congressional District Voting Electoral Votes

Nebraska					
Congressional District Voting			EVV		
Dem.	Rep.	Other	Dem.	Rep.	Other
2	38	0	15	24	1

Figure 6 – 4: EVV Electoral Votes

★ Election Test: Using EVV

The main tenet of this book is that we can, and should, save the Electoral College by using Equal Voice Voting (EVV). We do not have to discard a presidential election system that currently fails us. A rather small modification, neither requiring a U.S. Constitution amendment nor an interstate compact (agreement among states) is needed to remedy the problem. Further, should EVV be used for all of the governing jurisdictions (50 states and Washington, D.C.), the genius instituted within the Electoral College can be fully and finally realized.

EVV, as you now know, essentially removes WTA from the voting process and gives electoral vote representation on a state-by-state basis. It is fair to ask how our presidential elections, using EVV, would measure up against the standards.

EVV Voting Approach	
Standard	Grade
Fair	A
Equal	A
Inclusive	A
Engaging	A
Popular Voting	A
State Voting	A
Checks & Balances	A
Grade Point Average	**A**

Figure 6 – 5: EVV Voting Approach Grading

- **Fair** – The voting process is clear. A lot of attention has been given to ensure ballots are clear, easy to mark, and counted fairly. There would be no difference using EVV. **Grade: A**
- **Equal** – All votes matter. All votes cast for a viable candidate gain electoral vote representation. Every viable candidate also enjoys representation in every state in which they campaign. **Grade: A**
- **Inclusive** – In general, voters are not denied voting access. However, voter suppression has its negative effect. Since this is not due to the voting mechanism, per se, it is not reflected in the grade. (See note below.) **Grade: A**
- **Engaging** – Voters who may vote in opposition to the plurality of state voters would still experience fair voter representation. All

voters would be encouraged to vote, knowing their participation matters. **Grade: A**

Note: It should be noted that voter suppression emerges in various nefarious ways causing many to not be able to cast their ballots. No voting mechanism or approach alone can change this. Corruption and fraud have interfered with the nation's voting throughout its history. Such interference should be recognized for what it is, when it happens, and steps be taken to correct it. It is not part of this grading assessment though it certainly remains a challenge for a true democratic voting process.

This is an excellent grade. If the test were put on a four-point scale, as many college courses are, the national Grade Point Average (GPA) for presidential voting using EVV would be 4.0. Equal Voice Voting, for these four measures, gets an "A!"

Let's continue with the other three measures.

- **Capture the sentiment of the governed** (a popular vote result). The popular votes of the nation are captured and all of them matter. All votes for a viable candidate gain representation. All votes cast for a viable candidate gain electoral vote representation. **Grade: A**
- **Capture the sentiment of each state** (separate and equal voices). Each state weighs in with their respective voting voice, reflecting well the true sentiment of the state voters. **Grade: A**
- **Provide voting checks and balances.** The Electoral College system of checks and balances remain in place. The intermediary step of electing electors still functions as originally designed. The checks and balances to protect the voting process passes the stress test showing the disparity between the nation's popular voting and the electoral votes remains in balance. **Grade: A**

Three more "As" are added to the total bringing the presidential election process GPA to 4.0, a perfect score of "A." However, voter suppression remains as an imperfection of which we must be aware and continue to eradicate. While this is not a central part of the Electoral College, per se, a fair assessment must include it to show how much must yet be done to improve our levels of voter inclusion.

Of course, as mentioned earlier, this grading metric is somewhat subjective and you may not entirely agree with the grades given. Still, one can easily see that EVV is vastly superior to our current election process that employs WTA. EVV is also superior to congressional district voting because, again, WTA is not used. The measurement shows that there should be minimal support to retain WTA and that EVV clearly honors and preserves the Electoral College.

The point of this kind of assessment and comparison is that it serves as a good tool to ascertain the viability of the Electoral College or any other presidential election process. The election test will be used to measure the viability of the direct popular voting and the National Popular Voting (NPV) approaches in subsequent chapters.

★ Nonpartisanship Benefits

It's time to crush the egg shell just as Christopher Columbus did when he stood the hard-boiled egg on its end. While considering a voting process, simplicity is good. Clarity is good. But the cacophonous political noise that distracts us from our purpose in favor of picking a winner must be set aside. The push and pull of political parties to win, adhering to the always must win mantra, by elbowing others away or grasping political advantages must be set aside in favor of a method, a paradigm shift, that delivers more. The presidential voting process must meet one clear objective:

Listen to the voters.

Any piece of the process or any secondary diversion that obscures that objective must be seen as suspect and removed. Be it voter suppression or vote suppression by way of WTA, any silencing of voters and their disenfranchisement from the process, must be recognized and remedied. If the goal is simple, if it is clear, it is unjust to do otherwise.

The voting process is as important as the results when it positively meets the seven principles mentioned earlier. However, it is not enough to simply meet these principles and/or be satisfied with the result (i.e., the eventual winner). The process must also deliver the benefit of nonpartisanship.

Political party loyalty has caused the presidential voting process to retain the WTA handicap in the first place. For example, wanting a state's majority political party to retain its dominance prevents its politicians from considering a more inclusive and representative voting process. Conversely, recognizing that a majority party dominates in a state's legislature can restrain a minority party from attempting to change things. After all, the reasoning goes, a future election may find the minority party flipped so it has a new found majority status, enjoying the current voting advantage WTA provides.

EVV should be seen as enticing for states that are quite evenly divided between Democrats and Republicans. For example, in the 2016 election, had EVV been in place across the nation and the voting had been the same, seven states would have evenly split their electoral votes. It indicates how evenly divided those seven states are, from the voters' perspective. Further, for states having an odd number of electoral votes, 12 would have been separated by only one vote.

Likewise, the 2020 election would give us similar "close election" results. Ten states would have evenly split their electoral votes and another 15 states would have only a one electoral vote separation between Biden and Trump.

I am often asked who would have won a given past election if EVV had been used across the nation instead. The curiosity is normal but the question is the wrong one. It must be understood, again looking at the voting process from the voters' perspective, that a voting rule change will also change the election. Voter response will be different. Campaigning will be different. You can almost hear the chant:

Change the Game – Change the Campaign!

The nation's voting is more evenly divided between Democrats and Republicans than what is easily assumed when looking at the Electoral College election map results of blue and red states. Since our nation essentially had its governance formed on the notion that its power comes from the people, then EVV is the best approach to enable its collective voting voice to be raised and heard.

★ Swing States

Almost every presidential election finds the nation's attention focused on a handful of states that will tip the election scales one way or the other. The recent elections of this century have been close. There is just cause to pay attention to how a state's voting can *swing* to give advantage to either the Republican or Democrat candidate. As you now know, because of WTA, all of a state's electoral votes are cast for whichever candidate captures the plurality of a state's popular votes. A few votes can make the difference of a candidate winning the national election or not.

One of the consequences of this voting reality is that a few states capture all of the campaign attention. States that are known to easily go red (Republican) or blue (Democrat) are largely ignored by the counter candidate's campaign. For example, Republicans do not spend much time or resources campaigning in California since that's a state known to vote predominantly for the Democrat. Other examples would be the central states who are known to vote predominantly for the Republican candidate. They're commonly referred to as the *fly over* states because of the inattention they capture from the Democrats.

Let's use my home state of Oregon as an example. In recent elections, Oregon has cast all seven electoral votes for the Democrat candidate. The state is not considered to be electorally significant because it currently is assumed to be a democratic stronghold.

If Oregon had used EVV in 2020, it would have split its seven electoral votes giving four to Biden and three to Trump. Knowing this, one can easily imagine the Trump campaign giving more attention to this rather small (insignificant?) state to possibly increase the electoral vote capture to four.

Likewise, if Oklahoma had used EVV in 2020, it would have split its seven electoral votes giving two to Biden and five to Trump. Again, the campaigning would play out differently as Biden may have been able to increase the electoral voting there to three. The state would have become more significant in the election because of the possibility that more voting representation would have been realized.

Every state would suddenly become significant if EVV were used. The point here is not just about winning votes! If the campaigning can shift to include more states, the campaigning topics become more inclusive as well. As in our examples, Oregon and Oklahoma's concerns become more important and apparent as well. Campaign messaging becomes more than mere news – it transforms into becoming more home-grown, more significant across the nation.

★ Chapter Summary:

- Contingency elections are enacted when no candidate captures at least 270 electoral votes in the general election.
- Contingency elections are conducted by the U.S. House of Representatives to elect a president. Each state casts one vote for one of the three presidential candidates winning the most votes in the general election. The contingency election is repeated until a majority is reached.
- Contingency elections were only used in the 1800 and 1824 elections.
- Contingency elections are not often used, largely due to WTA. The sacrifice is the disenfranchisement of an average of 47.8% of the voters.
- One of the benefits of the Electoral College is that it provides checks and balances for the presidential election.
  - ➤ Each state selects electors to cast electoral votes to reflect the state's popular voting or used as a remedy when popular voting makes a poor choice.
  - ➤ The Electoral College requires that a consensus of voters (the popular vote) be captured across a coalition of states, thereby checking a small portion of the country dominating the election.
  - ➤ WTA weakens the Electoral College checks and balances, causing it to fail election stress tests.

- Election tests measure if voting processes are fair, equal, inclusive, and engaging. They also show if they capture the popular votes, capture the voting voice of individual jurisdictions, and provide checks and balances.
  - ➤ Election tests of the current voting process used by 48 states and Washington, D.C., show it does poorly. (Grade D)
  - ➤ Election tests of congressional district voting show it is an improvement over what we currently experience in the other jurisdictions (48 states and Washington, D.C.). (Grade C)
  - ➤ Election tests of EVV show it passes all of the voting standards.
  - ➤ (Grade A)
- Nonpartisanship is a major benefit EVV provides to presidential elections.
- The voice of the people must be heard in presidential elections.
- Swing states would not be relegated to a few, if EVV were used, as every state employing it would become significant in political campaigns.

CHAPTER 7
THE POPULAR VOTE

Let us never forget that government is ourselves and not an alien power over us. The ultimate rulers of our democracy are not a President and senators and congressmen and government officials, but the voters of this country.

FRANKLIN D. ROOSEVELT
(1982 - 1945, 32ND U.S. PRESIDENT)

Sensing that something is wrong with our presidential election voting results, setting aside candidate or political party preferences, why not simply start over? All that is needed is to eliminate the Electoral College and allow the voters to elect a president by a nation-wide popular vote decision.

It's not that simple. First, a U.S. Constitutional amendment needs to be passed. There are some assumptions that need to be addressed, too. Recognizing that we live in a republic of unified states under a federal umbrella means we must also recognize our differences. Our nation's diversity matters.

Our nation is a republic, made up of 50 sovereign states. Each state is a governmental jurisdiction unto itself, complete with Executive (Governor), Congressional, and Judicial branches, much the same as is exercised by our federal government. While each state is not considered to be a separate country, each state independently serves its constituents and deserves a similarly independent voting consideration.

Beyond the governing aspect of the many states, we must also recognize that ours is a vast nation made up of a myriad of mini-cultures, lifestyles, values, and perspectives. Far from being a homogeneous people, we bring a wide diversity of backgrounds, talents, and values to bear on the voting process for this important federal office – the only one elected by all voters across the nation.

We easily recognize that all states are not the same geographically. Some are large and some are small. Some are densely populated while others remain mostly rural with neighbors well beyond shouting distance. Viewing this kind of national landscape reveals that most voters, dwelling near each other in cities, could have a voting advantage over those more distant from each other. Minority rural voting voices could be silenced.

We are not a homogeneous nation. States differ widely on their respective laws formed across the span of their individual histories. Voting, for example, is not the same from one state to the next. Differences for voter registration, rights to vote, ability to vote early, and voting by mail are a few considerations that would have to be brought into nationwide alignment if a simple nation-wide popular vote were to be adopted for our presidential elections.

Assessing the popular vote approach using the principles set forth in Chapter 2 gives it an unfavorable grade. While the first impression of a popular vote approach may be appealing, it deserves a closer look. In light of our governmental principles and diversity of people, it fails to provide a truly democratic and sustainable voting mechanism upon which we can faithfully rely.

★ Democracy demands change

Many are not satisfied with presidential elections. Beyond an inability to select a favorite candidate, voters recognize that many are disenfranchised from the process. They sense something is wrong and either refuse to engage in the process or wish the process, the Electoral College, could be changed or eliminated altogether. Our democracy, wanting the voice of the people to be heard at the ballot box, cries out for a change. It seems to be past time to fix the process and cure the malady.

Our nation has experienced several close elections over the years. Two recent ones, 2000 and 2016, have caught our attention. It is especially aggravating if one candidate wins the most popular votes and still loses the race via the Electoral College.

Consider the Presidential election of 2016. The results of the election were touted as giving Trump a majority because, after all, he won more than 57.2% of the electoral votes compared with Clinton getting only 43.4%. It is easy for the winning political party and the media to focus on that difference – calling the Electoral College winning difference a mandate rather than an actual popular vote loss. Yet, the popular vote gave Clinton about a 2% popular vote edge.

In our nation's history, there have been three other instances wherein a candidate won the popular vote but significantly lost the Electoral College vote. These three are:

- **1876:** Samuel Tilden won fewer electoral votes but won 250,000+ more popular votes than Rutherford B. Hayes. Hayes won by only one electoral vote (185/184).
- **1888:** Grover Cleveland won 168 fewer electoral votes but won the popular vote. Benjamin Harrison won 233 electoral votes and became our president that year.
- **2000:** Al Gore won five fewer electoral votes than George Bush (271 electoral votes) but won the popular vote. One elector abstained from casting a ballot making 537 the Electoral College total.

Notice how significant a margin the second and third races noted above were won with the Electoral College versus the popular vote results. 1888 was 233 electoral votes versus 168. That's a 65 electoral vote difference! 2000 was 271 electoral votes versus 266. That's a five electoral vote difference! And both races identified the other contender as the popular vote winner!

It is reasonable, then, to look at our voting history and consider that a nationwide popular vote approach would work well for the country. The impulse to reject what we currently experience and reach for something better is appealing. The problem is that reaching for a popular voting solution hits some realities that demand a more sober assessment and response. These realities are:

- A U.S. Constitutional amendment is required.
- The United States is not homogeneous.

★ Amending the U.S. Constitution

Amending the U.S. Constitution is a challenge. Article V of the United States Constitution describes the process whereby it may be altered. Twenty-seven amendments have been added (appended) to the Constitution, so we know it can be done. The process is intentionally difficult because the Constitutional Framers knew that the document would have to withstand the tests of time made by corruption, fraud, and human whim.

Article V of the U.S. Constitution provides the remedy of an amendment should it be necessary to do so. It reads:

> The Congress, whenever two thirds of both houses shall deem it necessary, shall propose amendments to this Constitution, or, on the application of the legislatures of two thirds of the several states, shall call a convention for proposing amendments, which, in either case, shall be valid to all intents and purposes, as part of this Constitution, when ratified by the legislatures of three fourths of the several states, or by conventions in three fourths thereof, as the one or the other mode of ratification may be proposed by the Congress ... .

That is a long sentence made longer as it continues by addressing a concern that could have happened before 1808. The Framers were, by any measure, cautious. We should be thankful because changing the constitution is, in effect, changing the very core—the bones—of our national governance. Making changes to it should not be done lightly or without the significant consensus of those governed.

Essentially, the request for an amendment can begin either from the U.S. Congress or by the states. If the initiative comes from the U.S. Congress, then it must pass both chambers (Senate and House of Representatives) by two-thirds of its respective members. That means, today, 67 U.S. Senators would have to vote for it as would 292 U.S. Representatives. If the amendment passes both chambers with that number of supportive votes, it must still be ratified by the states. Ratification by the states means that both chambers (Senate and House of Representatives again) of 38 states (three-fourths of the 50-state total) would also have to pass the amendment.

The impetus can come from the states as well. If 34 states (two-thirds of the 50-state total) wish to have the U.S. Constitution amended, they can start the ball rolling without waiting for the U.S. Congress to make the first move. These 34 states can call for a convention, including the remaining 16 states, and propose amendments (there could be more than one issue of concern). Again, if 38 states ratify (agree to) the amendment, it is passed along to the U.S. Congress to get 2/3rds of both chambers to also agree to it.

Amending the U.S. Constitution can be done but when it comes to the Electoral College, things have not gone well. Alexander Keyssar noted in his book, "Why Do We Still Have the Electoral College?" that more than 800 amendments to the U.S. Constitution have been proposed in the U.S. Congress. None of these efforts ever were passed by both of the U.S. Congress chambers, thereby never facing the test of ratification by the states. Idiomatically speaking, amending the constitution for the Electoral College is a bridge too far or it's beyond our reach. In short, attempting to do so is just not practical.

Yes, an amendment to the U.S. Constitution to modify or eliminate the Electoral College "can" be done; but doing so would require tremendous interest, persuasion, and maybe some luck. Given the divide we witness today in our politics, it is probably a safe bet that gaining this kind of constitutional modification is not going to happen any time soon. Hoping that it will is simply not practical.

★ The United States is not homogeneous

Setting practicality aside and assuming a constitutional amendment regarding the Electoral College can be achieved, state lines will not matter if a popular vote approach is used for presidential elections. Imagine the country with the state lines removed, as shown below. It appears as a kind of empty expanse, being the same from coast to coast, sans topography of any kind – a country of sameness.

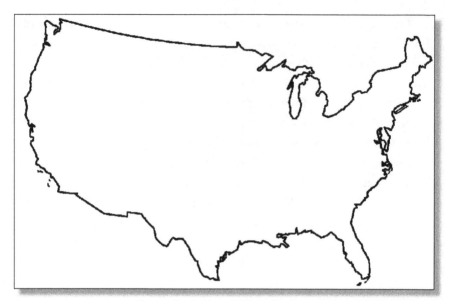

Figure 7 - 1: United States Outline

A fundamental premise of the popular vote is that the nation's population is quite homogenous and where it is not, it all balances out in the end. Therefore, it does not matter where people live, whether they live in cities or in the country, in the south or the north or along the coasts or in the central plains. The United State citizens are mostly the same in the aggregate because, after all, this country is often referred to as the "Great Melting Pot."

Statistical significance comes into play using this perspective. Statistical significance is the point of polling measurement wherein a small sample indicates the characteristics of the whole. For example, imagine you have a swimming pool and you want to measure the level of chlorine in the water. You do not need to analyze all of the water in the pool. Rather, you need only to take a very small sample (a few tablespoons will do) to be confident you know how concentrated the chlorine is in your swimming pool.

We witness such sampling in every presidential election when states are declared for a candidate with a very low percentage of the voters having been counted. Such declarations are estimates, of course, but usually they are accurate. Even with only 5% of the voters counted, an estimate of who will win can sometimes be declared. It can be done because of pre-election polling and the precinct-by-precinct assessments. Statistical probabilities become compelling.

Voter turnout has been low for many presidential elections. For example, voter turnout in 2016 was less than 70% of the registered voters. Using round numbers there were 198 million registered voters in that year and only 137 million voters participated. If all that is needed is a 5% sample, then when 6.9 million votes were counted, a presidential winner could be declared, if the leading candidate led by a clear margin.

Using that scenario, we can imagine a voting sampling that would work. But let's play it safe and, instead of a 5% threshold, we can bump it up a bit and use a 15% threshold for the statistical significance. Then the 15% sampling threshold would be 21 million voters. That is similar to the total voting in New York (7.7 million votes), Georgia (4.1 million votes), and Florida (9.4 million votes) for a total of 21.2 million votes in 2016. If that scenario were true, then voters from those three states would be all that was needed to confidently elect a president. It seems all voting could be done from one time zone.

A similar scenario would be to consider the voting citizens from the original 13 colonies. These states include: Connecticut, Delaware, Georgia, Maryland, Massachusetts, New Hampshire, New Jersey, New York, North Carolina, Pennsylvania, Rhode Island, South Carolina, and Virginia. If 2016 is used as an example; the votes from these 13 colonies would be 28% of the nation's votes. That sample would be statistically significant compared to the entire nation. Campaigning, for example, would be easier and the costs associated with the process would be greatly reduced. What could go wrong?

These ideas may not sit well with you, particularly if you do not live in any of the three example states discussed above or in one of the original 13 colonies. It would mean a large proportion of the nation becomes irrelevant. By the way, remember, 2016 had only 37.4% of the registered voters that counted due to WTA (Winner-Takes-All) used by the states to get the Electoral College results. If the 13-colony scenario bothers you, the current Electoral College results should too.

Take a step back and consider our nation from a macro view. Examine the map below and the ellipses. Consider what differences might be within those regions.

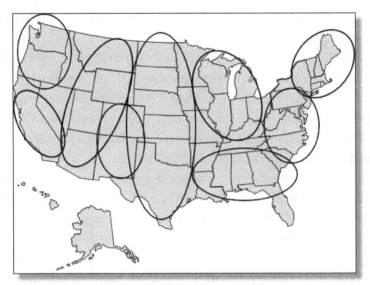

Figure 7 - 2: United States Regions

Think about the people who live in those regions and what they do for a living. Think about differences you may know regarding, for example, their regional histories, religious practices, ethnic makeup, natural resources, and types of industry.

Contrast each region with another that may not be similar. Compare the northwest region to the southeast. Compare the northeast with California. Compare the Rocky Mountains with the Great Lakes region. Compare the southwest with the Atlantic seaboard. Compare any region with the central plains area. Then throw in the extra-large state of Alaska and the islands of Hawaii.

The nation is a vast area encompassing almost 3.8 million square miles. "From sea to shining sea," as the "America the Beautiful" song goes, includes a lot of diversity both in what the country has to offer and the people that inhabit it. These regions with their contributing diversity matter, just as the citizens who live, work, and visit there do.

President Obama reminds us that:

> America is the first real experiment in building a large, multiethnic, multicultural democracy. And we don't know yet if that can hold. There haven't been enough of them around for long enough to say for certain that it's going to work.

Our hope and the hope of the Constitutional Framers is that the grand experiment will work, that we can absorb our diverse populations. There is much to consider when we seek to govern by "We the people."

Moving closer than the general regions identified above, we can take in the different states illustrated in the figure below. Each state is a sovereign governmental jurisdiction, as described earlier. Each has its own three governmental branches fashioned after what we have at the federal level: Executive branch (Governor), Congressional, and Judicial. While we do not consider each state to be a country unto itself, they remain independent of each other and have willingly come together under one governing umbrella, from which they collectively derive their name: United States of America.

It is for these reasons that electing a president of the United States is a unique exercise. It is the only federal office elected by the voters of the entire country. This one person must be able to address, guide, reassure, and lead an entire nation while at the same time represent this collection of states to the rest of the world. Picking a person suitable for this office demands more than a simple plurality of votes. The method used must, as the Framers knew and as was pointed out in Chapter 2, capture the consensus of the governed, attend to the voting voice of each state, and adhere to a method of checks and balances to guard against corruption and fraud.

As the Constitutional Framers crafted how our nation should be governed, they provided an outline of roles and responsibilities, differentiating governing powers between the federal government and states. Generally, the U.S. Constitution provides some specifics for federal governing powers and states claiming those that remain. Interpretations have varied broadly over time with some asserting an erosion of power from states and absorbed by the federal government. It is a constant balancing act, a political push-and-pull to achieve goals of life and liberty, and lest we forget, the pursuit of happiness. What remains intact is the reality of the national federal government and the individual sovereignty of states – our republic!

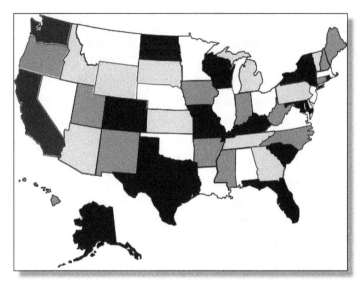

Figure 7 - 3: State Diversity

If we are to have a nation-wide popular vote, how these different states govern should be quite similar, if not totally homogenous. That is, the laws governing one state ought to coincide, at least generally, with the other 49. That is not reality, however. Just examining one perspective of law, voting, we can readily see there are distinct differences from one state to another.

The three examples that follow are excellent ways to illustrate how states are different from one another, at least insofar as voting practices are concerned. Not only do they clarify this diversity concept, they also force one to think about all the other areas in which states are distinct from one another, and therefor how important it is for our country's voting system to factor in these variations for the final result. It should be noted that the data used for these figures come from the National Conference of State Legislatures (NCSL) as they were presented in the summer of 2020. Time changes things and what is presented below may have changed in a given state due to the passage of new laws.

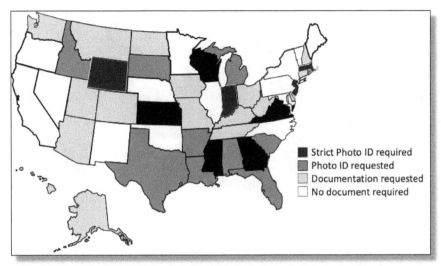

Figure 7 - 4: Voter ID Laws

When voters go to the polls to vote, they check in to ensure they are listed on the voter registration rolls. Different states have different rules for this important step. Some are quite strict, requiring either a photo to identify them such as a driver's license. Some are even more strict in that they require a special ID (Identification) with their photo to be used specifically for voting. Other states are more relaxed, either requiring a simple piece of documentation such as a utility bill or other address confirmation to ensure the voter is properly identified. Others require no such documentation. They usually are voting in very rural areas wherein they are easily identified by their friends and neighbors to validate who they are.

Figure 7 - 5: Early Voting Laws

When it comes time to vote for a president, it has been the custom for voters to cast their ballots at a precinct polling location. Finding that this can be a limitation for some voters, some states have enacted an ability to vote early, especially with mail-in voting as we saw in 2020. Other states insist that an absentee ballot be presented in person before the voting date. Other states (a growing number of them) not only allow early voting but encourage it by having their voting done by mailing in the ballots.

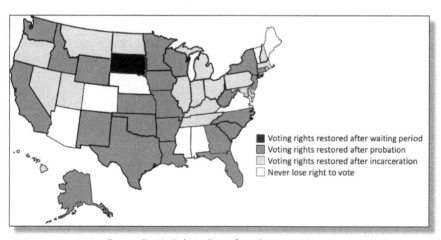

Figure 7 - 6: Felony Disenfranchisement Laws

Every state has law breakers who are classified as felons. These felons usually have their voting rights removed, but not always. Some states restore a felon's voting rights after they have been incarcerated. Other states restore these rights after a certain amount of time has passed. Other states restore the voting rights after the felon has completed their time of probation following their time of incarceration.

The point of showing these three state differences is not to necessarily inform you about the minute details of state-to-state voting rights, but to point out how varied the laws can be from state-to-state. The laws, and their relative nuances, form a complex patchwork quilt across this nation, further complicating the national landscape.

If a nationwide popular vote would be enacted instead of the Electoral College, these state differences (along with others) would need to be brought into alignment in order for there to be state-to-state voting equality. It would not be equal if some voters found it relatively easy to cast their ballots while others were more stringently restricted by a voter ID requirement. For example, it would not serve the nation well if some voters could take advantage of their state's early voting or mail-in voting options while other states demanded in-person voting. It would not be equal if some felons would be allowed to vote while others could not.

The United States citizenry is not homogeneous at all and we enjoy a great diversity among our people. We, as one nation, reflect different regions and different cultures and a lot of other diverse demographics. U.S. voters reflect a wide array of ethnic and racial backgrounds as well as philosophical perspectives. We are young and old, educated and not, white collar and blue collar, male and female, rich and poor, able and disabled, religious and not, and so on. Our diversity is a rich resource for talent and resourcefulness and future hope. It is also a source for many challenges. We do not all vote the same for a myriad of reasons!

Recognizing that our nation is truly a republic helps to square these and other state differences. Being a republic points to the fact that our nation is not a homogeneous one either by measure of its diversity but also by its state-by-state legal differences. These differences are more than a simple nuance. They remind us of our diversity. Because we all adhere to one U.S. Constitution, they remind us to embrace these differences knowing that they may be modified over time.

Some object to the idea of the Electoral College, pointing out that a direct popular vote in other countries works well. It seems like such an approach is more equal for all voters. The argument, again, hangs on the principle perception that our nation is homogeneous and that any state-by-state differences can be easily absorbed within a national election.

It should be remembered that there is a difference of geographic size of countries compared to the United States. For example, the U.S. encompasses 9,833,342 square kilometers while all of Europe (including the European portion of Russia) is 10,160,000 kilometers. That's a relative equality in size. However, the U.S. is divided into 50 states while Europe has 60 countries. European Russia at 3,960,000 square kilometers is an outsized country that is more than double our largest state of Alaska (1,723,337 square kilometers). The next largest state, Texas, is larger than the next largest European country of Ukraine. California is smaller than Sweden but larger than Norway. Montana is larger than Germany while the United Kingdom sits between Michigan and Minnesota in size.

The point in these comparisons is that our nation, these United States, are like no other European nation when it comes to size. Each state is comparable to a European nation in that it stands on its own, with its own governing structure and powers, providing its own distinct sovereignty that must be taken into account when voting for the nation's president.

One feature, if one can call it that, of our states is that their respective populations ebb and flow as people move around the country, by the additions made by births, and the subtractions incurred by deaths. The U.S. Census Bureau estimated in 2019 that my own state of Oregon grew 10.1% in population size since 2010. Texas grew by 15.3%, California by 6.1%, Florida by 14.2%. North Dakota, my childhood state, grew by 13.3%, and on it goes.

The reason this is important is because, once every ten years, a census is taken and state congressional districts are redrawn and the state representation in the U.S. House of Representatives changes state-by-state. While the total of U.S. Representatives remains the same, some states will gain representatives while others will lose some. Such representative shift is reflected in the Electoral College. A nationwide popular vote does not reflect such fluidity—it is what it is. Remembering that ours is a representative democracy, the Electoral College gives veracity to this voting aspect. A nation-wide popular vote does not.

As we consider the popular vote, it's a good idea to consider how the nation is populated from state-to-state. The map below shows how states vary in their population densities. The black and gray filled states are the most densely populated states. As you can see, the population is not evenly spread among states.

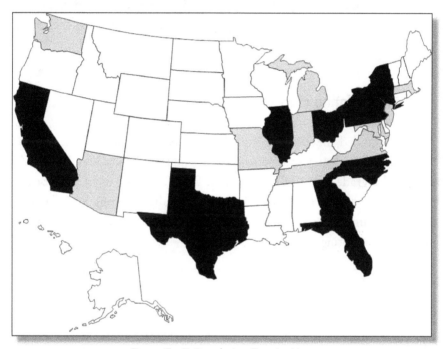

Figure 7 - 7: Population Density Map

The nine black states equal one half of our nation's population!

The 10 gray states equal one fourth of our nation's population!

The 31 white states and Washington, D.C. equal another sixth of our nation's population!

As you review the map, consider how presidential candidate campaign strategies would change if only the popular vote mattered. Most of the campaign attention would be focused on the most populated states and might also include the major cities in the lesser-populated states. Rural America would be largely ignored!

What happens when you are ignored? You may feel pushed away. It may seem that you do not matter. Your vote will not matter if the nation uses a purely popular vote approach and you live in rural America. Consider those who live in the 25 white states above. The popular vote approach simply won't serve them well when it comes time to pick their next president.

Essentially, the nine states shown in black above would be the primary focus for the candidates and would also be the key players in picking the next president. Since our country is so large, the geographic and cultural differences play a huge part in our collective experiences and responses during a presidential election. The popular vote approach fails the voting fairness test.

★ Popular Voting election test

We have graded the election approaches already discussed. The current election process using an Electoral College approach, shackled by WTA, rendered a grade of "D". Congressional District voting did a little better with a grade of "C". EVV set a high standard by attaining an "A" grade. Using the same comparison, we can now turn our attention to the nationwide popular voting approach.

Popular Vote	
Standard	Grade
Fair	A
Equal	F
Inclusive	A
Engaging	F
Popular Voting	A
State Voting	F
Checks & Balances	F
Grade Point Average	D

Figure 7 – 8: Popular Voting Grading

+ **Fair** – The voting process is clear. A lot of attention has been given to ensure ballots are clear, easy to mark, and counted fairly. **Grade: A**

+ **Equal** – Beyond voter suppression, picking a president by a nation-wide popular vote suffers equality because of the various voting rules established on a state-by-state basis, disenfranchising many and blocking an equal access to voting. Such rules prevent an equal election across the nation. **Grade: F**

+ **Inclusive** – In general, voters are not denied voting access. However, voter suppression emerges has its negative effect. Since this is not due to the voting mechanism, per se, it is not reflected in the grade. (See note below.) **Grade: A**

+ **Engaging** – Voters who are inclined to vote in opposition to the plurality of the nation's voters may easily recognize they are in the minority and not vote. Further, voting on a nation-wide basis as one among tens of millions may underscore a sense of being insignificant. **Grade: F**

> **Note:** It should be noted that voter suppression emerges in various nefarious ways causing many to not be able to cast their ballots. No voting mechanism or approach alone can change this. Corruption and fraud have interfered with the nation's voting throughout its history. Such interference should be recognized for what it is, when it happens, and steps be taken to correct it. It is not part of this grading assessment though it certainly remains a challenge for a true democratic voting process.

This is a passing grade. If the test were put on a four-point scale, as many college courses are, the national Grade Point Average (GPA) for presidential voting would be a an even 2.0. Popular voting gets a solid "C." Let's continue with the other three measures.

+ **Capture the sentiment of the governed** (a popular vote result). The popular votes are directly captured. **Grade: A**

- **Capture the sentiment of the state** (separate and equal voices). The state voting voice is silenced, giving no recognition to regional or state concerns. **Grade: F**
- **Provide voting checks and balances.** There are no checks and balances at work with a nation-wide popular vote process. An aggressive majority, localized in a relatively small geographic region of the country, could overwhelm the remaining national regions. **Grade: F**

One more "A" and two "Fs" are added to the total, lowering the presidential election process GPA to a solid 1.7 average, or a "D" grade. In other words, a nation-wide popular vote approach barely passes the test, even if it were available to do by amending the U.S. Constitution. Using a popular voting approach across the nation does not even meet the improved standard set by congressional district voting.

The grading comparisons we have thus far are:

- Current Voting Approach: D
- Congressional District Voting: C
- Popular Voting Approach: C-
- Equal Voice Voting Approach: A

You may not agree with the grades applied here but it is easy to recognize the spectrum of comparisons to each other based on the listed standards.

★ Chapter Summary:

- It is understandable that a presidential election process change is desired, given the disparity between the popular and Electoral College election results.
- To modify or eliminate the Electoral College requires an amendment to the U.S. Constitution, which requires a two-thirds acceptance by both chambers of the U.S. Congress and a ratification by 38 states' congresses. It is highly improbable that it can be enacted in the near future.

+ The United States is a republic and not a homogeneous nation. It is composed of different regions and sovereign states.

+ Different states use different voting rules, thereby making it impossible to implement the same kind of election nationwide. Voter registration, rights to vote, early voting, and voting by mail differences are examples of how states vary from each other.

+ States are comparable to European countries in their sizes and populations. The United States cannot be compared to individual European countries as to how to manage presidential elections.

+ Popular voting, conducted on a nationwide basis, barely meets the seven principles, failing tests of fairness, equality, inclusiveness, engagement, capturing the voting sentiment of voters as well as of the sovereign states, and providing checks and balances.

CHAPTER 8
NATIONAL POPULAR VOTE INTERSTATE COMPACT (NPVIC)

The American experiment with representative democracy has been a great success, but we need to realize that it needs to be a genuine representative democracy where ordinary people have a vote, have a voice in choosing the candidates who represent them.

RICHARD PAINTER

(B. 1961, FORMER WHITE HOUSE ETHICS LAWYER)

It is commendable when a problem is recognized. It is particularly so when solutions are sought and, be it luck or cleverness, a remedy is realized. On the other hand, ignoring a problem's cause and pushing to add a layer of complexity instead, invites embarrassment. And so it is with the National Popular Vote (NPVIC) approach.

NPVIC aims to correct what is perceived as an election mechanism failing with the Electoral College. Credibly, the NPVIC supporters point to the topsy-turvy results realized with the presidential elections of 2000 and again in 2016. Those elections resulted in a candidate winning a plurality of the nation's popular vote and still losing the election via the Electoral College results. These seemed, on their face, obvious failings that demand a voting approach correction for future elections.

The NPVIC idea is simple: form a compact of states that agree to cast all of their electoral votes for whichever candidate wins the nation's plurality of popular votes. The baseline requirement is that enough states, collectively, form the compact to meet the threshold of 270 electoral votes, as required by the U.S. Constitution, to cement a win.

One of the alluring features of NPVIC is that it does not require a U.S. Constitution amendment. The interstate compact of willing states can bypass the requirement for such a remedy, thereby cutting a shortcut past federal and state legislatures and their ratifications to comply.

There is more to NPVIC that usually goes unspoken. For one, as we saw in Chapter 4, popular and Electoral College voting result disparities still remain. In fact, there is a real danger that the voting disparities elicited by NPVIC can become worse. For another, though the candidate winning the popular vote is assured of winning the presidency, the NPVIC voting results will point to an erroneous voting story. Often, presidential wins are measured not only by who won and who lost, but also by giving attention to the margins of the win. Mandates may be indicated and, using NPVIC, they would be established on a false premise. The news media and the winning political parties would create and point to a false narrative which would misinform the public of the truth. In short, NPVIC can be shown to be ridiculous, radical, and dangerous.

NPVIC is ridiculous. The lack of a diagnosis to determine the cause for the existing voting approach problem distracts the public and political leaders to support a solution dressed up to capture attention rather than deliver a solid and sound election process. Much like a circus barker's audience, many are duped into "stepping right up" and becoming complicit as they throw their votes away.

NPVIC is radical. Ignoring the amendment remedy provided by the U.S. Constitution is disingenuous at best. At its worst, it can be likened to a colossal con. Further, NPVIC ignores state sovereignty and the fundamental fact that the United States is a republic. Individual states matter, as was acknowledged by the nation's Founding Fathers and protected by the U.S. Constitution itself. Finally, NPVIC severely puts ballots at an even greater risk of not being represented in the Electoral College due to the Winner-Takes-All (WTA) approach. The promised remedy fails.

There are additional concerns about NPVIC. Given that many elections turn out to be close elections, NPVIC does not identify how voting recounts would be conducted. Who would pay for such recounts? Which states would participate? These are just two of the questions that emerge unanswered with NPVIC. Noting that, sometimes, presidential elections experience disloyal electors, how would that reality affect an election using

NPVIC? Would all states within the interstate compact be required to pass laws that demanded all electors within the NPVIC compact remain loyal? Would such laws be constitutional? And what happens if, after a negative experience in one election, a state within the NPVIC compact withdraws, causing the compact to no longer meet the 270-vote threshold? Would the voters who remain in the compact feel cheated? Do the NPVIC compact states automatically return to the previous election method?

The current approach used when exercising the Electoral College already has earned a poor grade, as indicated in Chapter 6. Voting by congressional district is an improvement, grade-wise, while a popular vote is worse. Equal Voice Voting (EVV) earns the top marks and NPVIC settles in at the bottom of the list of five.

★ NPVIC Definition, Requirements, & the U.S. Constitution

NPVIC answers the call for a direct popular voting preference. It recognizes that the Electoral College prevents a nation-wide popular voting result from being the mainstay of the voting mechanism (never mind such prevention was the intent of the Constitutional Framers). NPVIC ushers in a clever side-step mechanism that avoids the constitutional restriction and chooses, instead, to gain an agreement among states for a nationwide popular voting result.

NPVIC requires that any state within its compact must cast all of its electoral votes for whichever candidate wins the nationwide popular vote. It is a form of WTA in that all of a state's electoral votes are cast for one presidential candidate. It does not matter if a plurality of voters within an NPVIC compact state prefers a different candidate from what a plurality of voters across the nation chooses. Their votes will not be represented in the Electoral College results. These voters will be disenfranchised from the election process.

As of this writing, 15 states and the District of Columbia have adopted the NPVIC idea. These states include: California, Colorado, Connecticut, Delaware, Hawaii, Illinois, Massachusetts, Maryland, New Jersey, New Mexico, New York, Oregon, Rhode Island, Vermont, and Washington. Together, they can contribute 196 electoral votes for a presidential election.

That means that NPVIC must yet be adopted by enough states to add another 74 electoral votes to reach the 270 electoral votes threshold before it can become enacted and ensure a candidate's win by the nation's popular voting total.

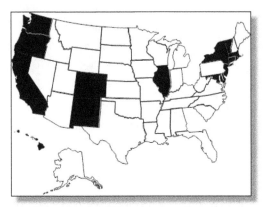

Figure 8 – 1: NPVIC Interstate Compact

NPVIC proponents insist that the election approach is a nonpartisan solution. Yet, reviewing the list of the states already included shows that these states typically, at least in recent elections, favor the Democratic candidates. That may be an unfair observation but it does indicate that these "Blue" states are at least inclined to favor NPVIC for some reason. Could the receptivity be because of the perception that there are more registered Democrats than Republicans? Could it be that ensuring the presidency is secured by a direct popular vote is preferable to allowing the Electoral College, including the checks and balances set in place by the Framers, have its controlling influence? The NPVIC workaround appears to ignore the cautions and safeguards set forth in the U.S. Constitution. It is especially so as it ignores the reality that the nation is a republic.

The NVPIC idea is a clever one in that it adopts a name which indicates most people already like and endorse it. It is the most popular after all, or so it is assumed. Add to that the mantra of "One person, one vote," what could be wrong? Everyone's vote would count, it is declared, unlike what we experience today. It sounds very inclusive. It sounds very democratic.

Chapter 7 pointed to what is required to amend the U.S. Constitution. It is not a simple remedy and deservedly so. The Framers recognized that the Constitution may need to be modified but it requires the agreement of specific majority margins of governing bodies at both the federal and state levels. History reveals that attempting to amend the Constitution in regards to the Electoral College is and promises to continue to be both a daunting and almost impossible task. As was stated in Chapter 7, Alexander Kessar noted in his book, "Why Do We Still Have the Electoral College?" that such an amendment has been attempted over 800 times and has never managed to pass in the U.S. Congress.

NPVIC comes to the rescue by submitting the idea that, if several states are in agreement, the Constitutional amendment remedy can effectively be set aside for this particular presidential election need. Cohesion among states, after all, is desirable and a consensus among many who hold a majority of electoral votes should hold sway, right?

The U.S. Constitution sheds some light on the topic, albeit in a tangential manner. Article I, Section 10, points out [bolding added for emphasis]:

> *No State shall, without the Consent of Congress, lay any Duty of Tonnage, keep Troops, or Ships of War in time of Peace, enter into any Agreement or* **Compact** *with another State, or with a foreign Power, or engage in War, unless actually invaded, or in such imminent Danger as will not admit of delay.*

While NPVIC requires an interstate compact among states, the U.S. Constitution points out that such agreement must first achieve the consent of the U.S. Congress. There are two things to consider here:

- **First:** The compact referred to in the Constitution directly refers to conditions of war. No shipping tonnage can be levied or troops or ships be controlled by a compact of states. That has nothing to do with electing a president.

  Yet, it cannot be overlooked that the "sentiment" outlined here refers to a prevention of a collection of states forming an advantage over other states, thereby avoiding a nationwide agreement. Does it apply for the forming of an interstate compact as NPVIC requires?

Is this an example of what the Constitutional Framers wished for the nation to avoid?

+ **Second**: The U.S. Congress has not, as of this writing, given its consent for an NPVIC compact. Suppose enough states come into agreement to reach the 270-vote electoral vote threshold, will they then seek and will they then be able to secure such federal consent from both chambers of the U.S. Congress? Without such assurance, forming the compact agreements beforehand seems to be risky at best.

Further concerns include the WTA aspect. As of this writing, four states (California, Massachusetts, Texas, and South Carolina) have brought forth suits at the district level, challenging the constitutionality of WTA. None of the cases have succeeded at the district level with the court consensus being that WTA is a state law and not part of the U.S. Constitution. All four cases are being appealed to the U.S. Supreme Court.

The plaintiffs in the lawsuits claim that state WTA laws violate the Equal Protection clause of the 14th Amendment as well as the First Amendment. The claim focuses on the 14th Amendment's assertion that, "No state shall … deny to any person within its jurisdiction the equal protection of the laws." Disenfranchising voters, in this writer's opinion, is a strong voice against its being a constitutional voting approach. A future Supreme Court decision will be notable.

The point of this discussion is that NPVIC is far from being accepted nationally, endorsed by the U.S. Congress, or found to be constitutional. While NPVIC "seems" to offer a viable voting option, it fails to meet expectations even in these fundamentals.

★ NPVIC Voting Results

A foundational tenet of NPVIC is the quest for a fair presidential election. It is the basis for the, "One person, one vote" rallying cry. What could be fairer than to have every voter cast a ballot and that it be counted? We are one nation, after all. Or so goes the thinking.

As has been emphasized earlier, the United States is a republic made up of 50 sovereign states. The Founding Fathers were adamant that it would be the basis for the best form of governance for the 13 colonies and it has proved to be strong as the nation expanded to the 50 states. Each sovereign state, so went their thinking, deserves to provide its own separate voting voice, proportionally, when selecting a president who serves us all. Resorting to a popular vote gathered across the nation, as NPVIC promises, obscures the state distinctions effectively erasing the sovereignty of states.

Capturing the sentiment of the governed – a popular vote – is desirable. We are electing a person to fulfill the duties of a president for all of us. Our collective voice is important. Yet, there is no need to dissolve the state borders, melding states together, and ignore the independence and diversity that a republic affords.

It must be remembered that NPVIC still includes the Electoral College. It does not replace the constitutional voting mechanism that has been in place since 1787. The key point about this is that all popular voting must be converted into electoral votes on a state-by-state basis. Doing so ensures a proportional voting representation across the 50 states and the District of Columbia.

It should also be recognized that engaging the NPVIC approach does not require a comprehensive acceptance by the entire nation. The result is that the NPVIC interstate compact in a sense forms a fictitious state of its own as it casts all of its electoral votes for the one candidate. It becomes another way for WTA to intercede, preventing a true voting result.

Voting results are important, of course. Below are some scenarios to consider had NPVIC been in place for the 2020 and 2016 elections.

2020 Election:

Imagine that enough states were added to the NPVIC interstate compact for each scenario. Imagine if, in addition to the 15 states and the District of Columbia noted above, a few more states were added to the compact. Adding Arizona, Georgia, Michigan, Minnesota, Nevada, and Virginia would provide the compact with 272 electoral votes, two more electoral votes than needed to ensure the presidential win.

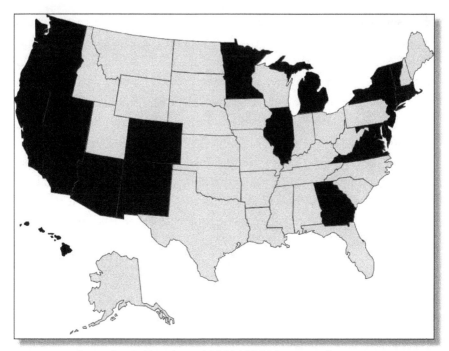

Figure 8 – 2: Hypothetical 2020 NPVIC Interstate Compact

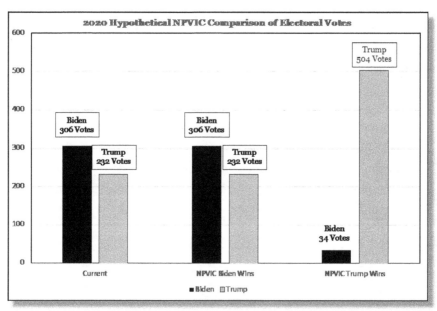

Figure 8 – 3: Hypothetical 2020 NPVIC Interstate Compact Graph

The actual 2020 voting results:

+ Biden wins popular vote by 4.48%
+ Electoral Votes: Biden 306 (56.88%), Trump 232, (43.12%)

If the NPVIC compact of states identified above had been in place:

+ Electoral Votes: Biden 306 (56.88%), Trump 232, (43.12%)

If the NPVIC compact of states identified above had been in place and Trump had won the popular vote instead:

+ Electoral Votes: Trump 504 (93.68%), Biden 34, (6.32%)

This reveals how volatile the NPVIC can be. It should be clear that the compact in effect forms a separate voting state, devoid of sovereignty, that competes against the states voting as separate governmental jurisdictions.

While the above example is bad, it can be worse. Let's use another hypothetical scenario and consider the 2016 election.

2016 Election:

Imagine that enough states were added to the NPVIC interstate compact for each scenario. Imagine if, in addition to the 15 states and the District of Columbia noted above, a few more states were added to the compact. Adding Indiana, Minnesota, Missouri, North Dakota, Oklahoma, Pennsylvania, and Virginia would provide the compact with exactly 270 electoral votes, enough to ensure the presidential win.

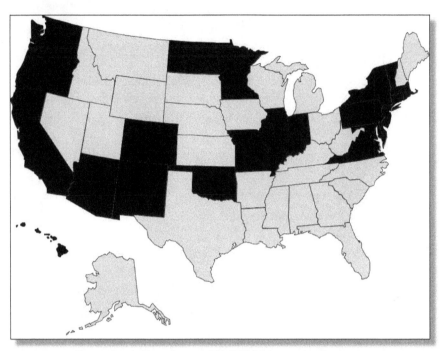

Figure 8 – 4: Hypothetical 2016NPVIC Interstate Compact

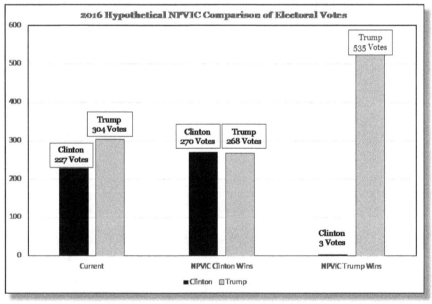

Figure 8 – 5: Hypothetical 2016 NPVIC Interstate Compact

The actual 2016 voting results:

+ Clinton wins popular vote by 2.02%
+ Electoral Votes: Trump 304 (56.51%), Clinton 227, (42.19%)
+ **Note:** Seven electoral votes were cast for other candidates.

If the NPVIC compact of states identified above had been in place:

+ Electoral Votes: Clinton 270 (50.19%), Trump 268, (49.81%)
+ **Note:** Assumes all electoral votes would be cast for only these candidates.

If the NPVIC compact of states identified above had been in place and Trump won the popular vote instead:

+ Electoral Votes: Trump 535 (99.44%), Clinton 3, (0.56%)
+ **Note:** Assumes all electoral votes would be cast for only these candidates.

The two election examples shown here, if examined closely, expose the fact that NPVIC does not solve the disenfranchisement issue. The Electoral College remains intact and as popular votes are translated into electoral votes, many voters cast ballots that are never represented. The NPVIC promise of "One person, one vote" soon dissipates into the ether. The number of disenfranchised voters (suppressed votes) in the two scenarios posed above actually increases vote suppression beyond what was currently experienced in these two elections.

> **NOTE:** The hypothetical Trump popular vote win scenario cannot provide an exact count because the change in winning margins if Trump won the popular vote cannot be exact.

As is evident with these hypothetical examples, based on actual elections, the NPVIC approach still disenfranchises tens of millions of voters by their not gaining Electoral College representation. The contrived workaround used to avoid the Electoral College results still cannot escape the perils WTA delivers.

One can play with multiple scenarios contriving various composites of NPVIC interstate compacts. As you saw in Chapter 4, popular vote and electoral vote result disparities can vary widely. Currently, such disparities, on average, vary by 31.39% in any given election. The point of any such speculative consideration is that NPVIC promises a popular vote winning candidate to succeed to win the presidency. Yet, the electoral vote margins are volatile and can swing widely making voting result disparities far wider than we currently experience. NPVIC can often enlarge those differences.

If the only objective is to pick a winner, as noted earlier in this book, any process will work. But process matters! If an election is close by popular voting measures (and many elections are), and the Electoral College voting delivers a large mismatch compared to the popular voting results, then a false narrative is created. The voting public is not treated to a factual voting result for the highest governmental office in the country.

★ Ridiculous, Radical, and Dangerous

Instead of simplifying the voting process, NPVIC adds hidden complexities that make this alternative voting process very unappealing. Succinctly put, NPVIC is a ridiculous, radical, and dangerous idea. Here's why:

NPVIC is ridiculous. Far from being laughable, the NPVIC ridiculousness emerges because it fails to accomplish what it sets out to do. It fails because it does not address the cause for any voting deficiency currently experienced. Further, NPVIC proponents cannot diagnose the problem, or worse if they can, they choose to ignore the implications of such a diagnosis.

For example, the Covid-19 pandemic made us painfully aware of how important symptoms can be. They must not be ignored and must be taken seriously. Suppose you had a fever. Is it a symptom of the virus? If you contact your doctor and report you are running a fever and your doctor advises you to take a cold shower, you probably would consider that ridiculous advice. Sure, the fever may abate with the cold shower but for how long and to what effect? Misdiagnosing the cause of the fever or, as in this example, ignoring it altogether, could cause you to die. It is serious! Ignoring a diagnostic step is a ridiculous approach to remedy a problem.

A less serious example would be if you took your car to an automotive technician with the complaint that it was getting poorer fuel efficiency than you expect. Instead of checking the engine and the vehicle's systems (a diagnosis), imagine your technician telling you that the problem can easily be remedied. The recommendation is that all you need to do to increase fuel efficiency is to be sure you drive downhill more than you drive uphill. It would be a ridiculous answer, right?

Likewise, NPVIC proponents recognize that there is a gross mismatch between popular and Electoral College vote results. The NPVIC approach is adopted, much like the recommendation for a cold shower or downhill driving, without any diagnoses. Either a diagnosis is not wanted and thereby cannot be ascertained, or it is totally ignored.

As pointed out in Chapter 3, the cause for the voting problem is the Winner-Takes-All (WPA) approach. The approach began in the early 1800s for some states, with all of them using it by 1880. WTA disenfranchises tens of millions of voters, even if NPVIC were applied. Further, WTA is not a part of the Electoral College and has wreaked havoc on our election system for almost all of our presidential elections. We have become so used to it that we fail to recognize its insidious nature and, as we do, we fail to relieve ourselves of the malady. WTA is the diagnosis – the cause – that NPVIC skips over.

NPVIC is radical. It is a fairly cleverly-crafted idea but manages to totally disrespect the fundamental principles put forth by our Constitutional Framers on three levels. First, NPVIC ignores the U.S. Constitution. As has been pointed out, the Framers instituted a remedy should any part of the constitution be deemed worthy of an amendment. Though it is an arduous task to realize an amendment, exercising a blatant workaround borders on the nefarious. It tramples on our rule of law while pretending to instill a more democratic device for the good of the country.

Second, NPVIC totally ignores that this nation is a republic as it ignores the sovereignty of states. It's not easy to ignore a state's sovereignty with its own governmental executive (Governor), congressional, and judicial institutions that mirror that of the U.S. federal government. The federal system that is reflected in the Electoral College requires each state to make an independent judgment on who should get its vote(s) for the nation's president. It follows that a state cannot abdicate its responsibility in this regard by delegating these voting powers to a group of states that form a compact to seize such control. Doing so discounts a state's separate voting voice, making it inconsequential and directly in opposition to the Framer's intent.

At no time does NPVIC give credence to an individual state's voting voice. Instead NPVIC furthers a mechanism that allows the popular vote to be the only prize. Further, it can be said, NPVIC actually forms a fake state with its interstate compact of states, forming a monster state that can easily overwhelm those less populated. Only votes cast for the candidate winning the nation's plurality of votes gain representation. All others are silenced by the colossal Winner-Takes-All (WTA) approach as campaigns focus on the more populous regions and urban areas of the country, as noted in Chapter 7.

Third, NPVIC puts voters at risk of having their ballots not be represented in the Electoral College. Since WTA has not been diagnosed as being the crux of the problem, NPVIC exacerbates the issue and can easily increase the number of voters who are disenfranchised. For example, in my home state of Oregon, Democrats have usually won in recent elections the plurality of votes for their candidate. Because of WTA, the votes for a Republican candidate fail to gain representation in the Electoral College and those voters are disenfranchised. If NPVIC were enacted and a Republican candidate won the nation's plurality of votes, all of the votes for the Democrat (usually the state plurality winner) would be unrepresented. In this case, disenfranchisement increases rather than decreases. Again, due to the radical diagnostic failure, no cure for the WTA is realized. Voter disenfranchisement (vote suppression) persists with NPVIC.

NPVIC is dangerous. As if all of the aforementioned were not severe enough, we must remember that there is more to an election story than merely who won the contest. Every presidential election drama is formed around the capturing of votes, both popular and electoral, until a full story unfolds. Winning vote margins are extolled and give credence to a candidate's claim to power or even a mandate. But is it the truth?

We have already seen how voting results can vary widely between what is realized by the popular vote as compared to what we see from the

Electoral College. If NPVIC uses a bypassing mechanism such that the Electoral College results mean little or nothing, the election story shifts to a false narrative. A close election can dissolve into a fake news story declaring a candidate winning by a landslide. While we may cringe at the idea of a close election being lost by a small percentage of votes, translating such elections into one of tens of percentage points difference (more than 80% in our earlier examples) should cause us to riot in the streets.

False narratives, while alarming, also render a quieter and more insidious aftermath. It has long been realized that disenfranchised voters are reluctant to vote in future elections. Many turn away from the ballot box entirely and fail to be politically engaged in this form of self-government we call representative democracy. While we currently experience a poor voter participation, NPVIC promises to make it worse. Some assessments assert that over 50% of eligible voters do not even register. Of that, another 40% do not vote. And, because of WTA, another 47.8% (on average) of the votes cast are not represented in the Electoral College. Dissuading additional voters via a false election news cycle is more than alarming – it is dangerous!

★ Additional Concerns

Imagine what would happen if NPVIC were in place and the nation's voting proved to be thinly won by a candidate. Normally, states conduct vote recounts to ensure a clear winner is called for the state as the WTA identifies who gets all of the electoral votes. Since that kind of scenario would not be in effect for the individual states within the NPVIC compact, how would a voting recount be conducted? Would there even be a recount?

Many other questions would surface in this kind of situation. Usually, voting recounts take place by states which are narrowly won or lost. Perhaps, though, a voting miscount, if there is one, could have been experienced by those voting in a state with a wide election margin. Voting recounts are costly so it would be important to predetermine which state(s) would be responsible to incur the voting recount costs. Would it be a shared cost by all states within the compact? Again, who or by which means would determine which state(s) should conduct a recount, given that errors could be found in any of the NPVIC participating states? Would it be satisfactory if a state not participating in the NPVIC compact conduct a recount to clarify its own records but the NPVIC states go unquestioned? By what appreciable nationwide winning margin percentage would determine the winning candidate? Would winning by one percent suffice? Would winning by only one vote, nationwide, seal the deal? Would some other confirmation of a winner be predetermined? And would such predetermination be beyond the reaches of fraud? Questions continue and voting confidence wanes.

We have already seen that disloyal electors have not historically been a large issue. The 2016 election provided the worst example with its seven disloyal electors. Even then, the election was not thrown off course by these few defectors. But given that NPVIC rests on the idea of the interstate compact states, collectively, ensure the winning threshold of 270 votes, such elector disloyalty could disrupt the entire election. If enough disloyal electors disrupt the election such that the threshold is not reached by the NPVIC compact states, would NPVIC then hold or would all of the participating states resort to their previous WTA results?

If NPVIC is used in one election but any of the interstate compact member states subsequently withdraw, the assumption is that NPVIC may not be able to deliver on its threshold of 270 electoral votes. If so, it would mean that the presidential election process would have to resort to their previous process. It could prove to be a fragile beginning for NPVIC, further eroding the confidence of the voting citizens. Such erosion can play havoc on subsequent voter turnout. Again, NPVIC would prove to be dangerous.

★ NPVIC Election Test

How does NPVIC measure up when assessed through the lens of the election test outlined in Chapter 6? Those tests provided grading for a voting approach should be:

- ◆ **Fair** – The voting options need to be clear, easy to understand, and the voting choices can be easily and accurately counted.
- ◆ **Equal** – The votes need to be equally represented so no advantage is given to any candidate or political party.

+ **Inclusive** – The opportunity to vote should not deny any voter access to the voting process.
+ **Engaging** – Voters should be motivated to vote having confidence that their vote will make a difference
+ Capture the sentiment of the governed (a popular vote result).
+ Capture the sentiment of each state (separate and equal voices).
+ Provide voting checks and balances.

The following shows the grading NPVIC would experience if measured against the standards put forth earlier.

National Popular Vote	
Standard	**Grade**
Fair	A
Equal	F
Inclusive	C
Engaging	F
Popular Voting	C
State Voting	F
Checks & Balances	F
Grade Point Average	F

Figure 8 – 6: NPVIC Grading

+ **Fair** – The voting process is clear. As is experienced currently, a lot of attention has been given to ensure ballots are clear, easy to mark, and counted fairly. Voting machine security is another pressing issue. Overall, across the nation, these concerns are aggressively addressed and corrections made when needed. Generally, it can be said that the election process would be fair. **Grade: A**
+ **Equal** – State electoral votes would still suffer the WTA process but could cause even larger percentages of voter representation to be forfeited than what is currently experienced. Further, NPVIC would cause viable candidate representation to be discarded. **Grade: F**

+ **Inclusive** – In general, voters are not denied voting access. However, voter suppression has its negative effect. Since this is not due to the voting mechanism, per se, it is not reflected in the grade. (See Note below.) NPVIC may or may not entice voter turnout given that some voters may perceive there is no chance their choice could win. **Grade: C**

+ **Engaging** – Voters who are inclined to vote in opposition to the plurality of state voters do not experience fair voter representation, due to WTA. Such disenfranchisement discourages voters from voting. **Grade: F**

> **Note:** It should be noted that voter suppression emerges in various nefarious ways causing many to not be able to cast their ballots. No voting mechanism or approach alone can change this. Corruption and fraud have interfered with the nation's voting throughout its history. Such interference should be recognized for what it is, when it happens, and steps be taken to correct it. It is not part of this grading assessment though it certainly remains a challenge for a true democratic voting process.

This is not a good grade. If the test were put on a four-point scale, as many college courses are, the national Grade Point Average (GPA) for presidential voting would be 1.5, or a "D+." NPVIC does not do well.

Let's continue with the other three measures.

+ **Capture the sentiment of the governed** (a popular vote result). The popular votes of the nation are captured but 47.8% of them are normally discarded, due to WTA, as they are converted into electoral votes. NPVIC can actually exacerbate this negative result creating a false voting result narrative. A true picture of the voting sentiment can be lost. **Grade: C**

+ **Capture the sentiment of each state** (separate and equal voices). Each state cannot weigh in with a respective voting voice because the NPVIC compact states are absorbed and act as one. **Grade: F**

+ **Provide voting checks and balances.** The Electoral College system of checks and balances are dissolved because of NPVIC's interstate compact. Consequently, the nation's voting results, ensuring a popular vote win, allows for greater corruption as minority voting voices become overwhelmed. **Grade: F**

Two more "Fs" and a "C" are added to the total bringing the presidential election process GPA to an embarrassing 0.86, an "F." While NPVIC may be appealing with its promise of a nationwide popular vote win, too many standards are missed to make it a viable option.

The five voting approaches covered in this book have now been graded. Again, as stated earlier, you may not agree with the grading provided here. However, comparing the five approaches and their respective grades, it is obvious which ones meet the standards and which do not. This kind of comparison shows how the voting approaches measure up in comparison to each other, providing a ranking according to performance. Congressional district voting passes. The current approach and the popular voting barely do while NPVIC clearly flunks. Only EVV shows it meets all of the standards.

Voting Approaches	Current Approach	Congressional District Voting	EVV	Direct Popular Voting	NPVIC
Standard	Grade	Grade	Grade	Grade	Grade
Fair	A	A	A	A	A
Equal	F	C	A	F	F
Inclusive	A	A	A	A	C
Engaging	F	C	A	F	F
Pop. Voting	F	C	A	A	F
State Voting	F	C	A	F	F
Checks & Balances	F	F	A	F	F
GPA	**D**	**C**	**A**	**D**	**F**

Figure 8 – 7: Voting Approaches Grading

The comparisons clearly point to the fact that we can do better with our presidential elections. We obviously suffer under the weight of WTA. Congressional district voting helps, a little, and the popular voting approach forfeits much of what our Constitutional Framers had in mind to the detriment of all of us. The worst proffered remedy is NPVIC as it remains ridiculous, radical, and dangerous.

★ Chapter Summary

- NPVIC requires an interstate compact of states collectively having at least 270 electoral votes.
- When enacted, NPVIC compact states agree to cast all of their electoral votes for whichever candidate wins the nation's plurality of popular votes.
- Currently, 15 states and the District of Columbia have agreed to the compact, able to contribute 196 electoral votes.
- NPVIC does not require a U.S. Constitution amendment.
- NPVIC ignores state sovereignty, a fundamental U.S. Constitution consideration.
- The Electoral College is still retained with NPVIC.
- NPVIC can exacerbate vote suppression.
- Disparities between popular and Electoral College voting results can (and often would) increase with NPVIC.
- NPVIC can create a false election result narrative causing the voting public to be misled and further erode future voter turnout.
- NPVIC is ridiculous, radical, and dangerous
  - ➤ NPVIC is ridiculous because its adherents either do not recognize the WTA problem or they ignore it.
  - ➤ NPVIC is radical because it defies the U.S. Constitution, ignores the sovereignty of states, and puts more voters at risk of not being represented by the Electoral College.
  - ➤ NPVIC is dangerous because it creates a false voting result narrative, thereby misinforming the public and discouraging voter turnout.

- NPVIC does not define voting recount rules, neither identifying which states conduct the recount nor how a recount is to be funded.
- NPVIC does not address the possibility of disloyal electors, failing to identify what may occur if the Electoral College 270 vote threshold is not met by the compact of states.
- NPVIC may be considered to be a partisan approach at this time because a nationwide popular vote might favor the Democratic party.
- NPVIC does not address the situation if states within the compact decide to break away from the agreement. What happens for the states remaining within the compact and their future voting process?
- NPVIC flunks the election tests identified above.

CHAPTER 9
AND NOW THIS

The classic rules of American politics are dying, if not dead, if you look at the last two presidential elections. An African-American could never be president until one was; a TV reality star couldn't become president until one was.

ERIC GARCETTI

(B. 1971, 42ND LOS ANGELES MAYOR)

Puzzled by the seeming complexity of the Electoral College voting mechanism, and the advantage Equal Voice Voting (EVV) brings, people will pursue their curiosity with questions about an assorted array of tangential issues. This curiosity is a natural response from those who express interest and merits attention. This chapter addresses three of the more common topics raised. The list is not exhaustive but it shows some of the concerns and shows how sweeping and necessary it is to give sober consideration to the election of a president.

The first discussion defines gerrymandering from a historical perspective and shows how it impacts elections today. An explanation follows of my own opinion as to how congressional districts should be drawn, based on line-drawing principles, and what results may be expected.

The second discussion addresses Ranked Choice Voting (RCV). Many have thought RCV competes with EVV. In some ways it does but one does not need to exclude the other. Instead, a modified RCV can be conjoined with EVV to elicit even greater exactness in voter preferences.

The entire book is about how we pick a president and making all votes matter. Discussions quickly turn to what we should look for in picking a president. What is the job description? What makes a good president? This last section is not definitive on what factors should guide you when picking a president so much as it is intended to spur you to consider some of the aspects listed here.

The presidency itself is discussed in light of what, in our constitutional and representative democracy, constitutes good governance. Many books have been written, studies made, courses delivered, and concerns addressed by revered intellectuals throughout history. I can humbly add only a little to this discussion. Basically, I emphasize the values and principles depicted in the earlier portions of this book.

As we herein have considered how our votes matter when picking a president, why we do is also an important topic to consider. The office of the presidency touches, influences, and enables almost every other aspect of our government. The presidential reach includes foreign and domestic policies, social justice directions, vision for our nation's future, along with the safety and nurturance of its citizens. The principles espoused in this book regarding the mechanism that brings the elected candidate to office also affect and enable the underpinnings for good governance from the Oval Office perspective to the homes of the governed.

★ Gerrymandering

Remember how I mentioned that our voting mechanism should be fair and equal? Congressional districts are notorious for being manipulated by whomever represents them when the district lines are redrawn (every 10 years). It's called gerrymandering. The following description, taken from www.wikipedia.com, describes how the process and the word came into being:

> The word gerrymander (originally written Gerry-mander) was used for the first time in the Boston Gazette on March 26, 1812. The word was created in reaction to a redrawing of Massachusetts state Senate election districts under the then-governor Elbridge Gerry (1744–1814). In 1812, Governor Gerry signed a bill that redistricted Massachusetts to benefit

his Democratic-Republican Party. When mapped, one of the contorted districts in the Boston area was said to resemble the shape of a salamander. The term was a portmanteau [combination] of the governor's last name and the word salamander.

Figure 9 - 1: Gerrymander Cartoon

Appearing with the term, and helping to spread and sustain its popularity, was a political cartoon depicting a strange animal with claws, wings and a dragon-like head satirizing the map of the odd-shaped district. This cartoon was most likely drawn by Elkanah Tisdale, an early 19th-century painter, designer, and engraver who was living in Boston at the time.

The word gerrymander was reprinted numerous times in Federalist newspapers in Massachusetts, New England, and nationwide during the remainder of 1812. This suggests some organized activity of the Federalists to disparage Governor Gerry, in particular, and the growing Democratic - Republican Party in general.

Gerrymandering soon began to be used to describe not only the original Massachusetts example, but also other cases of district-shape manipulation for partisan gain in other states. According to the Oxford English Dictionary, the word's acceptance was marked by its first publication in a dictionary (1848) and in an encyclopedia (1868).

In other words, congressional districts are often constructed to give the most favor to the political party that currently holds the most influence. These lines are redrawn whenever a new national census is taken. It is one of the primary reasons that incumbent representatives are so confident they will win the vote, term after term, to retain their seat in the House of Representatives. In effect, politicians are able to pick their constituents, rather than having voters pick their legislators. It's effectively an upending of the voting process. Such manipulation to control power and favor is not a good basis for forming a voting mechanism for our nation's Electoral College.

Here are two gerrymandered congressional districts to illustrate how convoluted districts can become:

Alabama's sixth Congressional District is currently held by a Republican U.S. Representative. Notice how it wraps around itself leaving a middle area to be included in another Congressional District (similar to the salamander cartoon above). The district definers strove to include the party-of-choice's voters and exclude others. Words like "Control," "Manipulation," and "Unfair" should spring to mind.

Figure 9 - 2: Alabama Congressional District #6

Another district, the one in which I live, is Oregon' fifth Congressional District. It is currently held by a Democrat U.S. Representative. Again, notice how the borders wrap around areas (avoiding voters?) and seem to extend to other areas (capturing voters?).

Figure 9 - 3: Oregon's Congressional District #5

It can be argued that Republicans take advantage of the gerrymandering to gain favor in their elections more than do Democrats. There is truth in that statement. Remember, though, that Democrats have also maneuvered the district border lines to their advantage. Neither political party can be proud of its gerrymandering history.

How Fairness Can Be Restored

Some efforts have been made to assemble panels of people who represent a mix of political and apolitical allegiances. The thinking is that these panels would oversee the process to ensure it is fair and not have districts turn into the dreaded salamanders noted earlier. The panels suggested are often large, including several members from the political parties involved and/ or from non-political groups. The inclusion of such large oversight panels (some being a dozen or more) could be a bit of an overkill in the quest for fairness. The districting defining process, using modern technology, is not an onerous process. Rather, a few people adept with the software can produce acceptable results. The panel, if one is used, would then simply confirm or deny the proffered districting plan according to their collective sense of fairness. It's a good first step in ensuring nefarious line-drawing is not exercised.

Remember how I pointed out in Chapter 2 that for any system to work well, it must follow some fundamental principles? For good election results, fairness and equal opportunity for voters to participate must be followed. Likewise, when identifying the boundaries of a congressional district, the principles agreed to should be followed.

The following discussion is a bit of a digression from the theme of this book but I bring it up to highlight the need for some simple principles (guidelines) to follow to ensure the results are fair for everyone. As we look at congressional districts across the country, many are confusing and render poor service simply because, again, they were drawn to capture a constituency – a political advantage.

While I'm not presenting the following as a prescription, I hope what is offered here adds some general guidelines to consider for improving the boundaries of future congressional districts. Think: people first, political advantage not at all.

The first step is to identify what constitutes a congressional district boundary. A boundary definition should make a boundary obvious and recognizable by everyone. It should be clear that the shape of the congressional district should also have some limitations. In other words, what shape should a district have without becoming out of control? This concern is simply answered by identifying the limits of how many boundary segments a congressional district can have. Here are some suggested parameters that could be so used:

1. A boundary segment is the distance between two angle points, or corners in the district's shape. Boundary segments includes any of the following examples:

   a. A straight line from one angle point or corner to the next.

   b. A major body of water such as an ocean, sea, bay, gulf, lake, canal, or river. Streams, ravines, and creeks would not suffice for a district boundary segment.

   c. Railroad tracks. If the boundary segment consists of more than one railroad track, each track would be considered a separate boundary segment.

   d. (**Note:** railroad tracks usually consist of two running in parallel to accommodate trains running in both directions. A boundary segment would include both tracks.)

   e. Freeways. If the boundary segment consists of more than one freeway, each freeway would be considered a separate boundary segment.

   f. County and state highways and roads. Each highway or road is counted as a boundary segment.

    g. City streets or avenues. Each street or avenue is counted as one boundary segment unless a given street or avenue is renamed along its pathway.

2. An angle point or corner is the juncture where two boundary segments join. For example, a straight-line boundary segment that meets the ocean (another boundary segment type) forms an angle point or corner. As long as there is an angle less than 180 degrees between two boundary segments, an angle point or corner is formed.

3. A district is composed of three to seven boundary segments and three to seven angle points or corners.

Shapes composed of three to seven sides and three to seven corners would be similar to the following examples:

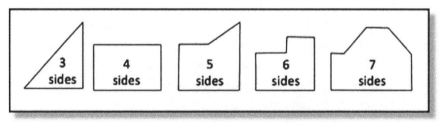

Figure 9 - 4: Example Congressional District Shapes

Districts would be drawn (started) from one corner (angle) of a state, using two joined boundary segments and their common angle as a starting point. The district boundary segments would then be drawn according to the rules above to include the number of citizens apportioned for one district.

For example, Oregon districts could be drawn starting from its southeast corner. Michigan's districts could start from the boundary segment formed by its southern border and Lake Michigan.

The next district would then be drawn using one of the initial district boundary segments. This process would continue until all of the state districts would be completed. Each district would have an equal proportion (or nearly so) of the state's citizens.

The point here is that congressional districts should be defined by their populations irrespective of their political preferences. Further, consideration for retaining homogeneity within a district in reference to the industries and human demographics may be impossible. A mix of each may actually be preferred. Yet the district lines should not be so convoluted that people are confused about which district they are in. Further, if districts jut out with extended territorial arms or become wrapped around islands of a population, it causes neighbors to be unnecessarily divided.

The Oregon district shown earlier in Figure 9 - 3, for example, includes some of the Oregon coastline, areas of low mountains and forests, valley areas for farming, and urban areas including multiple cities and towns. Included in this area we can find industries devoted to tourism, fishing, forestry, wineries, farming, and the plethora of concerns encountered within urban subdivisions and city centers. Such mixture is not a negative but contriving the borders to include and exclude constituents as it does, builds more distrust than inclusivity, counter to a good democracy.

Oregon's population is about 4,218,000, as of this writing, and has five congressional districts. Each district, then, should currently have approximately 843,600 citizens. If the 2020 Census shows that Oregon will add a congressional district, Oregon's total population will be divided by six so each district will have an average of 703,000 citizens. A margin of error, of course, would need to be acceptable allowing an over or under count of, say, 10% to make the district definition work well.

Why is all of this a concern when discussing the election of our nation's president? Two things come to mind: congressional district voting and contingency elections. Maine and Nebraska employ the congressional district voting approach. Inscribing with clear borders as much as possible would go far in eliciting a fair and equal proportioning of the state's citizens. Contingency voting, covered in Chapter 6, relies on a state's U.S. Representatives. If these legislators are elected by a fair process that includes well-drawn congressional districts, their votes in a contingency voting situation will better represent their constituents.

Again, this is merely offering up an approach to the congressional district-mapping problem that follows some common sense guidelines to ensure fairness is provided for all citizens and all political parties. As stated earlier, what is offered here is not meant to be prescriptive and I certainly realize others closer to the mapping process may have better solutions. Still, little success will be realized without fundamental principles used when redrawing the boundaries for state districts.

★ Ranked Choice Voting (RCV)

Ranked Choice Voting (RCV) is an approach designed to capture a more accurate picture of the consent of the governed. It accomplishes its goal well. Such accuracy is to be welcomed in our voting process, especially when so many vie for an elected office.

The method requires voters to rank the candidates running for an office according to their preference. For example, the candidate the voter most prefers would be ranked at the number one position. The second preferred candidate would be noted in second place, and so on, until all of the candidates are given a rank by the voter. Obviously, the approach is only applicable for election races for three or more candidates. If only two are running, RCV would not apply.

If one candidate captures a majority (not a plurality) of votes, there is no further calculation needed. The RCV approach when three candidates run for an office, includes six possible ballot variations, as shown in the table below. For example, two of the ballot variations will choose candidate "A" as the first choice, two others will choose candidate "A" as the second choice, and another two ballot variations will select candidate "A" as the third choice. The six variations show every possible voting combination possible.

Ballot Variations	Candidate Choices		
1	A	B	C
2	A	C	B
3	B	A	C
4	B	C	A
5	C	A	B
6	C	B	A

Figure 9 - 5: RCV First Round Example of Ballot Choices

However, if a majority winner is not realized from the first tabulation, the candidate with the fewest top-ranking votes is removed from consideration. The remaining candidate choices are then elevated one rank, if possible. The ballots are then retallied to elicit a majority winner. The removal of lowest ranked candidates and the counting process is repeated until a clear majority winner is revealed. A second-round change showing how "C" has been eliminated and the other candidates for those ballots are elevated in ranking, is shown in the table below. Notice that the third column is now blank because when candidate "C" is removed, other choices are moved up in rank.

Ballots	Candidate Choices		
1	A	B	
2	A	B	
3	B	A	
4	B	A	
5	A	B	
6	B	A	

Figure 9 - 6: RCV Second Round Example of Ballot Choices

If RCV were to be used for presidential elections, it would have to be employed on a state-by-state basis in order to honor the sovereignty of states and to adhere to the Electoral College structure. If so, the results would suffer like we experience today when we disenfranchise voters with the Winner-Takes-All (WTA) approach. It's already been shown in Chapter 3 that WTA causes a lot of unwanted problems as the approach ushers in vote suppression.

It is not necessary to completely discount RCV for presidential elections. RCV offers a positive reason for its consideration given that it elicits a more granular rendition of the sentiments revealed in an election. However, it must be modified if it is to render a proportional result via EVV suitable for a state-by-state presidential election.

The following explores some of the modified math needed to make RCV work with EVV. With an interest in keeping things simple, a couple of examples may suffice to explore RCV's possibilities.

RCV is modified in these examples because the goal is not to identify only one candidate but to award a proportion of electoral votes to all viable candidates. This approach honors the RCV intent while also continuing the proportional type of voting used by the Electoral College on a state-by-state basis.

An example state is used that is allocated 10 electoral votes to represent 3 million popular votes. The fictitious presidential election will include three candidates: "A," "B," and "C." Since there are more than two candidates, RCV could be used and will be compared with the current election process and EVV results.

<u>First Example</u>

Assume that Candidate "A" captures 46% (1,380,000 votes), Candidate "B" captures 30% (900,000 votes), and Candidate "C" captures 24% (720,000 votes).

Current election process = Candidate "A" wins 10 electoral votes due to WTA.

EVV election process = Popular Vote Value (PPV) = 300,000

> **NOTE:** PPV is derived by dividing the state's total popular votes by its allocated electoral votes. A candidate's electoral votes (using EVV) is determined by dividing the state's popular votes won by the candidate by the state's PPV.

- Candidate "A" = 4.6 rounded up to 5 electoral votes
- Candidate "B" = 3.0 is awarded 3 electoral votes
- Candidate "C" = 2.4 rounded down to 2 electoral votes

RCV election process

- Candidate "A" = First choice = 46%, Second choice 30%, Third choice 24%
- Candidate "B" = First choice = 30%, Second choice 40%, Third choice 30%
- Candidate "C" = First choice = 24%, Second choice 30%, Third choice 46%

The modified RCV approach includes six possible ballot choices, as was shown in table 9 – 1 above. Each ballot choice receives a ranked choice value that is an inverse of its ballot position. The figure below illustrates how ballots would be weighted with a modified RCV approach.

If a candidate is ranked as the top choice in a three-candidate race, that selection is given a ranked choice value of three. If a candidate is ranked second, he or she is given a ranked choice value of two. The last choice vote is given a ranked choice value of one. Each ballot, presenting the three candidates in ranked order, actually becomes six votes: three for the first-ranked candidate, two for the second-ranked candidate, and one for the last-ranked candidate. This process differentiates the value of each candidate according to the rank the voter gave him/her.

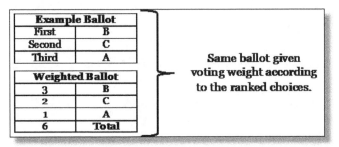

Figure 9 - 7: 1st Ballot Weighting Example for Modified RCV Approach

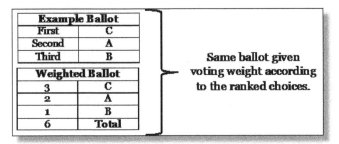

Figure 9 - 8: 2nd Ballot Weighting Example for Modified RCV Approach

Notice that both of the two example weighted ballots above, the vote weighted totals for the three candidates is different:

+ Candidate "A" = 1 (1st ballot) + 2 (2nd ballot) = 3
+ Candidate "B" = 3 (1st ballot) + 1 (2nd ballot) = 4
+ Candidate "C" = 2 (1st ballot) + 3 (2nd ballot) = 5

Each ballot's total weight (in this example) equals six. The total vote count then expands from 3 million votes to 18 million (6 X 3,000,000 = 18,000,000). Then, using the EVV method of conversion using the Popular Vote Value (PPV), this fictitious state election would have a PVV of 1,800,000. Without delving into all of the math involved, our example would show the following ranked choice values:

- Candidate "A" = 6,660,000 = 3.7 rounded up to 4 electoral votes
- Candidate "B" = 6,000,000 = 3.33 rounded down to 3 electoral votes
- Candidate "C" = 5,340,000 = 2.97 rounded up to 3 electoral votes

Already it is clear that a modified RCV approach can elicit a more accurate rendering of the voting outcome while still retaining the proportional aspect.

Second Example

The above example was not a close race. The second example shows what would occur with the election if two candidate campaigns run more neck-and-neck. Assume that Candidate "A" captures 46% (1,380,000 votes), Candidate "B" captures 42% (1,260,000 votes), and Candidate "C" captures 12% (360,000 votes).

Current election process = Candidate "A" wins 10 electoral votes due to WTA.

EVV election process = Popular Vote Value (PPV) = 300,000

- Candidate "A" = 4.6 rounded up to 5 electoral votes
- Candidate "B" = 4.2 rounded down to 4 electoral votes
- Candidate "C" = 1.2 rounded down to 1 electoral vote

RCV election process

- Candidate "A" = First choice = 46%, Second choice 40%, Third choice 14%
- Candidate "B" = First choice = 42%, Second choice 42%, Third choice 16%
- Candidate "C" = First choice = 12%, Second choice 18%, Third choice 70%

The total ranked vote values, given the ranked weighting, would still expand the three million votes to six million. Then, using the EVV method of conversion using the Popular Vote Value (PPV), this fictitious state election would have a PVV of 600,000. Our example would show the following ranked choice values:

- Candidate "A" = 6,960,000 = 3.87 rounded up to 4 electoral votes
- Candidate "B" = 6,780,000 = 3.77 rounded up to 4 electoral votes
- Candidate "C" = 4,260,000 = 2.37 rounded down to 2 electoral votes

Again, the modified RCV results show a more granular (more accurate) voting result than EVV, which relies on voters only selecting their top choice candidate. Here is a table comparing the results from these two approaches:

First Example	Electoral Votes		
	A	B	C
EVV	5	3	2
RCV	4	3	3
Second Example	Electoral Votes		
	A	B	C
EVV	5	4	1
RCV	4	4	2

Figure 9 - 9: Electoral Vote Award Comparisons

While the math by now has probably made your eyes cross, remember that it all takes place behind the scenes within the bowels of a computer. It may seem complex, and it is to a degree; the execution of a modified RCV method is not that difficult from a technological perspective.

However, RCV, whether it is the straightforward type now being used for some governing jurisdictions or the modified version exemplified above, harbors another challenge: humans. It is often amazing how simple things can become misconstrued and misunderstood. We humans can mess things up if we are given a chance.

Asking the general public to vote is the first challenge. There has been much written and many hands have been wrung over the worry caused by the nation's low voter turnout. Then, once they have their ballot in hand and are ready to vote, we ask them to rank their choices! Oh my!

Ranking our choices for a president does not come easy. We may know who we like but how do we compare those other two? Or, vice versa, we may know who we don't like but who should get top billing? For example, some voters will still only pick their top choice and leave the other two voting options blank. Perhaps repeated voting opportunities will help voters become more accustomed to this voting variance. Hopefully, too, they'll come to appreciate the intent of better capturing the intentions of the governed regardless of whether EVV is used alone or incorporates the modified RCV approach.

★ Picking a President

Political careers are built upon the science behind whatever makes a candidate successful in winning the presidency. The discipline is often constructed around strong assessments of the demographics of the governed on a state-by-state basis.

Factors of popularity and what goes into making a candidate appealing provide a huge chunk of consideration. Looks, especially height if the candidate is a man, their voice and how they speak, and even how they smile capture extra points. It is similar to the old sales perspective of not selling the steak so much as selling the steak's sizzle. Does the candidate come across as believable? Do we trust him/her? Would we expect he/she would listen to us or lead us well?

A winning candidate's list of attractions might include such considerations as experience, leadership, intelligence, emotional maturity, creativity, and the ability to make good decisions. At the very bottom of said list one may find the last entry to address the candidate's ability to form a good team. Perhaps, some would say, this should be at the top of the list. In other words, this election science seems to highlight the mass appeal more than the true capabilities needed to be the nation's president – the most powerful person in the world.

Still, we must decide. There is no real job description except a historical look at past presidents. We know that times change, history unfolds, new and unforeseen challenges appear. Is our voting no better than a guessing game? Should we simply rely on our gut instinct that informs us that this one – not that one – is the best choice?

Some voters rely exclusively on the political party with which they are registered and vote accordingly. People often register to vote according to the influence they experience from their family, their friends, and their neighbors. Soon they find themselves entrenched in a political camp without doing much choosing at all. The process becomes more of a confirmation of bias. For example, news media are selected because of their perceived political party favoritism. Stories are told reinforcing the common local narratives and attitudes that point to a favorite candidate. It is comforting to share such perspectives though they might cause us to ignore, even avoid, a truth that points to a competitor's strength or tarnishes our favored candidate.

Some voters pay close attention to the politics and remain engaged in the years leading up to an election. Some are one-issue voters and will vote for only a candidate who supports that one issue, regardless of other concerns. Others shut themselves off from the din of politics and make up their voting mind in the last days of an election campaign. Whatever strategy is used, the assurance that one's vote will always be the best choice is elusive.

There are dangers associated with presidential campaigns. There is fraud and corruption that can emerge in any political camp. None seem to be immune to such influence in spite of safeguards and good intentions. Recently, we have become aware of how outside influence from such powerful entities as Russia and China and others can leverage their way into the process. The general public is vulnerable to manipulation from a wide array of unsuspected fronts. There will be votes lost to such nefarious maneuverings, cast for candidates who may not be best for the task.

All of this is to point to the fact that picking the best presidential candidate for the next four years, regardless of what may come, is not easy. The preparation and perspective of one individual is not enough to fulfill this hiring step (and it is a hiring process). Rather, it takes as many eligible voters as possible to determine who is best to lead and serve this nation with its 50 states, Washington, D.C., and the five inhabited territories. In short, it must be remembered, picking a president begins with the people in our representative democracy.

Therefore, we come to one of the primary underpinnings (and the title) of this book: All Votes Matter! This nation can ill afford to disallow voters from gaining access to their voting privileges (voter suppression). Nor can it afford to throw away votes cast, via vote suppression, as we can plainly witness when WTA disallows the Electoral College from granting representation to almost half of the votes cast.

We must also consider the office of the presidency. There is no other like it. The reach and influence of this office touches almost every aspect of our existence and daily lives. Foreign policies affect wars and humanitarian efforts, global economies and global poverty, trade and scientific progress, human justice issues and diplomacy, and others are all interwoven to help our nation cooperate and exist with all of the other nations in the world. Domestically, the presidency pulls the levers of society to ensure we may be safe and prosper. Concerns about education, health, transportation, social justice, military, business, economy, agriculture, fishing, mining, forestry, environment, are some of the multi-faceted responsibilities of the president. In addition, this person must run the office such that it coordinates well with the other two branches of our federal government: Congress (both chambers) and the Justice system.

It is a political office that requires an ability to develop and hold a vision of success our nation can pursue within the mix of agendas put forth by others vying for power and control. The presidency must manage a realm of balance yet always be ready for the interruption of natural disasters, foreign attacks, economic failures, and societal breakdowns. It is not an office for the faint of heart.

Picking a president, then, is a huge responsibility for all of us. If you have ever hired someone you may have gone through the process of outlining the job description, taking in resumes from those applying for the job, reviewing them, and then interviewing the candidates. It is a process. And, as was noted about elections, the process is as important as the outcome. It is not enough to simply pick someone for the job. The hiring process should be thorough and intentional and serious.

None of us are prepared enough or know enough about either a candidate or the nation's future to pick a president entirely on our own. We may pick the very best person but, each of us, will do so with only a partial view of the situation. Each of us brings a different ability to pick the talent the nation needs. Accumulatively our aggregated votes point to the sentiment of the governed. Our form of government depends upon our picking our own leader by a process, the Electoral College, well-suited to deliver the best that *We the People* can, if we allow it to play out as it should.

Making all votes matter is a choice we have. Knowing now that we can be more inclusive in our election process. By removing WTA from the process and allowing the 46% of the votes cast we currently toss away to gain representation in the Electoral College, we can be more assured our presidential choosing process is, as Hamilton told us, "...at least excellent."

★ Chapter Summary

+ Gerrymandering is a nefarious way for politicians in power to choose those they want to govern and who will vote for them.
+ Congressional district boundaries are revisited and redrawn when the U.S. Census identifies state population densities.
+ Congressional district boundary drawing should be based on principles that limit the ability to exercise gerrymandering.
+ Ranked Choice Voting (RCV) is a good way to gain an accurate assessment of the voter preferences for three or more candidates.
+ RCV does not apply when only two candidates are on the ballot.
+ RCV allows one candidate to emerge with a majority vote win.
+ RCV would rely on WTA to pick a state-chosen presidential candidate (Electoral College remains intact).
+ RCV can be modified to work with Equal Voice Voting (EVV) so WTA is eliminated and an even more accurate electoral vote allocation is achieved.
+ A president affects almost every aspect of our lives as well as the domestic and foreign policies put forth by the nation.
+ Picking a president is an arduous and serious task entailing a plethora of considerations that make up a candidate's background, talent, education, values, and character.
+ Our nation is best served when neither voter suppression nor vote suppression is exercised. All Votes Matter!

CHAPTER 10
NEXT STEPS

It is my birthright, it is my political right, it is my democratic right, it is my constitutional right... that I must open my mouth... my voice... I can raise my voice.

MAMATA BANERJEE

(B. 1955, 8TH CHIEF MINISTER OF WEST BENGAL)

We need to talk!

Since you have now read most of this book, the next step is to discuss the ideas with others. You may be asking, "What should I say?" It can be a daunting challenge. However, there are some opportunities that present themselves. Presidential elections can stir a lot of emotions and people often have opinions – and are glad to share them. When they do, it's a perfect opportunity to raise some of these points:

- EVV provides a popular vote result.
- EVV makes all votes matter.
- The Electoral College is not antiquated nor racist. It is mostly misunderstood.
- The Electoral College is an ingenious voting system.
- EVV respects the Electoral College.
- The Electoral College respects that our nation is a federalist republic.
- The Winner-Takes-All (WTA) aspect throws minority votes away.
- It takes three registered voters to get one viable presidential ballot.
- Voter suppression affects tens of thousands of voters.

+ Vote suppression affects tens of millions of votes.
+ The National Popular Vote Interstate Compact (NPVIC) idea is ridiculous, radical, and dangerous.
+ EVV does not need a U.S. Constitution amendment.
+ EVV encourages greater voter turnout.

This book is about how we pick a president, focused primarily on how we convert, on a state-by-state basis, the popular votes into a nationwide electoral voting result. The Electoral College has been examined from a historical perspective, its structure, its purpose, and even its shortcomings. The Winner-Takes-All (WTA) aspect has been exposed as the cause of the extreme popular and electoral voting result disparities we experience in every presidential election. Equal Voice Voting (EVV) has been shown to be the best approach, compared to what we currently experience and to the National Popular Vote (NPV) idea.

The question is, "Now what?"

There are basically three steps that must take place before we realize a change in any governing process (our laws): **Awareness**, **Conversation**, and **Legislation**. You have taken the first step by becoming aware of EVV and what it promises. By reading this book, you are now challenged to join the conversation and tell others about it. As interest grows, it is hoped legislators will respond and bills will be sponsored and voted in to make EVV a reality in your state, a neighboring state, perhaps across the nation.

There is a political challenge that confronts the process. Some politicians will tell you that, "Winning is everything!" They mean that a political office must be captured, much like a flag on a hill. There is no room for a contender. If the status quo means a political party has an advantage, to entertain an idea that will erode that advantage is akin to being a traitor. Winning may be everything, but loyalty and allegiance are part of the process that gets you to where you want to go and stay.

Political parties notoriously lose state control when it comes to presidential elections. State citizens can often switch political party allegiance, election to election, as they vote their preferences for a new platform, a new promise, or a new popularity. Political parties, in spite of their best efforts, often cannot declare a state's victory before an election.

It is difficult, almost an impossible challenge, for politicians comfortably in power to consider a change that will ask that they trust all of their constituents. When they are asked to open the door to allow a mechanistic change that eradicates WTA and permits state-wide proportional voting, it is as if the people are asking for Pandora's box to be opened. There is a fear that power and control could slip away. It is a heavy task to ask politicians to vote for an idea that could challenge their very livelihood. It is especially so given that they then have to defend their vote to those opposed to it.

The challenge is an old one. It has to do with our innate sense of altruism. We humans are not usually wired to be naturally altruistic. Merriam Webster's Dictionary tells us that altruism is: *unselfish regard for or devotion to the welfare of others.* We, the governed, must recognize that the high calling of public service also demands a service type of leadership. The roles of power and control and, yes, greed, play their part in upending the expectations of the voters. It's easy, often too easy, to exclude others and participate in voter suppression and vote suppression to retain dominance.

A change in how we elect a president should be transparent. The people – a state's citizenry – should be apprised of what a fair, equal, inclusive, and an engaging presidential election can really look like. They should be aware of how vote suppression has served to erase their ballots, disenfranchise millions of voters, and provide a false voting result.

Thus, we are back at the beginning: Awareness. With awareness of EVV and the functioning of the Electoral College, the options to make change must also be put on the table. People can petition for change. They can petition to remove WTA from their state's presidential election. It would require, of course, a replacement mechanism so the popular votes are effectively converted into electoral votes. A petition to remove NPVIC might be brought if a state has already joined the interstate compact. Resistance for a petition might be eased if EVV can take NPVIC's place, knowing that a state's popular vote result would be easier to realize than waiting for NPVIC to take effect. And, if resistance persists, it might prove to be more acceptable to some if EVV were adopted with a sunset clause. Try the new approach for a while. It would be like taking the puppy home for a while to see if the family adjusts well to it (of course they will).

You have read the book, or about to finish the book, and the next step is in your hands. Don't simply put the book on a shelf and keep the idea to yourself. Too much is at stake for that. Tens of millions of voters across the nation will not matter if we cannot preserve the presidential elections with EVV. Tell someone about the idea. Share the book with them. Discuss it. Ask your legislators to consider sponsoring a bill.

The choice is yours to help our democracy by making all votes matter when we elect our next President of the United States.

★ Legislative Change Process

It was pointed out in the Introduction that process is as important as the results. We realize that picking someone to be a president can actually be an easy task. Have a congressional committee do it. Flip a coin. Roll some dice. Of course, those are frivolous ideas because our government rests on the foundation of *We the People* being where our governing power resides. Voting citizens must decide!

How citizens decide poses a tremendous challenge, especially in our federalist republic, a nation as large as the United States is, inclusive of its diverse ethnicities, religions, cultures, values, or priorities. The process must be transparent as it adheres to the principles put forth in the U.S. Constitution. The voting steps we take must be fair, equal, inclusive, and engaging. We must do the best we can to meet these expectations.

Sadly, many are not aware of the process. Many do not understand how or why the Electoral College functions as it does. Ignorance of this fundamental voting operation is pervasive and causes many to not respect it. A popular desire to discard it altogether is all too easily encouraged, resulting in a clamor to throw the baby out with the bathwater.

If one does not realize the three principles that the Electoral College is based upon, people cannot be aware of what is at stake. The idea that the voting mechanism captures the voting sentiment of the citizens (the popular vote), the sovereign voting voice of each state, and a provision for voting checks and balances must be recognized. It needs to be understood that the Electoral College does all of this via a proportional voting approach that allocates electoral votes on a state-by-state basis. The result is that our nationwide voting can avoid the pitfalls of mob rule inherent in a direct democracy, stumbling by casting a blind eye to state sovereignty, and negligently discarding a built-in opportunity for checks and balances.

We the people must be aware of these voting principles as we consider any change to how we vote for our President of the United States.

Awareness of the voting process is not a sole-sourced commodity. We gain awareness by learning from history, appreciating our governing structures and institutions, and reviewing of political criticisms. Our own critical thinking –the ability to connect the dots of reason and to question assumptions – may lead us to realize there is more than what meets the eye. For example, the 2020 electoral map depicted below, showing states won by Trump (Republican) in black and states won by Biden (Democrat) in gray should raise eyebrows. Maine and Nebraska are shown with stripes to show electoral votes were split between the two candidates. Surely, any given state is not totally for one or the other.

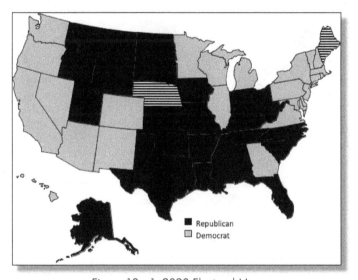

Figure 10 - 1: 2020 Electoral Map

Awareness is also acknowledging our gut reactions. We may not be cognizant of what is wrong, but we know something is. Something *feels* amiss. We vote and watch the nation's citizens cast their ballots, by the tens of millions, and it's all converted into these simple blocks of political party gains on a state-by-state basis. If you vote with the minority in your state, you can sense that your vote did not matter. You realize, you sense, that others were left out as well – again by the tens of millions.

Now you have read most of this book and you realize why we face the voting problems we do. You are also aware of how it can be fixed. You can realize how the simple black and gray map shown above can be more like the multiple shades of gray (Black = Republican, Gray = Democrat) shown below wherein the electoral votes are presented as a blend of voting sentiments.

This 2020 electoral map, had EVV been used across the nation, would have had two states entirely red (voting for Trump) and Vermont and Washington, D.C. entirely white (voting for Biden). The remaining states are made up of 25 different shades of gray to show how blended (and inclusive) the voting results could have been.

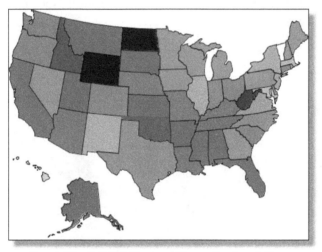

Figure 10 - 2: 2020 Electoral Map – Shades of Gray

Do you keep such awareness to yourself or do you tell others? There are many ways to inform those you know. You can correct them in conversation should the topic of Electoral College reform be brought up. You can initiate discussions with those you think might be interested. Debates might ensue as they wrestle with the new knowledge you share. Some of these discussions and debates may find favor among political activists, further enlarging the circle of informed citizens. Ideally, your state legislators, many who already are aware, will be encouraged that their constituency finds EVV to be an idea they favor.

Eventually, following the process, legislation will occur. It might begin with a simple petition to remove WTA from your state's presidential elections. Legislation might begin with a petition to remove NPVIC, if your state is already a part of the interstate compact. Perhaps your informed legislators will simply be better prepared to deny proposed legislation to adopt NPVIC for your state. Petitions could also be brought forth and signed to encourage your legislators to sponsor and pass a bill in favor of EVV for your state.

The point of this discussion is that process matters. It may take time but you have already begun by reading this book. You are far more aware than others who have not and you now have the opportunity to include others – inform them. Share the book with them. Buy a copy for your legislator. Start a conversation. Push for a change in how we elect our president.

★ Political Challenge

Let us assume your legislator(s) are informed and are encouraged to sponsor a bill for EVV in your state. What are you asking of them? We need to look at the political picture from their perspective.

Imagine that you are a legislator. You have run a successful campaign to win the election. Many, if not most, political races are hard-fought affairs with all candidates vying for dominance. You may have been advised that winning is everything! It took everything you had to win: your time, your money, your expertise, and the support of your family and close friends. Winning is now your mantra.

Suppose that you are of the political party that holds the majority in your state. The expectation may be that you can deliver your state, all of its electoral votes, to your party's presidential candidate. Your party, depending on your efforts, can deliver a message of significance to the entire nation about the viability of your presidential nominee and about your political party. Winning is everything. You do not want to forfeit any of this kind of control or power. To be on top is where it's at!

Now picture the scenario that some of your constituents of the minority party are encouraging you to adopt EVV. They say they want their votes to be represented in the Electoral College. To give in to this demand will mean that you will be forced to forfeit some of your political party's control and dominance when it comes to the next presidential election. You may be quite reluctant to give in to such demands, especially so if you know that not endorsing the idea does not cost you any political advantage.

The fact is political parties cannot always control how a presidential election will turn out. States have reversed political party loyalties in presidential elections numerous times. The following illustration shows how, over the previous 16 presidential elections, the election map has switched from one political party to the other.

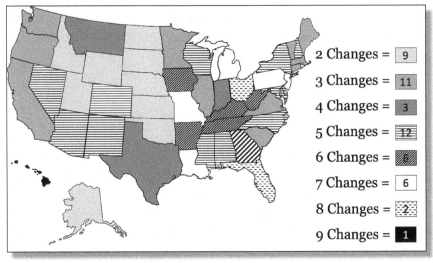

Figure 10 - 3: Political Party Changes in Presidential Elections

For example, my home state of Oregon has changed its political party choice three times since 1960. That year the state voted for Richard Nixon (Republican). The state switched to the Democrat nominee (Lyndon Johnson) in 1964. That's one change. Then the state switched parties again in 1968 and voted for Nixon (Republican). That's the second change. In 1984 Oregon voted for Reagan (Republican) but switched to the Democrat (Dukakis) in 1988 for the third switch.

While a legislator may be tempted to tout the political party line in hopes of preserving the party's election dominance, it becomes a false notion given historical reality. The truth causes the strategy to fold like a house of cards. It is time, long past time, to accept that any given state needs a better approach.

The question now becomes, "Who should be trusted?"

Actually, it's an old question dating back to that hot summer in 1787 when the Framers pondered its significance. Indeed, who should be trusted with something as precious as the voice of the people emerging as a simple voting ballot? Those men in that room wrestled with the significance, the vulnerabilities, the political exposure of allowing such decision-making to be gifted to *We the People*. They compromised, even back then, not fully letting their trust be vested into the citizens' hands. In a sense, their democratic trust had strings as they limited the voting powers to only white men who owned property, especially those who owned land.

Our nation is deserving of better than that. We have succeeded in lifting those restrictions and now rally together every four years to collect ballots from as many registered voters as possible. We call for every vote to be counted and to make all votes matter. Our nation deserves EVV to make it so.

Thus, we return to the concept of a paradigm shift mentioned in the Introduction. Recall how Columbus showed how a new idea, standing an egg on its end without assistance, can be done when it was thought it could not be. The egg was hard boiled and the egg shell's end crushed to support the egg in an upright position. Success was observed. The new idea, this paradigm shift, was accepted.

EVV requires a paradigm shift wherein presidential elections demand that we make all votes matter. The paradigm shift causes us to look at presidential elections from the perspective of the people – neither from the perspective of political party control nor from a vantage point of distrust. We cannot afford to disenfranchise voters, allowing vote suppression, while the nation sets forth on the sober task of picking a president. This book shows the paradigm shift can be accomplished with EVV. As simple as standing an egg on its end, revealing it can be done, the election paradigm shift allows us to recognize that we can free the Electoral College to deliver a fair, equal, inclusive, and engaging presidential election.

★ Challenges of Altruism

The paradigm shift begins with us – *We the People*. It is not enough to leave it to politicians for they represent us in this representative democracy. We, our values and priorities, are reflected in the bills they sponsor or vote against. It begins with what we want our elections to be. We must want what is best for us.

Are we up to this task? If you begin with the notion that you want your voice (your vote) to be heard, it is a small step to want fair representation. However, if you widen your circle and are willing to include those who do not vote as you do, the challenge of altruism presents a test.

We humans are hard-wired to protect ourselves and to secure what we think we rightfully own or control. Our existence, at least what we make of it, is ours to keep and preserve. Our society is full of examples of how we exclude others, separate ourselves from each other, and define barriers that send the message to keep away.

For example, properties are separated by fences. Some to identify what we own. Some to keep others away. Some to even prevent others from peering in. Some fences do all of the above, not to mention those fences built to control our pets and livestock. Their respective messaging tells us to, "Stay Away," or "Back Off," or "Beware!" None of them are invitations to enter and be welcomed and included.

Extending this perspective, we can see that separations can come in a wide array of conventions. Our cars separate us. Our clothes separate us. Our jobs separate us. Our religions separate us. The list goes on. None of this is bad, exactly, it just points to how much we live our lives as individuals, to show we are unique, to demarcate our personal safety zones. This bit of human nature, then, can bubble up seemingly out of our control or awareness and urge us to disallow others to get their way, even to the point of stifling their voices (votes). It may be a touch of nature, but it runs counter to democracy. Elections should include all voters.

Imagine the following scenario: Imagine that your neighbor is a real putz. You don't like him or her. You don't like how they look or how they act or what they say. You especially do not appreciate their views on life and how to live. Their values, their religion (if they practice any at all), and their politics are not yours. Would you defend their right to vote? Would you encourage them to vote? Would you give them a ride to the polling booth so they could cast their ballot?

If you are not willing to assist your neighbor in this way, you must ask yourself, "Why?" Reasons based on fear may come to mind as you may be fearful that their perspective, their voting wish, may come true. Maybe you prefer the status quo and do not want to give up an advantage or a sense of power. Maybe, if you are truly honest, your resisting the opportunity to assist your neighbor comes from your own greed. You do not want to pay taxes, for example, to help pay for the education of their bratty kids. Maybe you favor a tax cut that gives you deductions that your neighbor will not realize. Power, control, and greed are just a few of the reasons that emerge, preventing citizens from finding a full and inclusive democracy to be truly what they want.

Democracy is not easy because it is meant to include all voters. Since power comes from the people, repressing the voice of the people defeats democracy. Like it or not, your neighbor – that one you do not really like – is deserving of the freedom of voting just as you are. The altruistic demand is that everyone sacrifices something, sometime, for the gain of liberty for everyone. It might mean your allowing, even supporting, the freedom of voting by those with whom you disagree. Everyone must matter! All votes must matter!

★ Changing the Rules

One of the goals of this book is to encourage you to do something to change the rules. Much has already been shown here to identify the problems we currently endure with presidential elections. As the book began, "It's not working." Something must be done and you are being asked to get started.

What can you do?

At the start of this chapter, I noted that there are, essentially, three steps to change laws. They are: Awareness, Conversation, and Legislation. That is the correct order of progression for an idea to turn into a bill to be voted upon and result into becoming law. You are already in the midst of the awareness phase since you have now read most of this book. The following discussion then jumps to the legislative step, outlining what must be done to enable a bill to be passed. Since this chapter is about "Next Steps," the chapter ends on that note – what can be done next – starting a conversation.

Awareness does not always emerge all at once. Unlike opening our eyes and seeing clearly one sunny morning, our attention may become focused and our observation made clearer over time. It is like some kind of phenomenon that seeps in rather than something spilling over and washing through our mind.

It has often been said that repetition is the mother of learning. To belabor the point, I'll say it again, "Repetition is the mother of learning." It's true. You did not learn your ABC's by one quick glance, unless you're some kind of rare savant who has photographic memory. You do not learn a skill by practicing it once. You do the same thing over and over and over. Perfection demands practice.

Advertisers know this. It is not enough to put an ad on TV once. They must do it repeatedly. They do so not just to reach a wider audience. They repeat the ad because they know that we need to hear and see the message again and again and again. They know that if we need or want to buy something, that repeated message will come to the forefront and entice us to reach for their product.

Likewise, it is not enough to just read this book. You may have to thumb back-and-forth through some of the pages and chapters to ponder the messages a few more times. Even then, it is not enough. You need to consider the messaging and compare it to other points of view and consider the advantages and disadvantages of each. This comparing is a form of repetition and it is important if progress is to be made.

Conversation is critical to reinforce an idea. I once had a professor of philosophy who told his class that if you cannot say what you mean, you don't know what you mean. The lesson was regarding semantics and he was pressing upon us the importance of being exact and clear and confident in how we express an idea. Thinking of an idea and expressing the idea are two different things.

Saying what we think can either be expressed verbally or it can be in a written form. The important aspect of this step is that the idea is shared with someone else. It takes a bit of courage to do this kind of sharing as it invites debate and disagreement. It is how ideas get tested, reinforced, and eventually accepted.

You are invited to tell others about EVV. You may not feel comfortable or conversant with it at this point, but the subject can still be brought up as discussions revolve around a yearning for a better democracy. Others may not have heard of EVV at all, or maybe you will be surprised that they have. Do the numbers brought forth in this book and on the EVV website measure up? Do they support the narrative, the notion that this election change is needed and is worth pursuing? Do you think it can be brought to fruition? It's worth talking about.

As separate individuals, you and I may not have much power to change things. Collectively, though, much can happen. The invitation here is for you to contact others who may be connected to still others. The current presidential voting mechanism, you now know, uses the Winner-Takes-All (WTA) approach as an add-on to each state's election process. It favors only voters casting their ballots for a candidate winning the plurality of votes in each state. Thus, the appeal of EVV is for those voting in the minority in each state. Voters who recognize that their vote really doesn't currently matter, will be most likely to take notice of what EVV offers.

The minority entities in each state should be strongly considered. Which is the minority political party in your state? Which political parties do you think will NOT prevail in your state for an upcoming presidential election? Common minority political parties may be more numerous than you realize. For example, in my home state of Oregon, the following political parties are recognized by the Oregon State Elections Division:

+ American Elect Party
+ Constitution Party
+ Democratic Party
+ Independent Party
+ Libertarian Party
+ Pacific Green Party
+ Progressive Party
+ Republican Party
+ Working Families Party

These represent a rather wide assortment of voters. Your state may actually have others and/or even more. Any voters, in any given year, may find themselves aligning with a candidate who captures a minority share of votes. These voters, as you now know, will be disenfranchised from the voting process. Their votes will not matter! These entities are the voters who will take the most interest in EVV because it promises to legitimize their ballots.

Of course, even if one is aligned with the political party that captures a majority of votes for their presidential candidate, their sense of being fair and equal – honoring our sense of democracy – may welcome what EVV offers. All votes matter!

What can you say to entice others to consider EVV? Here are a few lead-in facts and phrases that may help you get started (they were briefly listed at the chapter's beginning):

- EVV provides a popular vote result without a U.S. Constitution amendment.
- (See Chapter 4: Equal Voice Voting)
- EVV makes all votes matter.
- (See Chapter 4: Equal Voice Voting)
- The Electoral College is neither antiquated nor racist. It is mostly misunderstood.
- (See Chapter 1: Constitutional History, Chapter 5: Interference)
- The Electoral College is an ingenious system because it captures the popular vote, respects the voting voice of the sovereign states, and provides a system of checks and balances. (See Chapter 1: Constitutional History, Chapter 2: Electoral College Purpose, Chapter 3: Consistency Matters)
- EVV respects the Electoral College, honoring the U.S. Constitution.
- (See Chapter 3: Consistency Matters, Chapter 7: The Popular Vote)
- The Electoral College honors the fact that our nation's form of government is a federalist republic. Each state is sovereign.
- (See Chapter 1: Constitutional History)
- The Winner-Takes-All (WTA) aspect throws minority votes away, disenfranchising 47.8% of voters through vote suppression.
- (See Chapter 3: Consistency Matters)
- It takes three registered voters to get one viable presidential ballot. Usually, over 40% of registered voters don't vote. We ignore 47.8% of the votes cast.
- (See Chapter 3: Consistency Matters)
- Voter suppression affects tens of thousands of voters. Vote suppression affects tens of millions of voters. Both are bad and need to stop.

- (See Chapter 5: Interference)
- We remove around 47.8% of the votes cast so they gain no representation in the Electoral College. That is vote suppression and it affects tens of millions of votes.
- (See Chapter 5: Interference)
- The National Popular Vote Interstate Compact (NPVIC) idea is ridiculous, radical, and dangerous.
- (See Chapter 8: The National Popular Vote Interstate Compact)
  - ➤ Ridiculous – NPV fails to diagnose the election results problem. WTA disenfranchises millions of voters. NPVIC does not correct it.
  - ➤ Radical—NPVIC defies the U.S. Constitution (it can only be changed by an amendment). It ignores the sovereignty of states by forming an interstate compact. It puts votes at greater risk of not being represented due to WTA.
  - ➤ Dangerous – NPVIC's voting results can produce even wider disparities between the popular and electoral voting results than what we experience already. This leads to false messaging about elections which egregiously misleads the public and erodes trust in the voting process.
- EVV does not need a U.S. Constitutional amendment.
- (See Chapter 7: The Popular Vote)
- EVV encourages greater voter turnout.
- (See Chapter 4: Interference)

One resource beyond this book is the Equal Voice Voting website. The website provides information, including the weekly blog, to help promote the EVV message. Share the blogs with others and encourage them to access the website at: www.equalvoicevoting.com

Legislation can take many paths. Each state has its own process for how an idea becomes law. An example, taken from Oregon's legislative website, is provided in Appendix A. A presentation about initiatives, taken from Oregon's Secretary of State's website, is also provided in the Appendix.

It should be noted that all states are not the same in how ideas become law. For example, many western states (my home state of Oregon being one) have an initiative process enabling citizens to begin the process. The

Secretary of State oversees the process including: ensuring a certain number of signatures are collected, that a ballot title is created, etc.

Contacting your legislators, individually, to let them know you favor EVV will be received but there is no assurance it will be heard. An email is good. A phone call is better. A personal visit with your legislator is best. Still, your plea may not gain much traction because, well, your concern has not reached a tipping point that indicates to your legislator that your concern and suggested remedy is ready for political consumption. That is, it is perceived as having little chance of winning. It is difficult for a politician to attach his/her name to a bill (sponsor) if it has little chance of capturing more votes.

Thus, initiatives become a popular way to gain attention. The point of an initiative is to draw attention to and gain support for an idea. If the idea and its description is simple and easy to understand, the signing exercise thereof, by similarly concerned citizens, can be simple as long as the idea seems to be an obvious need for the common good. If the idea is more complicated, probably requiring multiple pages of explanation, getting people to sign it is more arduous.

To get legislation initiated can take a convoluted path and may not happen quickly. Patience and persistence are certainly requirements for success. Resistance may come from political party adherents who currently enjoy a majority advantage in a state's congress. Greater acceptance may be realized by the political party adherents of a state's minority party. If enough attention is drawn to the shortcomings of our current election process and to the advantages of EVV, greater acceptance may also be realized by those less committed to a political party, causing the issue and remedy to reach a political acceptance tipping point in a state.

★ Conclusion

The next steps that can be taken, now that you have read the book, are to encourage others to become aware of EVV, join in conversations surrounding the election process issue, and strive to encourage your legislators to sponsor a bill. These are not easy steps and may seem to take more time than expected. Remember, the task is to call for a paradigm shift – a call to do something we have not done before. It is a request for people to change their perspectives and seek a greater democratic process when electing our U.S. President. EVV is a new vision that simply sees that all votes matter!

★ Chapter Summary

+ Three steps are required to make a new law:
+ Awareness, Conversation, and Legislation.
+ Political challenges that resist change include:
  ➢ Retaining political power (winning is everything!)
  ➢ Unwillingness to trust the voting population (retaining control)
+ Political resistance is natural. It preserves the status quo, retains power and control, and leverages greed.
+ Passing new laws is complicated. Initiatives, in some states, can be made. Legislative sponsorship is required and popular acceptance (winning the vote) must reach a tipping point for an idea to gain acceptance and passage as a bill.
+ Share the blogs with others and encourage them to visit the website at: www.equalvoicevoting.com

★ Choices

Life is about choices. We make several each and every day. Voting choices, though, are rare and even more so when it comes time to elect a President of the United States. Such choices are precious. As U.S. Representative from Georgia, John Lewis, advised us, "The vote is the most powerful nonviolent change agent you have in a democratic society. You must use it because it is not guaranteed. You can lose it."

Essentially, when considering using our voting power, we have three perspectives from which to make our voting choices:

1. You, not me
2. Me, not you
3. We

You, not me is a reference to how many individuals consider their voting power. It's essentially saying that "you" are more deserving than am I to participate in our democracy. The "you" in this case is any other person who votes. It's not a good perspective, not a healthy form of patriotism, and not a positive choice. It's a perspective that essentially says, "My vote does not matter!" Many in our society do not register to vote though they are eligible to do so. Many others register but do not vote though recent voting law changes have expanded their opportunity to do so. It's a posture that forfeits an individual's power to others. It's unfortunate but common.

The *Me, not you* is a reference to those who vote but also encourage other willing voters to be excluded from the voting act (voter suppression) or have their votes not matter (vote suppression).

Voter suppression is fraudulent and points to its enablers as being weak, corrupt, and nefarious. Voter suppression is a pox upon our representative democracy. It's a blight of character as well as an exercise that nullifies patriotism.

Since WTA is a part of the U.S. Presidential election process, most voters are unaware of their participation in vote suppression. Yet, it persists and effectively disenfranchises tens of millions of voters. It nullifies the ballots of voters who may not choose as we do in every presidential election. It's an egregious affront to our nation's democracy and to its people. It's a voting limitation that, as this book attests, does not need to be accepted. We must choose to end its prevalence in our elections.

The *We* reference is a voting perspective that allows, even encourages all voters to cast their ballots in our free society. All of us have different perspectives, our values may not coincide, our needs and desires may vary. Still, through the shared power of the vote, we can share in our governance for the mutual benefit of everyone. Our vote is a fundamental strength, a basis for our democratic government. We must acknowledge and protect the tenet that *All Votes Matter*. It's a perspective that requires a paradigm shift away from "Winning is everything!" to a more inclusive perspective. We must decide to preserve this *All Votes Matter* principle, exercise it, and then trust it will serve to provide us the life, liberty, and pursuit of happiness that was promised in the Preamble to the Constitution that begins with:

We the people...

One thing I believe profoundly: We make our own history. The course of history is directed by the choices we make, and our choices grow out of the ideas, the beliefs, the values, the dreams of the people. It is not so much the powerful leaders that determine our destiny as the much more powerful influence of the combined voice of the people themselves.

Eleanor Roosevelt (1884 – 1962, First Lady of the United States and First Chair of the United Nations Commission on Human Rights

TURNING AN IDEA INTO LAW

The following steps and diagram are taken from the Oregon's legislature website:

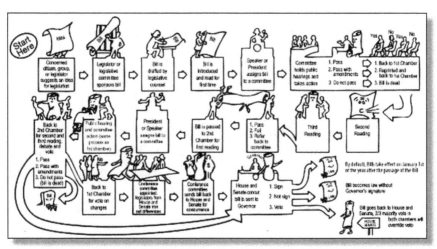

Figure A - 1: Bill Becomes Law in Oregon

★ Steps of How Ideas Become Law

+ An idea to change, amend, or create a new law is presented by a concerned citizen or group to a Representative.
+ The Representative decides to sponsor the bill and introduce it to the House of Representatives, and requests that the attorneys in

the Legislative Counsel's office draft the bill in the proper legal language.

+ The bill is then presented to the Chief Clerk of the House, who assigns the bill a number and sends it back to the Legislative Counsel's office to verify it is in proper legal form and style.

+ The bill is then sent to the State Printing Division, where it is printed and returned to House of Representatives for its first reading.

+ After the bill's first reading, the Speaker refers it to a committee. The bill is also forwarded to the Legislative Fiscal Officer and Legislative Revenue Officer to determine fiscal or revenue impact.

+ The committee reviews the bill, and holds public hearings and work sessions.

+ In order for the bill to go to the House floor for a final vote, or be reported out of committee, a committee report is signed by the committee chair and delivered back to the Chief Clerk.

+ Any amendments to the bill are printed, and the bill may be reprinted to include the amendments (engrossed bill).

+ The bill, now back in the house of origin (House), has its second reading.

+ The measure then has its third reading, which is its final recitation before the vote. This is the time the body debates the measure. To pass, the bill must receive aye votes of a majority of members (31 in the House, 16 in the Senate).

+ If the bill is passed by a majority of the House members, it is sent to the Senate.

+ The bill is read for the first time, and the Senate President assigns it to committee. The committee reports the bill back to the Senate where the bill is given the second and third readings.

+ If the bill is passed in the Senate without changes, it is sent back to the House for enrolling.

+ If the bill is amended in the Senate by even one word, it must be sent back to the House for concurrence. If the House does not concur with the amendments, the presiding officers of each body appoint a conference committee to resolve the differences between the two versions of the bill.

- After the bill has passed both houses in the identical form, it is signed by three officers: The Speaker of the House, the Senate President, and the Chief Clerk of the House or Secretary of the Senate, depending on where the bill originated.
- The enrolled bill is then sent to the Governor who has five days to take action. If the Legislative Assembly is adjourned, the Governor has 30 days to consider it.
- If the Governor chooses to sign the bill, it will become law on January 1 of the year after the passage of the act or on the prescribed effective date. In 1999, the Legislative Assembly adopted ORS 171.022, which reads, "Except as otherwise provided in the Act, an Act of the Legislative Assembly takes effect on January 1 of the year after passage of the Act." The Governor may allow a bill to become law without his/her signature, or the Governor may decide to veto the bill. The Governor's veto may be overridden by a two-thirds vote of both houses.
- The signed enrolled bill, or act, is then filed with the Secretary of State, who assigns it an Oregon Laws chapter number.
- Staff in the Legislative Counsel's office insert the text of the new laws into the existing Oregon Revised Statutes in the appropriate locations and make any other necessary code changes.

★ Initiatives

In some instances, an idea can be brought forth to a state's congress by way of an initiative. The explanation below is taken from Wikipedia, noting an initiative's purpose and history in the United States.

> An initiative (also known as a popular or citizens' initiative) is a means by which a certain minimum number of registered voters can force a government to choose to either enact a law or hold a public vote. In the United States, a popular vote on a measure is referred to as a referendum only when originating

with the legislature. An initiative may be called a "ballot measure," "initiative measure," or "proposition."

The United States has no initiative process at the national level, but the initiative is in use at the level of state government in 24 states and the District of Columbia, and is also in common use at the local government level.

The modern system of initiative and referendum originated in the state of South Dakota, which adopted initiative and referendum in 1898 by a popular vote of 23,816 to 16,483. Oregon was the second state to adopt and did so in 1902, when the Oregon Legislative Assembly adopted it by an overwhelming majority. The "Oregon System," as it was at first known, subsequently spread to many other states, and became one of the signature reforms of the Progressive Era (1890s-1920s).

The next page shows an initiative process chart taken from Oregon's Secretary of State's website. It shows the decision points through which an initiative progresses or is rejected. The chart, as the website cautions, is intended to help explain the initiative process. It is only a summary that does not include all legal requirements. Please refer to the State Initiative and Referendum Manual for legal requirements.

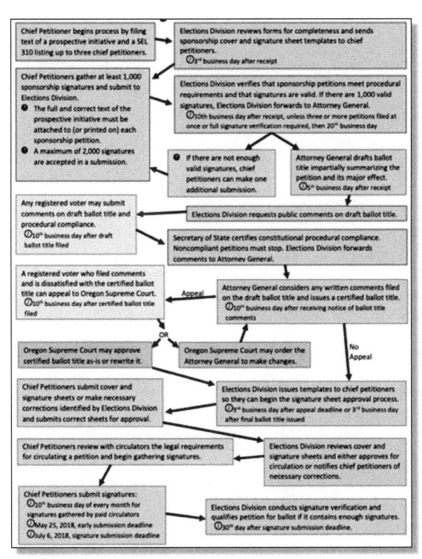

Figure A - 2: Oregon Initiative Process Chart

1960 – 2020 ELECTION DATA

The tables below provide the data gathered for the 16 elections spanning the years of 1960 through 2020. Each state's data are shown, giving how the popular votes were cast for each candidate and how, if EVV were used instead, those popular votes would have been converted into electoral votes.

States that show an even split between two candidates, using EVV, are highlighted in gray. The electoral vote cell is highlighted in black if one state would have cast all of its electoral votes to one candidate at the exclusion of any other.

Some election year anomalies include:

+ 1960 – There were 15 unpledged electors: six in Alabama, all eight in Mississippi, and one in Oklahoma. The total electoral votes were 537.
+ 1972 – One non-loyal Nixon elector cast one vote for John Hospers. The total electoral votes shown on the 1972 table is 537 instead of 538.
+ 2016 – There were seven unpledged electors: One in Hawaii, two in Texas, and four in the state of Washington.

The election results are gleaned from multiple sources, as per the following:

The 2020 election results were provided by Reuters Graphics found on their website at: https://graphics.reuters.com/USA-ELECTION/RESULTS-LIVE-US/jbyprxelqpe/

Some election 2020 results were also captured at individual Secretary of State websites.

Election results from 1984 through 2016 were provided by the Federal Election Commission on their website at:

https://www.fec.gov/introduction-campaign-finance/election-and-voting-information/

Election results from 1960 through 1980 were found on Dave Leip's Atlas of U.S. Presidential Election Results found on their website at: https://uselectionatlas.org/RESULTS/

Much appreciation is extended to these resources not only for the data provided but for the meticulousness and patience required to provide such accuracy. It must be recognized that such data is gathered from 51 governmental jurisdictions (50 states and Washington, D.C.). Such endeavors serve all of us well.

States	Popular Vote	Electoral Votes	PVV	Biden Pop. Votes	Biden	Biden EVV Electoral Votes	Trump Pop. Votes	Trump	Trump EVV Electoral Votes
AK	359,530	3	119,843	153,778	1.28	1	189,951	1.58	2
AL	2,309,900	9	256,656	843,473	3.29	3	1,434,159	5.59	6
AR	1,219,014	6	203,169	423,916	2.09	2	760,613	3.74	4
AZ	3,385,845	11	307,804	1,672,143	5.43	6	1,661,686	5.40	5
CA	17,272,400	55	314,044	11,016,457	35.08	36	5,931,349	18.89	19
CO	3,256,952	9	361,884	1,804,352	4.99	5	1,364,607	3.77	4
CT	1,824,317	7	260,617	1,080,680	4.15	4	715,291	2.74	3
DC	344,356	3	114,785	317,323	2.76	3	18,586	0.16	0
DE	504,010	3	168,003	296,268	1.76	2	200,603	1.19	1
FL	11,067,456	29	381,636	5,297,045	13.88	14	5,668,731	14.85	15
GA	4,998,566	16	312,410	2,474,507	7.92	8	2,461,837	7.88	8
HI	574,469	4	143,617	366,130	2.55	3	196,864	1.37	1
IA	1,690,871	6	281,812	759,061	2.69	3	897,672	3.19	3
ID	868,105	4	217,026	287,021	1.32	1	554,118	2.55	3
IL	6,033,774	20	301,943	3,471,915	11.50	12	2,446,891	8.10	8
IN	3,033,198	11	275,745	1,242,495	4.51	5	1,729,852	6.27	6
KS	1,334,330	6	222,388	551,199	2.48	2	753,370	3.39	4
KY	2,136,768	8	267,096	772,474	2.89	3	1,326,646	4.97	5
LA	2,148,062	8	268,508	856,034	3.19	3	1,255,776	4.68	5
MA	3,631,473	11	330,134	2,382,202	7.22	7	1,167,202	3.54	4
MD	3,037,030	10	303,703	1,985,023	6.54	7	976,414	3.22	3
ME	816,428	4	204,107	431,277	2.11	2	360,446	1.77	2
MI	5,544,102	16	346,506	2,804,039	8.09	8	2,649,852	7.65	8
MN	3,277,270	10	327,727	1,717,177	5.24	5	1,484,065	4.53	5
MO	3,025,962	10	302,596	1,253,014	4.14	4	1,718,736	5.68	6
MS	1,315,240	6	219,207	539,494	2.46	2	756,731	3.45	4
MT	605,750	3	201,917	244,786	1.21	1	343,602	1.70	2
NC	5,524,813	15	368,321	2,684,302	7.29	7	2,758,775	7.49	8
ND	361,819	3	120,606	114,902	0.95	0	235,595	1.95	3
NE	951,390	5	190,278	374,362	1.97	2	556,331	2.92	3
NH	804,430	4	201,108	424,921	2.11	2	365,654	1.82	2
NJ	4,551,202	14	325,086	2,599,245	8.00	8	1,876,252	5.77	6
NM	923,676	5	184,735	501,474	2.71	3	401,828	2.18	2
NV	1,405,376	6	234,229	703,486	3.00	3	669,890	2.86	3
NY	8,597,485	29	296,465	5,230,985	17.64	18	3,244,798	10.94	11
OH	5,922,202	18	329,011	2,679,165	8.14	8	3,154,834	9.59	10
OK	1,560,699	7	222,957	550,890	2.47	2	1,020,280	4.58	5
OR	2,374,321	7	339,189	1,340,383	3.95	4	958,448	2.83	3
PA	6,915,265	20	345,763	3,455,528	9.99	10	3,373,911	9.76	10
RI	517,757	4	129,439	307,486	2.38	2	199,922	1.54	2
SC	2,513,329	9	279,259	1,091,541	3.91	4	1,385,103	4.96	5
SD	422,609	3	140,870	150,471	1.07	1	261,043	1.85	2
TN	3,049,514	11	277,229	1,139,376	4.11	4	1,849,820	6.67	7
TX	11,323,963	38	297,999	5,261,055	17.65	18	5,891,778	19.77	20
UT	1,487,677	6	247,946	560,282	2.26	2	865,140	3.49	4
VA	4,456,310	13	342,793	2,413,582	7.04	7	1,962,614	5.73	6
VT	367,428	3	122,476	242,820	1.98	3	112,704	0.92	0
WA	4,087,631	12	340,636	2,369,612	6.96	7	1,584,651	4.65	5
WI	3,297,434	10	329,743	1,630,716	4.95	5	1,610,151	4.88	5
WV	794,204	5	158,841	235,847	1.48	1	545,051	3.43	4
WY	276,765	3	92,255	73,491	0.80	0	193,559	2.10	3
Totals	158,102,477	538		81,179,205		273	74,103,782		265
				Popular Vote Percentage		51.35%			46.87%
				Electoral Votes / (Percentage)		306 / (56.88%)			232 / (43.12%)
				Equal Voice Vote Percentage		50.74%			49.26%

Table B - 1: 2020 Example Election Results if EVV Were Used

States	Popular Vote	Electoral Votes	PVV	Clinton Pop. Votes	Clinton EVV Electoral Votes	Trump Pop. Votes	Trump EVV Electoral Votes	Johnson Pop. Vote	Johnson EVV Electoral Votes	Stein Pop. Votes	Stein EVV Electoral Votes
AK	318,608	3	106,203	116,454	1	163,387	2	18,725		5,735	
AL	2,123,372	9	235,930	729,547	3	1,318,255	6	44,467		9,391	
AR	1,130,676	6	188,446	380,494	2	684,872	4	29,829		9,473	
AZ	2,573,165	11	233,924	1,161,167	5	1,252,401	6	106,327		34,345	
CA	14,181,604	55	257,847	8,753,792	35	4,483,814	17	478,500	2	278,657	1
CO	2,780,247	9	308,916	1,338,870	5	1,202,484	4	144,121		38,437	
CT	1,644,920	7	234,989	897,572	4	673,215	3	48,676		22,841	
DC	311,268	3	103,756	282,830	3	12,723	0	4,906		4,258	
DE	443,814	3	147,938	235,603	2	185,127	1	14,757		6,103	
FL	9,420,039	29	324,829	4,504,975	14	4,617,886	15	207,043		64,399	
GA	4,114,732	16	257,171	1,877,963	7	2,089,104	9	125,306		7,674	
HI	428,937	4	107,234	266,891	3	128,847	1	15,954		12,737	
IA	1,566,031	6	261,005	653,669	3	800,983	3	59,186		11,479	
ID	690,255	4	172,564	189,765	1	409,055	3	28,331		8,496	
IL	5,536,424	20	276,821	3,090,729	12	2,146,015	8	204,491		74,112	
IN	2,734,958	11	248,633	1,033,126	4	1,557,286	7	133,993		7,841	
KS	1,184,402	6	197,400	427,005	2	671,018	4	55,406		23,506	
KY	1,924,149	8	240,519	628,854	3	1,202,971	5	53,752		13,913	
LA	2,029,032	8	253,629	780,154	3	1,178,638	5	37,978		14,031	
MA	3,325,046	11	302,277	1,995,196	7	1,090,893	4	138,018		47,661	
MD	2,781,446	10	278,145	1,677,928	7	943,169	3	79,605		35,945	
ME	747,927	4	186,982	357,735	2	335,593	2	38,105		14,251	
MI	4,799,284	16	299,955	2,268,839	8	2,279,543	8	172,136		51,463	
MN	2,944,813	10	294,481	1,367,716	6	1,322,951	4	112,972		36,985	
MO	2,808,605	10	280,861	1,071,068	4	1,594,511	6	97,359		25,419	
MS	1,209,357	6	201,560	485,131	2	700,714	4	14,435		3,731	
MT	497,147	3	165,716	177,709	1	279,240	2	28,037		7,970	
NC	4,741,564	15	316,104	2,189,316	7	2,362,631	8	130,126		12,105	
ND	344,360	3	114,787	93,758	0	216,794	3	21,434		3,780	
NE	844,227	5	168,845	284,494	2	495,961	3	38,946		8,775	
NH	744,296	4	186,074	348,526	2	345,790	2	30,827		6,416	
NJ	3,874,046	14	276,718	2,148,278	8	1,601,933	6	72,477		37,772	
NM	798,319	5	159,664	385,234	3	319,667	2	74,541		9,879	
NV	1,125,385	6	187,564	539,260	3	512,058	3	37,384		0	
NY	7,721,442	29	266,257	4,556,118	18	2,819,533	11	176,598		107,934	
OH	5,496,487	18	305,360	2,394,164	8	2,841,005	10	168,599		44,310	
OK	1,452,992	7	207,570	420,375	2	949,136	5	83,481		0	
OR	2,001,336	7	285,905	1,002,106	4	782,403	3	94,231		50,002	
PA	6,165,478	20	308,274	2,926,441	9	2,970,733	11	146,715		49,941	
RI	464,144	4	116,036	252,525	2	180,543	2	14,746		6,220	
SC	2,103,027	9	233,670	855,373	4	1,155,389	5	49,204		13,034	
SD	370,093	3	123,364	117,458	0	227,721	3	20,850		0	
TN	2,508,027	11	228,002	870,695	4	1,522,925	7	70,397		15,993	
TX	8,969,226	38	236,032	3,877,868	16	4,685,047	21	283,492	1	71,558	
UT	1,131,430	6	188,572	310,676	2	515,231	4	39,608		9,438	
VA	3,984,631	13	306,510	1,981,473	7	1,769,443	6	118,274		27,638	
VT	315,067	3	105,022	178,573	3	95,369	0	10,078		6,758	
WA	3,317,019	12	276,418	1,742,718	8	1,221,747	4	160,879		58,417	
WI	2,976,150	10	297,615	1,382,536	5	1,405,284	5	106,674		31,072	
WV	714,423	5	142,885	188,794	1	489,371	4	23,004		8,075	
WY	255,849	3	85,283	55,973	0	174,419	3	13,287		2,515	
Totals	136,669,276	538		65,853,514	267	62,984,828	267	4,478,267	3	1,452,485	1
Popular Vote Percentage				48.18%		46.09%		3.28%		1.06%	
Electoral Votes / (Percentage)				227 / (42.19%)		304 / (56.51%)		0 / (0%)		0 / (0%)	
EVV Electoral Votes Percentage				49.63%		49.63%		0.56%		0.19%	

Table B - 2: 2016 Example Election Results if EVV Were Used

States	Popular Vote	Electoral Votes	PVV	Obama Pop. Votes	Obama EVV Electoral Votes	Romney Pop. Votes	Romney EVV Electoral Votes
AK	300,495	3	100,165	122,640	1	164,676	2
AL	2,074,338	9	230,482	795,696	3	1,255,925	6
AR	1,069,468	6	178,245	394,409	2	647,744	4
AZ	2,299,254	11	209,023	1,025,232	5	1,233,654	6
CA	13,038,547	55	237,064	7,854,285	35	4,839,958	20
CO	2,569,522	9	285,502	1,323,102	5	1,185,243	4
CT	1,558,960	7	222,709	905,083	4	634,892	3
DC	293,764	3	97,921	267,070	3	21,381	0
DE	413,921	3	137,974	242,584	2	165,484	1
FL	8,474,179	29	292,213	4,237,756	15	4,163,447	14
GA	3,900,050	16	243,753	1,773,827	7	2,078,688	9
HI	434,697	4	108,674	306,658	3	121,015	1
IA	1,582,180	6	263,697	822,544	3	730,617	3
ID	652,274	4	163,069	212,787	1	420,911	3
IL	5,242,014	20	262,101	3,019,512	12	2,135,216	8
IN	2,624,534	11	238,594	1,152,887	5	1,420,543	6
KS	1,159,971	6	193,329	440,726	2	692,634	4
KY	1,797,212	8	224,652	679,370	3	1,087,190	5
LA	1,994,065	8	249,258	809,141	3	1,152,262	5
MA	3,167,767	11	287,979	1,921,290	7	1,188,314	4
MD	2,707,327	10	270,733	1,677,844	6	971,869	4
ME	713,180	4	178,295	401,306	2	292,276	2
MI	4,730,961	16	295,685	2,564,569	9	2,115,256	7
MN	2,936,561	10	293,656	1,546,167	5	1,320,225	5
MO	2,757,323	10	275,732	1,223,796	4	1,482,440	6
MS	1,285,584	6	214,264	562,949	3	710,746	3
MT	484,048	3	161,349	201,839	1	267,928	2
NC	4,505,372	15	300,358	2,178,391	7	2,270,395	8
ND	322,627	3	107,542	124,827	1	188,163	2
NE	794,379	5	158,876	302,081	2	475,064	3
NH	710,972	4	177,743	369,561	2	329,918	2
NJ	3,640,292	14	260,021	2,125,101	8	1,477,568	6
NM	783,758	5	156,752	415,335	3	335,788	2
NV	1,014,918	6	169,153	531,373	3	463,567	3
NY	7,081,159	29	244,178	4,485,741	19	2,490,431	10
OH	5,580,847	18	310,047	2,827,709	9	2,661,437	9
OK	1,334,872	7	190,696	443,547	2	891,325	5
OR	1,789,270	7	255,610	970,488	4	754,175	3
PA	5,753,670	20	287,684	2,990,274	11	2,680,434	9
RI	446,049	4	111,512	279,677	3	157,204	1
SC	1,964,118	9	218,235	865,941	4	1,071,645	5
SD	363,815	3	121,272	145,039	1	210,610	2
TN	2,458,577	11	223,507	960,709	4	1,462,330	7
TX	7,993,851	38	210,365	3,308,124	16	4,569,843	22
UT	1,017,440	6	169,573	251,813	1	740,600	5
VA	3,854,489	13	296,499	1,971,820	7	1,822,522	6
VT	299,290	3	99,763	199,239	3	92,698	0
WA	3,125,516	12	260,460	1,755,396	7	1,290,670	5
WI	3,068,434	10	306,843	1,620,985	5	1,407,966	5
WV	670,438	5	134,088	238,269	2	417,655	3
WY	249,061	3	83,020	69,286	0	170,962	3
Totals	129,085,410	538		65,915,795	275	60,933,504	263
			Popular Vote Percentage		51.06%		47.20%
			Electoral Votes / (Percentage)		332 / (61.71%)		206 / (38.29%)
			Equal Voice Vote Percentage		51.12%		48.88%

Table B - 3: 2012 Example Election Results if EVV Were Used

States	Popular Vote	Electoral Votes	PVV	Obama Pop. Votes	Obama EVV Electoral Votes	McCain Pop. Votes	McCain EVV Electoral Votes
AK	326,197	3	108,732	123,594	1	193,841	2
AL	2,099,819	9	233,313	813,479	3	1,266,546	6
AR	1,086,617	6	181,103	422,310	2	638,017	4
AZ	2,293,475	10	229,348	1,034,707	5	1,230,111	5
CA	13,561,900	55	246,580	8,274,473	35	5,011,781	20
CO	2,401,462	9	266,829	1,288,633	5	1,073,629	4
CT	1,646,794	7	235,256	997,772	4	629,428	3
DC	265,853	3	88,618	245,800	3	17,367	0
DE	412,412	3	137,471	255,459	2	152,374	1
FL	8,390,744	27	310,768	4,282,074	14	4,045,624	13
GA	3,924,486	15	261,632	1,844,123	7	2,048,759	8
HI	453,568	4	113,392	325,871	3	120,566	1
IA	1,537,123	7	219,589	828,940	4	682,379	3
ID	903,150	4	225,788	236,440	1	403,012	3
IL	5,522,371	21	262,970	3,419,348	13	2,031,179	8
IN	2,751,054	11	250,096	1,374,039	6	1,345,648	5
KS	1,235,872	6	205,979	514,765	3	699,655	3
KY	1,826,620	8	228,328	751,985	3	1,048,462	5
LA	1,960,761	9	217,862	782,989	4	1,148,275	5
MA	3,080,985	12	256,749	1,904,097	8	1,108,854	4
MD	2,631,596	10	263,160	1,629,467	6	959,862	4
ME	731,163	4	182,791	421,823	2	295,273	2
MI	5,001,766	17	294,222	2,872,579	10	2,048,639	7
MN	2,910,369	10	291,037	1,573,354	6	1,275,409	4
MO	2,925,205	11	265,928	1,441,911	5	1,445,814	6
MS	1,289,865	6	214,978	554,662	3	724,597	3
MT	490,302	3	163,434	231,667	1	242,763	2
NC	4,310,789	15	287,386	2,142,651	8	2,128,474	7
ND	316,621	3	105,540	141,278	1	168,601	2
NE	801,281	5	160,256	333,319	2	452,979	3
NH	710,970	4	177,743	384,826	2	316,534	2
NJ	3,868,237	15	257,882	2,215,422	9	1,613,207	6
NM	830,158	5	166,032	472,422	3	346,832	2
NV	967,848	5	193,570	533,736	3	412,827	2
NY	7,640,931	31	246,482	4,804,945	20	2,752,771	11
OH	5,708,350	20	285,418	2,940,044	11	2,677,820	9
OK	1,462,661	7	208,952	502,496	2	960,165	5
OR	1,827,864	7	261,123	1,037,291	4	738,475	3
PA	6,013,272	21	286,346	3,276,363	12	2,655,885	9
RI	471,766	4	117,942	296,571	3	165,391	1
SC	1,920,969	8	240,121	862,449	4	1,034,896	4
SD	381,975	3	127,325	170,924	1	203,054	2
TN	2,599,749	11	236,341	1,087,437	5	1,479,178	6
TX	8,077,795	34	237,582	3,528,633	15	4,479,328	19
UT	952,370	5	190,474	327,670	2	596,030	3
VA	3,723,260	13	286,405	1,959,532	7	1,725,005	6
VT	325,046	3	108,349	219,262	3	98,974	0
WA	3,036,878	11	276,080	1,750,848	7	1,229,216	4
WI	2,983,417	10	298,342	1,677,211	6	1,262,393	4
WV	713,451	5	142,690	303,857	2	397,466	3
WY	254,658	3	84,886	82,868	0	164,958	3
Totals	131,561,845	538		69,498,516	291	59,948,323	247
	Popular Vote Percentage			52.83%			45.57%
	Electoral Votes / (Percentage)			365 / (67.84%)			173 / (32.16%)
	Equal Voice Vote Percentage			54.09%			45.91%

Table B - 4: 2008 Example Election Results if EVV Were Used

States	Popular Vote	Electoral Votes	PVV	Kerry Pop. Votes	Kerry EVV Electoral Voes	Bush Pop. Votes	Bush EVV Electoral Voes
AK	312,598	3	104,199	111,025	1	190,889	2
AL	1,883,449	9	209,272	693,933	3	1,176,394	6
AR	1,054,945	6	175,824	469,953	3	572,898	3
AZ	2,012,585	10	201,259	893,524	4	1,104,294	6
CA	12,421,852	55	225,852	6,745,485	31	5,509,826	24
CO	2,130,330	9	236,703	1,001,732	4	1,101,255	5
CT	1,578,769	7	225,538	857,488	4	693,826	3
DC	227,586	3	75,862	202,970	3	21,256	0
DE	375,190	3	125,063	200,152	2	171,660	1
FL	7,609,810	27	281,845	3,583,544	13	3,964,522	14
GA	3,301,875	15	220,125	1,366,149	6	1,914,254	9
HI	429,013	4	107,253	231,708	2	194,191	2
IA	1,506,908	7	215,273	741,898	3	751,957	4
ID	598,447	4	149,612	181,098	1	409,235	3
IL	5,274,322	21	251,158	2,891,550	12	2,345,946	9
IN	2,468,002	11	224,364	969,011	4	1,479,438	7
KS	1,187,756	6	197,959	434,993	2	736,456	4
KY	1,795,882	8	224,485	712,733	3	1,069,439	5
LA	1,943,106	9	215,901	820,299	4	1,102,169	5
MA	2,912,388	12	242,699	1,803,800	8	1,071,109	4
MD	2,386,678	10	238,668	1,334,493	6	1,024,703	4
ME	740,752	4	185,188	396,842	2	330,201	2
MI	4,839,252	17	284,662	2,479,183	9	2,313,746	8
MN	2,828,387	10	282,839	1,445,014	5	1,346,695	5
MO	2,731,364	11	248,306	1,259,171	5	1,455,713	6
MS	1,152,145	6	192,024	458,094	2	684,981	4
MT	450,445	3	150,148	173,710	1	266,063	2
NC	3,501,007	15	233,400	1,525,849	7	1,961,166	8
ND	312,833	3	104,278	111,052	1	196,651	2
NE	778,186	5	155,637	254,328	2	512,814	3
NH	677,738	4	169,435	340,511	2	331,237	2
NJ	3,611,691	15	240,779	1,911,430	8	1,670,003	7
NM	756,304	5	151,261	370,942	2	376,930	3
NV	829,587	5	165,917	397,190	2	418,690	3
NY	7,391,036	31	238,421	4,314,280	19	2,962,567	12
OH	5,627,908	20	281,395	2,741,167	10	2,859,768	10
OK	1,463,758	7	209,108	503,966	2	959,792	5
OR	1,836,782	7	262,397	943,163	4	866,831	3
PA	5,769,590	21	274,742	2,938,095	11	2,793,847	10
RI	437,134	4	109,284	259,760	2	169,046	2
SC	1,617,730	8	202,216	661,699	3	937,974	5
SD	388,215	3	129,405	149,244	1	232,584	2
TN	2,437,319	11	221,574	1,036,477	5	1,384,375	6
TX	7,410,765	34	217,964	2,832,704	13	4,526,917	21
UT	927,844	5	185,569	241,199	1	663,742	4
VA	3,198,367	13	246,028	1,454,742	6	1,716,959	7
VT	312,309	3	104,103	184,067	2	121,180	1
WA	2,859,084	11	259,917	1,510,201	6	1,304,894	5
WI	2,997,007	10	299,701	1,489,504	5	1,478,120	5
WV	755,887	5	151,177	326,541	2	423,778	3
WY	243,428	3	81,143	70,776	0	167,629	3
Totals	122,295,345	538		59,028,439	258	62,040,610	277

	Kerry	Bush
Popular Vote Percentage	48.27%	50.73%
Electoral Votes / (Percentage)	251 / (46.65%)	286 / (51.12%)
Equal Voice Vote Percentage	47.96%	51.49%

Table B - 5: 2004 Example Election Results if EVV Were Used

States	Popular Vote	Electoral Votes	PVV	Gore Pop. Votes	Gore EVV Electoral Votes	Bush Pop. Votes	Bush EVV Electoral Votes	Nader Pop. Votes	Nader EVV Electoral Votes
AK	285,560	3	95,187	79,004	0	167,398	3	28,747	0
AL	1,666,272	9	185,141	692,611	4	941,173	5	18,323	0
AR	921,781	6	153,630	422,768	3	472,940	3	13,421	0
AZ	1,532,016	8	191,502	685,341	4	781,652	4	45,645	0
CA	10,965,856	54	203,071	5,861,203	30	4,567,429	22	418,707	2
CO	1,741,368	8	217,671	738,227	3	883,748	5	91434	0
CT	1,459,525	8	182,441	816,015	5	561,094	3	64,452	0
DC	201,894	3	67,298	171,923	3	18,073	0	10,576	0
DE	327,622	3	109,207	180,068	2	137,288	1	8,307	0
FL	5,963,110	25	238,524	2,912,253	12	2,912,790	13	97,488	0
GA	2,596,804	13	199,754	1,116,230	6	1,419,720	7	13,432	0
HI	367,951	4	91,988	205,286	2	137,845	2	21,623	0
IA	1,315,563	7	187,938	638,517	4	634,373	3	634,373	3
ID	501,621	4	125,405	138,637	1	336,937	3	12,292	0
IL	4,742,123	22	215,551	2,589,026	13	2,019,421	9	103,759	0
IN	2,199,302	12	183,275	901,980	5	1,245,836	7	18,531	0
KS	1,072,218	6	178,703	399,276	2	622,332	4	36,086	0
KY	1,544,187	8	193,023	638,898	3	872,492	5	23,192	0
LA	1,765,656	9	196,184	792,344	4	927,871	5	20,473	0
MA	2,702,984	12	225,249	1,616,487	8	878,502	4	173,564	0
MD	2,025,480	10	202,548	1,145,782	6	813,797	4	53,768	0
ME	651,817	4	162,954	319,951	2	286,616	2	37,127	0
MI	4,232,501	18	235,139	2,170,418	10	1,953,139	8	84,165	0
MN	2,438,685	10	243,869	1,168,266	5	1,109,659	5	126,696	0
MO	2,359,892	11	214,536	1,111,138	5	1,189,924	6	38,515	0
MS	994,184	7	142,026	404,614	3	572,844	4	8,122	0
MT	410,997	3	136,999	137,126	1	240,178	2	24,437	0
NC	2,911,262	14	207,947	1,257,692	6	1,631,163	8		0
ND	288,256	3	96,085	95,284	0	174,852	3	9,486	0
NE	697,019	5	139,404	231,780	2	433,862	3	24,540	0
NH	569,081	4	142,270	266,348	2	273,559	2	22,198	0
NJ	3,187,226	15	212,482	1,788,850	9	1,284,173	6	94,554	0
NM	598,605	5	119,721	286,783	3	286,417	2	21,251	0
NV	608,970	4	152,243	279,978	2	301,575	2	15,008	0
NY	6,821,999	33	206,727	4,107,697	20	2,403,374	12	244,030	1
OH	4,655,256	21	221,679	2,186,190	10	2,351,209	11	117,857	0
OK	1,234,229	8	154,279	474,276	3	744,337	5		0
OR	1,533,968	7	219,138	720,342	4	713,577	3	77,357	0
PA	4,913,119	23	213,614	2,485,967	12	2,281,127	11	103,392	0
RI	409,112	4	102,278	249,508	3	130,555	1	25,052	0
SC	1,382,717	8	172,840	565,561	3	785,937	5	20,200	0
SD	316,269	3	105,423	118,804	1	190,700	2		0
TN	2,076,181	11	188,744	981,720	5	1,061,949	6	19,781	0
TX	6,407,637	32	200,239	2,433,746	12	3,799,639	20	137,994	0
UT	770,754	5	154,151	203,053	1	515,096	4	35,850	0
VA	2,739,447	13	210,727	1,217,290	6	1,437,490	7	59,398	0
VT	294,308	3	98,103	149,022	2	119,775	1	20,374	0
WA	2,487,433	11	226,130	1,247,652	6	1,108,864	5	103,002	0
WI	2,598,607	11	236,237	1,242,987	6	1,237,279	5	94,070	0
WV	648,124	5	129,625	295,497	2	336,475	3	10,680	0
WY	218,351	3	72,784	60,481	0	147,947	3	4,625	0
Totals	105,354,899	538		50,999,897	266	50,456,002	266	3,487,954	6

	Popular Vote Percentage	48.41%		47.89%		3.31%
	Electoral Votes / (Percentage)	266 / (49.44%)		271 / (48.70%)		0 / (0%)
	Equal Voice Vote Percentage	49.44%		49.44%		1.12%

Table B - 6: 2000 Example Election Results if EVV Were Used

States	Popular Vote	Electoral Votes	PVV	Clinton Pop. Votes	Clinton EVV Electoral Votes	Dole Pop. Votes	Dole EVV Electoral Votes	Perot Pop. Votes	Perot EW Electoral Votes
AK	241,620	3	80,540	80,380	1	122,746	2	26,333	0
AL	1,534,349	9	170,483	662,165	4	769,044	5	92,149	0
AR	884,262	6	147,377	475,171	4	325,416	2	69,884	0
AZ	1,404,405	8	175,551	653,288	4	622,073	4	112,072	0
CA	10,019,484	54	185,546	5,119,835	29	3,828,380	21	697,847	4
CO	1,510,704	8	188,838	671,152	4	691,848	4	99,629	0
CT	1,392,614	8	174,077	735,740	5	483,109	3	139,523	0
DC	185,726	3	61,909	158,220	3	17,339	0	4,780	0
DE	270,845	3	90,282	140,355	2	99,062	1	28,719	0
FL	5,303,794	25	212,152	2,546,870	12	17,339	11	4,780	2
GA	2,299,071	13	176,852	1,053,849	6	1,080,843	7	146,337	0
HI	360,120	4	90,030	205,012	3	113,943	1	27,358	0
IA	1,234,842	7	176,406	620,258	4	492,644	3	105,159	0
ID	491,719	4	122,930	165,443	1	256,595	3	62,518	0
IL	4,311,391	22	195,972	2,341,744	12	1,587,021	8	346,408	2
IN	2,135,842	12	177,987	887,424	5	1,006,693	6	224,299	1
KS	1,074,300	6	179,050	387,659	2	583,245	4	92,639	0
KY	1,388,708	8	173,589	636,614	4	387,659	4	92,639	0
LA	1,783,959	9	198,218	927,837	5	712,586	4	123,293	0
MA	2,556,786	12	213,066	1,571,763	8	718,107	3	227,217	1
MD	1,789,870	10	178,987	966,207	6	681,530	4	115,812	0
ME	605,897	4	151,474	312,788	3	186,378	1	85,970	0
MI	3,848,844	18	213,825	1,989,653	9	1,481,212	7	336,670	2
MN	2,192,640	10	219,264	1,120,438	5	766,476	4	257,704	1
MS	893,857	7	127,694	394,022	3	439,838	4	52,222	0
MO	2,158,065	11	196,188	1,025,935	5	890,016	5	217,188	1
MT	407,261	3	135,754	167,922	1	179,652	2	55,229	0
NC	2,515,807	14	179,701	1,107,849	6	1,225,938	8	168,059	0
ND	266,411	3	88,804	106,905	1	125,050	2	32,515	0
NE	677,415	5	135,483	236,761	2	363,467	3	71,278	0
NH	499,175	4	124,794	246,214	2	196,532	2	48,390	0
NJ	3,075,807	15	205,054	1,652,329	9	1,103,078	5	262,134	1
NM	556,074	5	111,215	273,495	3	232,751	2	32,257	0
NV	464,279	4	116,070	203,974	2	199,244	2	43,986	0
NY	6,316,129	33	191,398	3,756,177	20	1,933,492	10	503,458	3
OH	4,534,434	21	215,925	2,148,222	10	1,859,883	9	483,207	2
OK	1,206,713	8	150,839	488,105	3	582,315	5	130,788	0
OR	1,377,760	7	196,823	659,641	4	538,152	3	121,221	0
PA	4,506,118	23	195,918	2,215,819	12	1,801,169	9	430,984	2
RI	390,284	4	97,571	233,050	3	104,683	1	43,723	0
SC	1,151,689	8	143,961	506,283	4	573,458	4	64,386	0
SD	323,826	3	107,942	139,333	1	150,543	2	31,250	0
TN	1,894,106	11	172,191	909,146	6	863,530	5	105,918	0
TX	5,611,644	32	175,364	2,459,683	14	2,736,167	16	378,537	2
UT	665,629	5	133,126	221,633	2	361,911	3	66,461	0
VA	2,416,642	13	185,896	1,091,060	6	1,138,350	7	201,003	0
VT	258,449	3	86,150	137,894	3	80,352	0	31,024	0
WA	2,253,837	11	204,894	1,123,323	6	840,712	4	201,003	1
WI	2,196,169	11	199,652	1,071,971	6	845,029	4	227,339	1
WV	636,459	5	127,292	327,812	3	233,946	2	71,639	0
WY	211,571	3	70,524	77,934	1	105,388	2	25,929	0
Totals	96,287,402	538		47,412,357	278	36,735,934	231	7,620,866	26
			Popular Vote Percentage	49.24%		38.15%			7.91%
			Electoral Votes / (Percentage)	379 / (70.45%)		159 / (29.55%)			0 / (0%)
			Equal Voice Vote Percentage	51.67%		42.94%			4.83%

Table B - 7: 1996 Example Election Results if EVV Were Used

States	Popular Vote	Electoral Votes	PVV	Clinton Pop. Votes	Clinton EVV Electoral Votes	Bush Pop. Votes	Bush EVV Electoral Votes	Perot Pop. Votes	Perot EVV Electoral Votes
AK	258,506	3	86,169	78,294	0	102,000	3	73,481	0
AL	1,688,060	9	187,562	690,080	4	804,283	5	183,109	0
AR	950,653	6	158,442	505,823	4	337,324	2	99,132	0
AZ	1,486,975	8	185,872	543,050	3	572,086	3	353,741	2
CA	11,131,721	54	206,143	5,121,325	25	3,630,574	18	2,296,006	11
CO	1,569,180	8	196,148	629,681	3	562,850	3	366,010	2
CT	1,616,332	8	202,042	682,318	3	578,313	3	348,771	2
DC	227,572	3	75,857	192,619	3	20,698	0	9,681	0
DE	289,735	3	96,578	126,055	2	102,313	1	59,213	0
FL	5,314,492	25	212,580	2,072,798	10	2,173,310	10	1,053,067	5
GA	2,321,125	13	178,548	1,008,966	6	995,252	6	309,657	1
HI	372,842	4	93,211	179,310	3	136,822	1	53,003	0
IA	1,354,607	7	193,515	586,353	3	504,891	3	253,468	1
ID	482,142	4	120,536	137,013	1	202,645	2	130,395	1
IL	5,050,157	22	229,553	2,453,350	11	1,734,096	8	840,515	3
IN	2,305,871	12	192,156	848,420	4	989,375	6	455,934	2
KS	1,157,236	6	192,873	390,434	2	449,951	2	312,358	2
KY	1,492,900	8	186,613	665,104	4	617,178	3	203,944	1
LA	1,790,017	9	198,891	815,971	4	733,386	4	211,478	1
MA	2,773,664	12	231,139	1,318,639	8	805,039	3	630,731	3
MD	1,985,046	10	198,505	988,571	5	707,094	4	281,414	1
ME	679,499	4	169,875	263,420	2	206,504	1	206,820	1
MI	4,274,673	18	237,482	1,871,182	8	1,554,940	7	824,813	3
MN	2,347,947	10	234,795	1,020,997	5	747,841	3	562,506	2
MS	981,793	7	140,256	400,258	3	487,793	4	85,626	0
MO	2,391,565	11	217,415	1,053,873	5	811,159	4	518,741	2
MT	410,611	3	136,870	154,507	2	144,207	1	107,225	0
NC	2,611,850	14	186,561	1,114,042	6	1,134,661	6	357,864	2
ND	308,133	3	102,711	99,168	0	136,244	3	71,084	0
NE	739,283	5	147,857	217,344	1	344,346	3	174,687	1
NH	537,945	4	134,486	209,040	2	202,484	2	121,337	0
NJ	3,343,594	15	222,906	1,436,206	7	1,356,865	6	521,829	2
NM	569,986	5	113,997	261,617	3	212,824	2	91,895	0
NV	506,318	4	126,580	189,148	2	175,828	1	132,580	1
NY	6,926,933	33	209,907	3,444,450	17	2,346,649	11	1,090,721	5
OH	4,939,964	21	235,236	1,984,942	9	1,894,310	8	1,036,426	4
OK	1,390,359	8	173,795	473,066	3	592,929	3	319,878	2
OR	1,462,643	7	208,949	621,314	3	475,757	2	354,091	2
PA	4,959,810	23	215,644	2,239,164	11	1,791,841	8	902,667	4
RI	453,478	4	113,370	213,302	3	131,605	1	105,051	0
SC	1,202,527	8	150,316	479,514	3	577,507	5	138,872	0
SD	336,254	3	112,085	124,888	1	136,718	2	73,295	0
TN	1,982,638	11	180,240	933,521	5	841,300	5	199,968	1
TX	6,154,018	32	192,313	2,281,815	12	2,496,071	13	1,354,781	7
UT	743,999	5	148,800	183,429	1	322,632	3	203,400	1
VA	2,558,665	13	196,820	1,038,650	5	1,150,517	6	348,639	2
VT	289,701	3	96,567	133,592	3	88,122	0	65,991	0
WA	2,288,228	11	208,021	993,039	5	731,235	4	541,801	2
WI	2,531,114	11	230,101	1,041,066	5	930,855	4	544,479	2
WV	683,711	5	136,742	331,001	3	241,974	2	108,829	0
WY	200,587	3	66,862	68,160	1	79,347	2	51,263	0
Totals	**104,426,659**	**538**		**44,909,889**	**242**	**39,104,545**	**212**	**19,742,267**	**84**
			Popular Vote Percentage		43.01%		37.45%		18.91%
			Electoral Votes / (Percentage)		370 / (68.77%)		168 / (31.23%)		0 / (0%)
			Equal Voice Vote Percentage		44.98%		39.41%		15.61%

Table B - 8: 1992 Example Election Results if EVV Were Used

States	Popular Vote	Electoral Votes	PVV	Dukakis Pop. Votes	Dukakis EVV Electoral Votes	Bush Pop. Votes	Bush EVV Electoral Votes
AK	200,116	3	63,945	72,584	1	119,251	2
AL	1,378,476	9	151,676	549,506	4	815,576	5
AR	827,738	6	135,969	349,237	3	466,578	3
AZ	1,171,873	7	165,224	454,029	3	702,541	4
CA	9,887,065	47	207,599	4,702,233	23	5,054,917	24
CO	1,372,394	8	168,704	621,453	4	728,177	4
CT	1,443,394	8	178,353	676,584	4	750,241	4
DC	192,877	3	62,332	159,407	3	27,590	0
DE	249,891	3	82,762	108,647	1	139,639	2
FL	4,302,313	21	203,450	1,656,701	8	2,618,885	13
GA	1,809,672	12	149,677	714,792	5	1,081,331	7
HI	354,461	4	87,747	192,364	2	158,625	2
IA	1,225,614	8	151,989	670,557	4	545,355	4
ID	408,968	4	100,288	147,272	1	253,881	3
IL	4,559,120	24	188,620	2,215,940	12	2,310,939	12
IN	2,168,621	12	179,867	860,643	5	1,297,763	7
KS	993,044	7	139,526	422,636	3	554,049	4
KY	1,322,517	9	146,072	580,368	4	734,281	5
LA	1,628,202	10	160,116	717,460	4	883,702	6
MA	2,632,805	13	199,696	1,401,415	7	1,194,635	6
MD	1,714,358	10	170,247	826,304	5	876,167	5
ME	555,035	4	137,675	243,569	2	307,131	2
MI	3,669,163	20	182,063	1,675,783	9	1,965,486	11
MN	2,096,790	10	207,181	1,109,471	5	962,337	5
MS	931,527	7	131,687	363,921	3	557,890	4
MO	2,093,713	11	189,688	1,001,619	5	1,084,953	6
MT	365,674	4	89,837	168,936	2	190,412	2
NC	2,134,370	13	163,648	890,167	5	1,237,258	8
ND	297,261	3	98,099	127,739	1	166,559	2
NE	661,465	5	131,438	259,235	2	397,956	3
NH	451,074	4	111,308	163,696	1	281,537	3
NJ	3,099,553	16	191,134	1,320,352	7	1,743,192	9
NM	521,287	5	102,968	244,497	2	270,341	3
NV	350,067	4	84,695	132,738	2	206,040	2
NY	6,485,683	36	178,604	3,347,882	19	3,081,871	17
OH	4,393,699	23	189,399	1,939,629	10	2,416,549	13
OK	1,171,036	8	145,224	483,423	3	678,367	5
OR	1,201,694	7	168,047	616,206	4	560,126	3
PA	4,536,251	25	179,801	2,194,944	12	2,300,087	13
RI	404,620	4	100,721	225,123	2	177,761	2
SC	986,009	8	122,125	370,554	3	606,443	5
SD	312,991	3	103,858	145,560	1	165,415	2
TN	1,636,250	11	147,912	679,794	5	947,233	6
TX	5,427,410	29	185,847	2,352,748	13	3,036,829	16
UT	647,008	5	127,159	207,343	2	428,442	3
VA	2,191,609	12	180,747	859,799	5	1,309,162	7
VT	243,328	3	80,035	115,775	1	124,331	2
WA	1,865,253	10	183,735	933,516	5	903,835	5
WI	2,191,608	11	197,663	1,126,794	6	1,047,499	5
WV	653,311	6	108,514	341,016	3	310,065	3
WY	176,551	3	57,993	67,113	1	106,867	2
Totals	91,594,809	538		41,809,074	246	48,886,097	289
			Popular Vote Percentage		45.65%		53.37%
			Electoral Votes / (Percentage)		111 / (20.63%)		426 / (79.18%)
			Equal Voice Vote Percentage		45.72%		53.72%

Table B - 9: 1988 Example Election Results if EVV Were Used

States	Popular Vote	Electoral Votes	PVV	Mondale Pop. Votes	Mondale EVV Electoral Votes	Reagan Pop. Votes	Reagan EVV Electoral Votes
AK	207,605	3	69,202	62,007	0	138,377	3
AL	1,441,713	9	160,190	551,899	3	872,849	6
AR	884,406	6	147,401	338,646	2	534,774	4
AZ	1,025,897	7	146,557	333,854	2	681,416	5
CA	9,505,423	47	202,243	3,922,519	19	5,467,009	28
CO	1,295,380	8	161,923	454,975	3	821,817	5
CT	1,466,900	8	183,363	569,597	3	890,877	5
DC	211,288	3	70,429	180,408	3	29,009	0
DE	254,572	3	84,857	101,656	1	152,190	2
FL	4,180,051	21	199,050	1,448,816	7	2,730,350	14
GA	1,776,120	12	148,010	706,628	5	1,068,722	7
HI	335,846	4	83,962	147,154	2	185,050	2
IA	1,319,805	8	164,976	605,620	4	703,088	4
ID	411,144	4	102,786	108,510	1	297,523	3
IL	4,819,088	24	200,795	2,086,499	10	2,707,103	14
IN	2,233,069	12	186,089	841,481	5	1,377,230	7
KS	1,021,991	7	145,999	333,149	2	677,296	5
KY	1,369,345	9	152,149	539,539	4	821,702	5
LA	1,706,822	10	170,682	651,586	4	1,037,299	6
MA	2,559,453	13	196,881	1,239,606	6	1,310,936	7
MD	1,675,873	10	167,587	787,935	5	879,918	5
ME	553,144	4	138,286	214,515	2	336,500	2
MI	3,801,658	20	190,083	1,529,638	8	2,251,571	12
MN	2,084,449	10	208,445	1,036,364	5	1,032,603	5
MO	2,122,771	11	192,979	848,583	4	1,274,188	7
MS	940,192	7	134,313	352,192	3	581,477	4
MT	384,377	4	96,094	146,742	2	232,450	2
NC	2,175,361	13	167,335	824,287	5	1,346,481	8
ND	308,971	3	102,990	104,429	1	200,336	2
NE	652,090	5	130,418	187,866	1	460,054	4
NH	389,066	4	97,267	120,395	1	267,051	3
NJ	3,217,862	16	201,116	1,261,323	6	1,933,630	10
NM	514,370	5	102,874	201,769	2	307,101	3
NV	286,667	4	71,667	91,655	1	188,770	3
NY	6,806,810	36	189,078	3,119,609	17	3,664,763	19
OH	4,547,619	23	197,723	1,825,440	9	2,678,560	14
OK	1,255,676	8	156,960	385,080	2	861,530	6
OR	1,226,527	7	175,218	536,479	3	685,700	4
PA	4,844,903	25	193,796	2,228,131	12	2,584,323	13
RI	410,492	4	102,623	197,106	2	212,080	2
SC	968,529	8	121,066	344,459	3	615,539	5
SD	317,867	3	105,956	116,113	1	200,267	2
TN	1,711,994	11	155,636	711,714	5	990,212	6
TX	5,397,571	29	186,123	1,949,276	11	3,433,428	18
UT	829,856	5	125,931	155,369	1	469,105	4
VA	2,146,635	12	178,886	796,250	4	1,337,078	8
VT	234,561	3	78,187	95,730	1	135,865	2
WA	1,883,910	10	188,391	807,352	4	1,051,670	6
WI	2,211,689	11	201,063	995,740	5	1,198,584	6
WV	735,742	6	122,624	328,125	3	405,483	3
WY	188,968	3	62,989	53,370	0	133,241	3
Totals	92,651,918	538		37,577,185	215	54,454,175	323
		Popular Vote Percentage			40.56%		58.77%
		Electoral Votes / (Percentage)			13 / (2.42%)		525 / (97.58%)
		Equal Voice Vote Percentage			39.96%		60.04%

Table B - 20: 1984 Example Election Results if EVV Were Used

States	Popular Vote	Electoral Votes	PVV	Carter Pop. Votes	Carter EVV Electoral Votes	Reagan Pop. Votes	Reagan EVV Electoral Votes	Anderson Pop. Votes	Anderson EVV Electoral Votes
AK	158,445	3	52,815	41,842	0	86,112	3	11,156	0
AL	1,341,929	9	149,103	636,730	4	654,192	5	16,481	0
AR	857,098	6	142,850	398,041	3	403,164	3	22,468	0
AZ	873,945	6	145,658	246,843	2	529,688	4	76,952	0
CA	8,609,351	45	191,319	3,083,652	16	4,524,858	25	739,832	4
CO	1,184,415	7	169,202	367,973	2	652,264	5	130,633	0
CT	1,406,285	8	175,786	541,732	3	677,210	5	171,807	0
DC	173,889	3	57,963	130,231	3	23,213	0	18,131	0
DE	235,668	3	78,556	105,754	1	111,252	2	16,288	0
FL	3,687,026	17	216,884	1,419,475	7	2,046,951	10	189,692	0
GA	1,597,467	12	133,122	890,955	7	654,168	5	36,055	0
HI	303,287	4	75,822	135,879	2	130,112	2	32,021	0
IA	1,317,661	8	164,708	508,672	3	676,026	5	115,633	0
ID	437,431	4	109,358	110,192	1	290,699	3	27,058	0
IL	4,749,721	26	182,682	1,981,413	11	2,358,049	13	346,754	2
IN	2,242,033	13	172,464	844,197	5	1,255,656	8	111,639	0
KS	979,795	7	139,971	326,150	2	566,812	5	68,231	0
KY	1,294,627	9	143,847	616,417	4	635,274	5	31,127	0
LA	1,548,591	10	154,859	708,453	5	792,853	5	26,345	0
MA	2,524,298	14	180,307	1,057,631	6	1,056,223	6	382,539	2
MD	1,540,496	10	154,050	726,161	6	680,606	4	119,537	0
ME	523,011	4	130,753	220,974	2	238,522	2	53,327	0
MI	3,909,725	21	186,177	1,661,532	9	1,915,225	11	275,223	1
MN	2,051,953	10	205,195	954,173	6	873,268	4	174,997	0
MO	2,099,824	12	174,985	931,182	5	1,074,181	7	77,920	0
MS	892,620	7	127,517	429,281	3	441,089	4	12,036	0
MT	363,952	4	90,988	118,032	1	206,814	3	29,281	0
NC	1,855,833	13	142,756	875,635	6	915,018	7	52,800	0
ND	301,545	3	100,515	79,189	0	193,615	3	23,640	0
NE	640,854	5	128,171	166,424	1	419,214	4	44,854	0
NH	383,999	4	96,000	108,864	1	221,705	3	49,693	0
NJ	2,975,684	17	175,040	1,147,364	7	1,546,557	9	234,632	1
NM	456,237	4	114,059	167,826	1	250,779	3	29,459	0
NV	247,885	3	82,628	66,666	0	155,017	3	17,651	0
NY	6,201,959	41	151,267	2,728,372	18	2,893,831	20	467,801	3
OH	4,283,603	25	171,344	1752414	10	2,206,545	15	25,472	0
OK	1,198,741	8	149,843	402,026	3	695,570	5	38,284	0
OR	1,181,516	6	196,919	456,890	2	571,044	4	112,389	0
PA	4,561,501	27	168,944	1,933,740	11	2,261,872	14	292,921	2
RI	449,335	4	112,334	198,342	3	154793	1	59,819	0
SC	890,083	8	111,260	428,220	4	439,277	4	13,868	0
SD	327,703	4	81,926	103,855	1	198,343	3	21,431	0
TN	1,617,616	10	161,782	783,051	5	787,761	5	35,991	0
TX	4,541,637	26	174,678	1,881,147	11	2,510,705	15	111,613	0
UT	604,222	4	151,056	124,266	0	439,687	4	30,284	0
VA	1,866,032	12	155,503	752,174	5	989,609	7	95,418	0
VT	213,207	3	71,069	81,891	1	94,628	2	31,761	0
WA	1,742,394	9	193,599	650,193	3	865,244	6	185,073	0
WI	2,273,221	11	206,656	981,584	5	1,088,845	6	160,657	0
WV	737,715	6	122,953	367,462	3	334,206	3	31,691	0
WY	176,713	3	58,904	49,427	0	110,700	3	12,072	0
Totals	86,633,778	538		35,480,589	220	43,899,046	303	5,490,437	15
			Popular Vote Percentage	40.95%		50.67%			6.47%
			Electoral Votes / (Percentage)	49 / (9.11%)		489 / (90.89%)		0 / (0%)	
			Equal Voice Vote Percentage	40.89%		56.32%			2.79%

Table B - 31: 1980 Example Election Results if EVV Were Used

States	Popular Vote	Electoral Votes	PVV	Carter Pop. Votes	Carter EVV Electoral Votes	Ford Pop. Votes	Ford EVV Electoral Votes
AK	123,574	3	41,191	44,058	1	71,555	2
AL	1,182,850	9	131,428	659,170	5	504,070	4
AR	769,396	6	128,233	499,614	2	268,753	4
AZ	742,719	6	123,787	295,602	4	418,642	2
CA	7,867,117	45	174,825	3,742,284	21	3,882,244	24
CO	1,081,135	7	154,448	460,353	3	584,367	4
CT	1,381,526	8	172,691	647,895	4	719,261	4
DC	168,830	3	56,277	137,818	3	27,873	0
DE	235,834	3	78,611	122,596	2	109,831	1
FL	3,150,631	17	185,331	1,636,000	9	1,469,531	8
GA	1,467,458	12	122,288	979,409	8	483,743	4
HI	291,301	4	72,825	147,375	2	140,003	2
IA	1,279,306	8	159,913	619,931	4	632,863	4
ID	340,932	4	85,233	126,549	1	204,151	3
IL	4,718,833	26	181,494	2,271,295	13	2,364,269	13
IN	2,220,362	13	170,797	1,014,714	6	1,183,958	7
KS	957,845	7	136,835	430,421	3	502,752	4
KY	1,167,142	9	129,682	615,717	5	531,852	4
LA	1,278,439	10	127,844	661,365	5	587,446	5
MA	2,547,558	14	181,968	1,429,475	8	1,030,276	6
MD	1,432,273	10	143,227	759,612	5	672,661	5
ME	483,208	4	120,802	232,279	2	236,320	2
MI	3,653,749	21	173,988	1,696,714	10	1,893,742	11
MN	1,949,931	10	194,993	1,070,440	6	819,395	4
MO	1,953,600	12	162,800	998,387	6	927,443	6
MS	769,360	7	109,909	381,309	4	366,846	3
MT	328,734	4	82,184	149,259	2	173,703	2
NC	1,677,906	13	129,070	927,365	7	741,960	6
ND	297,094	3	99,031	136,078	1	153,470	2
NE	607,668	5	121,534	233,692	2	359,705	3
NH	339,618	4	84,905	92,479	1	101,273	3
NJ	3,014,472	17	177,322	1,444,653	8	1,509,688	9
NM	418,590	4	104,148	201,148	2	211,419	2
NV	201,876	3	67,292	92,479	1	101,273	2
NY	6,534,420	41	159,376	3,389,558	22	3,100,791	19
OH	4,111,873	25	164,475	2,011,621	13	2,000,505	12
OK	1,092,251	8	136,531	532,442	4	545,708	4
OR	1,029,876	6	171,646	490,407	3	492,120	3
PA	4,620,787	27	171,140	2,328,677	14	2,205,604	13
RI	411,170	4	102,793	227,636	2	181,249	2
SC	802,594	8	100,324	450,825	5	346,140	3
SD	300,678	4	75,170	147,068	2	151,505	2
TN	1,476,346	10	147,635	825,879	6	633,969	4
TX	4,071,884	26	156,611	2,082,319	14	1,953,300	12
UT	541,198	4	135,300	182,110	1	337,908	3
VA	1,697,094	12	141,425	813,896	6	836,554	6
VT	187,855	3	62,618	81,044	1	102,085	2
WA	1,555,534	9	172,837	717,323	4	777,732	5
WI	2,101,336	11	191,031	1,040,232	6	1,004,987	5
WV	750,674	6	125,112	435,914	3	314,760	3
WY	156,343	3	52,114	62,239	1	92,717	2
Totals	81,540,780	538		40,776,725	273	39,063,972	265
Popular Vote Percentage					50.01%		47.91%
Electoral Votes / (Percentage)					297 / (55.20%)		240 / (44.61%)
Equal Voice Vote Percentage					50.74%		49.26%

Table B - 42: 1976 Example Election Results if EVV Were Used

States	Popular Vote	Electoral Votes	PVV	McGovern Pop. Votes	McGovern EVV Electoral Votes	Nixon Pop. Votes	Nixon EVV Electoral Votes
AK	95,219	3	31,740	32,967	1	55,349	2
AL	1,006,093	9	111,788	256,923	2	728,701	7
AR	647,666	6	107,944	198,899	2	445,751	4
AZ	653,505	6	108,918	198,540	2	402,812	4
CA	8,367,862	45	185,952	3,475,847	19	4,602,096	26
CO	953,884	7	136,269	329,980	2	597,189	5
CT	1,384,277	8	173,035	555,498	3	810,763	5
DC	163,421	3	54,474	127,827	3	35,226	0
DE	235,516	3	78,505	92,283	1	140,357	2
FL	2,583,283	17	151,958	718,117	5	1,857,759	12
GA	1,174,772	12	97,898	289,529	3	881,496	9
HI	270,274	4	67,569	101,409	1	168,865	3
IA	1,225,944	8	153,243	496,206	3	706,207	5
ID	310,379	4	77,595	80,826	1	199,384	3
IL	4,723,236	26	181,663	1,913,472	11	2,788,179	15
IN	2,125,529	13	163,502	708,568	4	1,405,154	9
KS	916,095	7	130,871	270,287	2	619,812	5
KY	1,067,499	9	118,611	371,159	3	676,446	6
LA	1,051,491	10	105,149	298,142	3	686,852	7
MA	2,458,756	14	175,625	1,332,540	8	1,112,078	6
MD	1,353,812	10	135,381	505,781	4	829,305	6
ME	417,271	4	104,318	160,584	2	256,458	2
MI	3,490,325	21	166,206	1,459,435	9	1,961,721	12
MN	1,741,652	10	174,165	802,346	5	898,269	5
MO	1,852,589	12	154,382	698,531	5	1,154,058	7
MS	645,963	7	92,280	126,782	1	505,125	6
MT	317,603	4	79,401	120,197	2	183,976	2
NC	1,518,612	13	116,816	438,705	4	1,054,889	9
ND	280,514	3	93,505	100,384	1	174,109	2
NE	576,289	5	115,258	169,991	1	406,298	4
NV	181,766	3	60,589	66,016	1	115,750	2
NH	334,059	4	83,515	116,435	1	213,724	3
NJ	2,997,229	17	176,308	1,102,211	6	1,845,502	11
NM	385,931	4	96,483	141,084	1	235,606	3
NY	7,161,830	41	174,679	2,951,084	17	4,192,778	24
OH	4,094,787	25	163,791	1,558,889	10	2,441,827	15
OK	1,029,900	8	128,738	247,147	2	759,025	6
OR	927,946	6	154,658	392,760	3	486,686	3
PA	4,592,105	27	170,078	1,796,951	11	2,714,521	16
RI	415,808	4	103,952	194,645	2	220,383	2
SC	677,880	8	84,735	189,270	2	478,427	6
SD	307,415	4	76,854	139,945	2	166,476	2
TN	1,201,182	10	120,118	357,293	3	813,147	7
TX	3,472,714	26	133,566	1,154,291	9	2,298,896	17
UT	478,476	4	119,619	126,284	1	323,643	3
VA	1,457,019	12	121,418	438,887	4	988,493	8
VT	186,946	3	62,315	68,174	1	117,149	2
WA	1,470,847	9	163,427	568,334	3	837,135	6
WI	1,852,890	11	168,445	810,174	5	989,430	6
WV	762,399	6	127,067	277,435	2	484,964	4
WY	145,570	3	48,523	44,358	0	100,464	3
Totals	77,744,030	538		29,173,222	199	47,168,710	339
Popular Vote Percentage					37.52%		60.67%
Electoral Votes / (Percentage)					17 / (3.16%)		520 / (96.65%)
Equal Voice Vote Percentage					36.99%		63.01%

Table B - 53: 1972 Example Election Results if EVV Were Used

States	Popular Vote	Electoral Votes	PVV	Humphrey Pop. Votes	Humphrey EVV Electoral Votes	Nixon Pop. Votes	Nixon EVV Electoral Votes	Wallace Pop. Votes	Wallace EVV Electoral Votes
AK	83,035	3	27,678	35,411	1	37,600	2	10,024	0
AL	1,049,917	10	104,992	196,579	2	146,923	1	691,425	7
AR	609,590	6	101,598	184,901	2	189,062	2	235,627	2
AZ	486,936	5	97,387	170,514	2	266,721	3	46,573	0
CA	7,251,587	40	181,290	3,244,318	18	3,467,664	19	487,270	3
CO	811,199	6	135,200	335,174	2	409,345	4	60,813	0
CT	1,256,232	8	157,029	621,561	4	556,721	4	76,650	0
DC	170,578	3	56,859	139,566	3	31,012	0	0	0
DE	214,367	3	71,456	89,194	1	96,714	2	28,459	0
FL	2,187,805	14	156,272	676,794	4	886,804	6	624,207	4
GA	1,250,266	12	104,189	334,440	3	380,111	4	535,550	5
HI	236,218	4	59,055	141,324	2	91,425	2	3,469	0
IA	1,167,931	9	129,770	476,699	4	619,106	5	66,422	0
ID	291,183	4	72,796	89,273	1	165,369	3	36,541	0
IL	4,619,749	26	177,683	2,039,814	11	2,174,774	13	390,958	2
IN	2,123,597	13	163,354	806,659	5	1,067,885	7	243,108	1
KS	872,783	7	124,683	302,996	2	478,674	5	88,921	0
KY	1,055,893	9	117,321	397,541	3	462,411	4	193,098	2
LA	1,097,450	10	109,745	309,615	3	257,535	2	530,300	5
MA	2,331,752	14	166,554	1,469,218	9	766,844	5	87,088	0
MD	1,235,039	10	123,504	538,310	5	517,995	4	178,734	1
ME	392,936	4	98,234	217,312	2	169,254	2	6,370	0
MI	3,306,250	21	157,440	1,593,082	10	1,370,665	9	331,968	2
MN	1,588,510	10	158,851	857,738	6	658,643	4	68,931	0
MO	1,809,502	12	150,792	791,444	5	811,932	6	206,126	1
MS	654,509	7	93,501	150,644	2	88,516	0	415,349	5
MT	274,404	4	68,601	114,117	2	138,835	2	20,015	0
NC	1,587,493	13	122,115	464,113	4	627,192	5	496,188	4
ND	247,882	4	61,971	94,769	2	138,669	2	14,244	0
NE	536,851	5	107,370	170,784	2	321,163	3	44,904	0
NH	297,299	4	74,325	130,589	2	154,903	2	11,173	0
NJ	2,875,395	17	169,141	1,264,206	7	1,325,467	8	262,187	2
NM	327,281	4	81,820	130,081	2	169,692	2	25,737	0
NV	154,218	3	51,406	60,598	1	73,188	2	20,432	0
NY	6,790,066	43	157,909	3,378,470	22	3,007,932	19	358,864	2
OH	3,959,698	26	152,296	1,700,586	11	1,791,014	12	467,495	3
OK	943,086	8	117,886	301,658	3	449,697	4	191,731	1
OR	819,622	6	136,604	358,866	3	408,433	3	49,683	0
PA	4,747,928	29	163,722	2,259,405	14	2,090,017	13	378,582	2
RI	385,000	4	96,250	246,518	3	122,359	1	15,678	0
SC	666,982	8	83,373	197,486	2	254,062	3	215,430	3
SD	281,264	4	70,316	118,023	2	149,841	2	13,400	0
TN	1,248,617	11	113,511	351,233	3	472,592	4	424,792	4
TX	3,079,406	25	123,176	1,266,804	10	1,227,844	10	584,269	5
UT	422,568	4	105,642	156,665	1	238,728	3	26,906	0
VA	1,361,491	12	113,458	442,387	4	590,319	5	321,833	3
VT	161,404	3	53,801	70,255	1	85,142	2	5,104	0
WA	1,304,281	9	144,920	616,037	5	588,510	4	96,990	0
WI	1,691,538	12	140,962	748,804	5	809,997	7	127,835	0
WV	754,206	7	107,744	374,091	4	307,555	3	72,560	0
WY	127,205	3	42,402	45,173	1	70,927	2	11,105	0
Totals	73,199,999	538		31,271,839	228	31,783,783	241	9,901,118	69
		Popular Vote Percentage		42.72%		43.42%			13.53%
		Electoral Votes / (Percentage)		191 / (35.50%)		301 / (55.95%)			46 / (8.55%)
		Equal Voice Vote Percentage		42.38%		44.80%			12.83%

Table B - 64: 1968 Example Election Results if EVV Were Used

States	Popular Vote	Electoral Votes	PVV	Johnson Pop. Votes	Johnson EVV Electoral Votes	Goldwater Pop. Votes	Goldwater EVV Electoral Votes
AK	67,259	3	22,420	44,329	2	22,930	1
AL	689,817	10	68,982	0	0	479,085	10
AR	560,426	6	93,404	314,197	3	243,264	3
AZ	480,770	5	96,154	237,753	2	242,535	3
CA	7,057,586	40	176,440	4,171,877	24	2,879,108	16
CO	776,986	6	129,498	476,024	4	296,767	2
CT	1,218,578	8	152,322	826,269	5	390,996	3
DC	198,597	3	66,199	169,796	3	28,801	0
DE	201,320	3	67,107	122,704	2	78,078	1
FL	1,854,481	14	132,463	948,540	7	905,941	7
GA	1,139,336	12	94,945	522,557	6	616,584	6
HI	207,271	4	51,818	163,249	4	44,022	0
IA	1,184,539	9	131,615	733,030	6	449,148	3
ID	292,477	4	73,119	148,920	2	143,557	2
IL	4,702,841	26	180,879	2,796,833	15	1,905,946	11
IN	2,091,606	13	160,893	1,170,848	7	911,118	6
KS	857,901	7	122,557	464,028	4	386,579	3
KY	1,046,105	9	116,234	669,659	6	372,977	3
LA	896,293	10	89,629	397,068	4	509,225	6
MA	2,344,798	14	167,486	1,786,422	11	549,727	3
MD	1,116,457	10	111,646	730,912	7	385,495	3
ME	381,221	4	95,305	262,264	3	118,701	1
MI	3,203,102	21	152,529	2,136,615	14	1,060,152	7
MN	1,554,462	10	155,446	991,117	6	559,624	4
MO	1,817,879	12	151,490	1,164,344	8	653,535	4
MS	409,146	7	58,449	52,618	0	356,528	7
MT	278,628	4	69,657	164,246	2	113,032	2
NC	1,424,983	13	109,614	800,139	7	624,844	6
ND	258,389	4	64,597	149,784	2	108,207	2
NE	584,154	5	116,831	307,307	3	276,847	2
NH	288,093	4	72,023	184,064	3	104,029	1
NJ	2,846,770	17	167,457	1,867,671	11	963,843	6
NM	327,615	4	81,904	194,017	2	131,838	2
NV	135,433	3	45,144	79,339	2	56,094	1
NY	7,166,015	43	166,652	4,913,156	30	2,243,559	13
OH	3,969,196	26	152,661	2,498,331	16	1,470,865	10
OK	932,499	8	116,562	519,834	4	412,665	4
OR	786,305	6	131,051	501,017	4	282,779	2
PA	4,822,690	29	166,300	3,130,954	19	1,673,657	10
RI	390,091	4	97,523	315,463	4	74,615	0
SC	524,756	8	65,595	215,700	3	309,048	5
SD	293,118	4	73,280	163,010	2	130,108	2
TN	1,143,946	11	103,995	634,947	6	508,965	5
TX	2,626,811	25	105,072	1,663,185	16	958,566	9
UT	400,310	4	100,078	219,628	2	180,682	2
VA	1,042,267	12	86,856	558,038	6	481,334	6
VT	163,089	3	54,363	108,127	2	54,942	1
WA	1,258,556	9	139,840	779,881	6	470,366	3
WI	1,691,815	12	140,985	1,050,424	7	638,495	5
WV	792,040	7	113,149	538,087	5	253,953	2
WY	142,716	3	47,572	80,718	2	61,998	1
Totals	70,641,539	535		43,129,040	319	27,175,754	216
			Popular Vote Percentage		61.05%		38.47%
			Electoral Votes / (Percentage)		485 / (90.84%)		52 / (9.72%)
			Equal Voice Vote Percentage		59.63%		40.37%

Table B - 75: 1964 Example Election Results if EVV Were Used

States	Popular Vote	Electoral Votes	PVV	Kennedy Pop. Votes	Kennedy EVV Electoral Votes	Nixon Pop. Votes	Nixon EVV Electoral Votes
AK	60,762	3	20,254	29,809	1	30,953	2
AL	564,473	11	51,316	318,303	6	237,981	5
AR	428,509	8	53,564	215,049	5	184,508	3
AZ	398,491	4	99,623	176,781	2	221,241	2
CA	6,506,578	32	203,331	3,224,099	16	3,259,722	16
CO	736,246	6	122,708	330,629	3	402,242	3
CT	1,222,883	8	152,860	657,055	4	565,813	4
DE	196,683	3	65,561	99,590	2	96,373	1
FL	1,544,176	10	154,418	748,700	5	795,476	5
GA	733,349	12	61,112	458,638	8	274,472	4
HI	184,705	3	61,588	92,410	2	92,295	1
IA	1,273,810	10	127,381	550,565	4	722,381	6
ID	300,450	4	75,113	138,853	2	161,597	2
IL	4,757,409	27	176,200	2,377,846	14	2,368,988	13
IN	2,135,360	13	164,258	952,358	6	1,175,120	7
KS	928,825	8	116,103	363,213	3	561,474	5
KY	1,124,462	10	112,446	521,855	5	602,607	5
LA	807,891	10	80,789	407,339	7	230,980	3
MA	2,469,480	16	154,343	1,487,174	10	976,750	6
MD	1,055,349	9	117,261	565,808	5	489,538	4
ME	421,773	5	84,355	181,159	2	240,608	3
MI	3,318,097	20	165,905	1,687,269	10	1,620,428	10
MN	1,541,887	11	140,172	779,933	6	757,915	5
MO	1,934,422	13	148,802	972,201	7	962,221	6
MS	298,171	8	37,271	108,362	5	73,561	2
MT	277,579	4	69,395	134,891	2	141,841	2
NC	1,368,556	14	97,754	713,136	7	655,420	7
ND	278,431	4	69,608	123,963	2	154,310	2
NE	613,095	6	102,183	232,542	2	380,553	4
NH	295,761	4	73,940	137,772	2	157,989	2
NJ	2,773,111	16	173,319	1,385,415	8	1,363,324	8
NM	311,107	4	77,777	156,027	2	153,733	2
NV	107,267	3	35,756	54,880	2	52,387	1
NY	7,291,079	45	162,024	3,830,085	24	3,446,419	21
OH	4,161,859	25	166,474	1,944,248	12	2,217,611	13
OK	903,150	8	112,894	370,111	3	533,039	5
OR	776,421	6	129,404	367,402	3	408,060	3
PA	5,006,541	32	156,454	2,556,282	16	2,439,956	16
RI	405,535	4	101,384	258,032	3	147,502	1
SC	386,688	8	48,336	198,129	4	188,558	4
SD	306,487	4	76,622	128,070	2	178,417	2
TN	1,051,792	11	95,617	481,453	5	556,577	6
TX	2,311,084	24	96,295	1,167,567	12	1,121,310	12
UT	374,709	4	93,677	169,248	2	205,361	2
VA	771,449	12	64,287	362,327	6	404,521	6
VT	167,324	3	55,775	69,186	1	98,131	2
WA	1,241,572	9	137,952	599,298	4	629,273	5
WI	1,729,082	12	144,090	830,805	6	895,175	6
WV	837,781	8	104,723	441,786	4	395,995	4
WY	140,782	3	46,927	63,331	1	77,451	2
Totals	68,832,483	537		34,220,984	276	34,108,157	261

Popular Vote Percentage	49.72%	49.55%
Electoral Votes / (Percentage)	303 / (56.42%)	219 / (40.78%)
Equal Voice Vote Percentage	51.40%	48.60%

Table B - 86: 1960 Example Election Results if EVV Were Used

ACKNOWLEDGEMENTS

Many kind and generous friends have contributed to the creation of, "All Lives Matter." Further, their contributions have been gratefully received over a span of time – often over several years. I could not have ventured into this endeavor without them. Encouragement and support take many forms. Sometimes it might simply have been a comment or a seemingly small suggestion that prompted further research or manuscript modification. Other times, the criticism might have pushed me to alter my approach or to rethink my perspective. To say the book evolved is an accurate assessment of its birth and development. To all who have participated, I owe a deep gratitude.

I became intrigued with presidential elections before I was eligible to vote. The political conventions and their contests caught my attention and inspired my thinking at an early age. When I became aware of how the elections seemed to fail the capture of voter sentiment, I was challenged to find an alternative method. When I developed the EVV method (the answer to the challenge) I decided to write a book about it. It launched me into a serious endeavor that has now spanned almost a decade.

This is actually the third version of the book. Early attempts (two) were mostly collections of data from earlier elections and comparisons to what would have happened had EVV been used across the nation instead. They were, essentially, data dumps and were, in truth, rather laborious and boring reads. Yes, I had a few friends who made this painfully plain to see. I owe that honesty a nod of thanks as well.

"All Votes Matter" emerged as a desire to make the election story clearer and a more entertaining read than the first two attempts. I reached out to friends who I trusted to help with their expertise and their honesty to make the effort better. They delivered!

The following is not presented in any particular order except for an alphabetical listing of their names.

F. Gerald Brown has been a wonderful encourager from the early years of the process. Known as an astute critical thinker, Gerry aided me by pointing me to studies made by the League of Women Voters, thereby challenging my own assumptions and expanding my perspectives.

Larry Chasteen, PhD and Management Professor at the University of Texas, Dallas, has become an email acquaintance. He noted some errors made earlier and brought attention to a central tenet of the book: how EVV voting results compares with what we currently experience. His advice has made the message stronger, for which I owe him my sincere appreciation.

Jim Dana has probably known me the longest in this list of supporters, other than my wife. While he admits to not being overly political, his input has been important to the structure of the book so it teaches as it proceeds. You, dear reader, owe him gratitude for he's made it easier to get through some of these details.

Bill Denney has been a constant voice of support, prompting me to further my reading of history and being apprised of current events. Our discussions have often been a solace and a valued prompt to keep going in spite of common disappointment. Bill has taught me a lot and especially has encouraged an eagerness to learn more history!

Louisa Gonyou has helped edit the works and, most importantly, been a great encourager from the beginning. Now retired, Louisa once was the Executive Assistant to Michigan's Supreme Court Justice Dennis W. Archer. Her attention to law and detail was invaluable.

Eric Griswold has given me "eyes" to see my work from a perspective I hadn't had earlier. He is the one that pointed out how key it is to welcome a change of perspective – a paradigm shift – when discussing the Electoral College. He, as a retired photographer, is also responsible for my personal photo. My apologies, Eric, you can only do so much with what you have to work with.

Steve Hammond, Executive Creative Director for H2R Marketing, is a neighbor with an artistic talent that makes one picture worth thousands of words. His cover creation helps make the book stand out among the many giving it the visual gravitas it needed. His creative work helps make the book come alive.

Jim Mattis is a true confidence builder. Known as an expert in his own right, his grasp of law and history and how EVV can make a difference has been encouraging. Jim has introduced me to wider audiences and allowed me to face political realities without giving daylight to any kind of despair.

Steve Toft, a former boss and long-time friend, is one of the finest writers I know. He brought his writing skills to bear on the manuscript, helping it become grammatically correct and the message clearer. Steve helped make an otherwise difficult read and fun walk of discovery in the park of politics and governance.

Most of all, none of this would have emerged if it hasn't been for my wife, **Jane.** She is the one who has read everything I've written and been honest enough and brave enough to set me straight when I've gone astray. She's listened to my complaints, to my off-the-rails exuberance when new discoveries are made, and still calmly supports what I'm doing. As an editor, she is remarkable. She quickly points out when one though fails to follow another or when some notion is ill-supported or failed to be proved. In other words, she's helped make the book a comprehensive and focused read. My thanks to her and for her will never be enough.

I must also acknowledge those who have disagreed with my idea. There have been, and probably will be, several. I've been told to give it up! I've been told that EVV doesn't have a chance of being accepted. It's probably sage advice but I cannot deter from the path I've chosen. What do we, as a nation, suffer when tens of millions of patriotic citizens cast their ballots for a president and yet are ignored? Do they not deserve to be heard, to be represented in the Electoral College? Others have decried the EVV concept saying that would be better to eliminate the Electoral College (never mind they never suggest with what to replace it) or they align their allegiance behind the national popular vote idea. I can understand their frustration, though it be rather unfounded. I find their criticism encouraging, rather than off-putting. Such rebuke has encouraged me to further my resolve which, at times, wanes when few seem interested in true reform that gives voice to so many. To this bit of conflict, and to those who engender it, I offer my thanks.

ABOUT THE AUTHOR

Jerry Spriggs, B.A., M.S., is a retired instructional designer, having designed curricula and developed training strategies and materials for the U.S. Air Force, U.S. Navy, and numerous Fortune 500 corporations. His career stemmed from his interest in game design. How we elect our president via the Electoral College began as a curiosity, grew into a hobby, developed into a passion, and is now a *beast of truth* he must water and feed every day. Jerry and his wife live in Oregon.

CPSIA information can be obtained
at www.ICGtesting.com
Printed in the USA
BVHW080939250221
600957BV00001B/62